2022 SUPPLEMENT
CASES AND MATERIALS ON

CONSTITUTIONAL LAW

THEMES FOR THE CONSTITUTION'S THIRD CENTURY

Sixth Edition

■ ■ ■

Daniel A. Farber
Sho Sato Professor of Law
University of California, Berkeley

William N. Eskridge Jr.
John A. Garver Professor of Jurisprudence
Yale Law School

Jane S. Schacter
William Nelson Cromwell Professor of Law
Stanford Law School

AMERICAN CASEBOOK SERIES®

**WEST
ACADEMIC**
PUBLISHING

American Casebook Series is a trademark registered in the U.S. Patent and Trademark Office.

© 2021 LEG, Inc. d/b/a West Academic
© 2022 LEG, Inc. d/b/a West Academic
444 Cedar Street, Suite 700
St. Paul, MN 55101
1-877-888-1330

West, West Academic Publishing, and West Academic are trademarks of West Publishing Corporation, used under license.

Printed in the United States of America

ISBN: 978-1-63659-900-7

TABLE OF CONTENTS

TABLE OF CASES

The principal cases are in bold type.

2022 SUPPLEMENT TO CASES AND MATERIALS ON

CONSTITUTIONAL LAW

THEMES FOR THE CONSTITUTION'S THIRD CENTURY

Sixth Edition

CHAPTER 1

A PROLOGUE ON CONSTITUTIONAL HISTORY

■ ■ ■

APPENDIX: RECENT JUSTICES

The Roberts Court

Page 72. Insert at the bottom of the page:

Amy Coney Barrett was born in New Orleans. She graduated from Notre Dame Law School, practiced law in Washington, D.C., and then returned to Notre Dame as a faculty member. She was appointed to the Seventh Circuit by President Trump. She was then nominated by President Trump to fill the seat vacated as a result of Justice Ruth Bader Ginsburg's death during the final months of the Trump Administration. Her nomination was controversial for two reasons. First, her nomination was only two months before the next presidential election. Republicans had previously refused to consider a nomination made by President Obama during the year of a presidential election, but they saw no barrier to voting on Barrett's nomination. Second, her nomination was seen as decisively cementing conservative control of the Supreme Court for years to come. She was confirmed by a vote of 52–48.

Ketanji Brown Jackson was born in Washington, D.C., and raised in Miami. She attended Harvard for both college and law school. In the interim between the two, she worked as a journalist and researcher for Time magazine. After clerkships and some years of practice as a public defender, she joined the U.S. Sentencing Commission and then served eight years as district court judge and then briefly on the D.C. Circuit. Her best known ruling on the trial bench rejected President Trump's effort to prevent a former aide from testifying before Congress. President Biden nominated to fill the position of Justice Breyer when his announced retirement took place. Her nomination was reported out of committee by voice vote. She confirmed by a 53–47 margin, with three Republicans voting in her favor.

CHAPTER 3

THE CONSTITUTION AND RACIAL DISCRIMINATION

■ ■ ■

SECTION 2. THE STATE ACTION DOCTRINE AS A LIMIT ON THE JUDICIAL POWER TO ADDRESS RACIAL DISCRIMINATION

B. THE PUBLIC/PRIVATE DISTINCTION TODAY

1. Private Actors and Public Functions

Page 263. Insert after the final paragraph:

In *Manhattan Community Access Corporation v. Halleck*, 139 S.Ct. 1921 (2019), the Supreme Court, by a 5–4 vote, underscored that the public functions doctrine offers an exceedingly narrow route to establishing state action. In *Halleck*, two public producers for a public access cable channel were suspended after a film they made aired and generated complaints. They claimed the channel abridged their free speech by suspending them based on the content of their film. The question was whether this public access channel on Time Warner's cable system in Manhattan was a state actor for purposes of the First Amendment. Although state regulations *required* New York City to ensure that a cable system would provide public access channels if the city granted it a cable franchise, the public access channel itself was operated by a private entity. "It is not enough that the federal, state, or local government exercised the function in the past, or still does," said Justice Kavanaugh for the majority, nor is it sufficient that "the function serves the public good or public interest in some way." Instead, the government must have "traditionally *and* exclusively performed the function," and " 'very few' functions fall into that category." In justifying its restrictive approach to public functions, the Court offered a full-throated normative defense of the state-action requirement, noting that "[n]umerous private entities in American obtain government licenses, government contracts, or government-granted monopolies" and subjecting them to constitutional constraints would be inconsistent with what the Court took to be the normative underpinnings of the state action doctrine: "enforc[ing] a critical boundary between the government and the individual," "protect[ing]" a robust sphere of individual liberty" and avoiding principles that "would expand governmental control while restricting individual liberty and private enterprise." In her dissent, Justice Sotomayor emphasized that the public access channel was not a garden-variety private actor operating "against a regulatory backdrop," but instead a private actor specifically delegated a "constitutional responsibility" to operate a public forum for purposes of the First Amendment (see Chapter 6, § 4A). Having been legally tasked to operate a such a forum, she argued, the public access station must "be accountable to the Constitution's demands."

CHAPTER 4

SEX AND GENDER DISCRIMINATION AND OTHER EQUAL PROTECTION CONCERNS

■ ■ ■

SECTION 3. WHAT LEVEL OF SCRUTINY FOR OTHER "SUSPICIOUS" CLASSIFICATIONS?

B. LANGUAGE AND ETHNICITY

Page 448. Insert at the end of Note 1:

In a highly charged recent case, the Court emphasized the relevance of just this sort of comparative inquiry about how prospective jurors had been questioned. In *Flowers v. Mississippi*, 139 S.Ct. 2228 (2019), the Court, by a 7–2 margin, upheld the *Batson* claim of Curtis Flowers, a black defendant who was convicted of murder and had challenged the prosecution's peremptory strikes against five of six black prospective jurors. This was the sixth trial for Flowers on the murder charge, and all but one of those past trials had involved *Batson* claims challenging the same prosecutor's use of race-based strikes. Recently, the case had garnered considerable media attention. In an extended analysis reaffirming the link between *Batson* and the Fourteenth Amendment's core ban on race discrimination, Justice Kavanaugh included among the factors judges may consider in assessing *Batson* challenges "disparate questioning and investigation of black and white prospective jurors in the case." In a further effort to clarify how a trial judge can identify pretextual justifications as part of the inquiry, the majority also included as relevant factors:

- statistical evidence of a prosecutor's disparate questioning and investigation of black and white prospective jurors in the case;
  * * *

- a prosecutor's misrepresentations of the record when defending the strikes during the *Batson* hearing;

- relevant history of the State's peremptory strikes in past cases; or

- other relevant circumstances that bear upon the issue of racial discrimination.

The Kavanaugh opinion drew a sharply worded dissent from Justice Thomas, who argued that Flowers' conviction should stand, and that *Batson* is a misguided doctrine that wrongly limits the use of peremptory strikes. Rather than being seen as discriminatory, Thomas argued that race-based strikes should be legitimate trial strategy that can help all litigants, including black defendants who wish to strike "potentially hostile white jurors."

D. SEXUAL ORIENTATION

Page 483. Insert after Problem 4-6:

PROBLEM 4-7:
BOSTOCK V. CLAYTON COUNTY: *WHAT IMPLICATIONS FOR EQUAL PROTECTION CLAIMS?*

Title VII of the Civil Rights Act of 1964 bans discrimination in employment based on race and sex, among other protected characteristics. Its language does not specifically refer to discrimination based on sexual orientation or gender identity. In *Bostock v. Clayton County*, 140 S.Ct. 1731 (2020), the Supreme Court interpreted the language of Title VII to mean that an employer who fires an employee for being gay or transgender has fired that employee "because of" sex. The landmark ruling means that LGBT employees now have federal protection against employment discrimination.

Bostock is a statutory interpretation decision that emphasizes the force of the text rather than the unwritten purpose or expectations of the lawmakers who passed the law in 1964. It is not a constitutional holding. But the dissenting justices emphasized its potential impact on equal protection claims involving sexual orientation and gender identity. Consider what impact the decision may have in the constitutional domain.

The first thing to note is the decision's reasoning. Writing for a 6–3 majority, Justice Gorsuch reasoned that:

An individual's homosexuality or transgender status is not relevant to employment decisions. That's because it is impossible to discriminate against a person for being homosexual or transgender without discriminating against that individual based on sex. Consider, for example, an employer with two employees, both of whom are attracted to men. The two individuals are, to the employer's mind, materially identical in all respects, except that one is a man and the other a woman. If the employer fires the male employee for no reason other than the fact he is attracted to men, the employer discriminates against him for traits or actions it tolerates in his female colleague. Put differently, the employer intentionally singles out an employee to fire based in part on the employee's sex, and the affected employee's sex is a but-for cause of his discharge. Or take an employer who fires a transgender person who was identified as a male at birth but who now identifies as a female. If the employer retains an otherwise identical employee who was identified as female at birth, the employer intentionally penalizes a person identified as male at birth for traits or actions that it tolerates in an employee identified as female at birth. Again, the individual employee's sex plays an unmistakable and impermissible role in the discharge decision.

In the opinion, Gorsuch focused on the language in Title VII banning discrimination "because of" sex and relied on previous case law applying the but-for causation test to that statutory language. While that approach flows from law developed under Title VII, it has potentially significant implications for the many other federal statutes that ban sex discrimination. Indeed, in a vigorous dissent, Justice Alito collected over 100 such statutes in an appendix and said that, because of them, it was "virtually certain" that the holding would have "far reaching consequences." As a statutory holding, then, *Bostock* worked a significant change to the legal landscape for LGBT persons.

Does the logic of *Bostock* dictate that discrimination by government based on sexual orientation and gender identity are also per se forms of sex discrimination, and thus subject to intermediate scrutiny? The majority opinion was silent on this question. But Justice Alito's dissent argued that the decision "may exert a gravitational pull in constitutional cases" because "[b]y equating discrimination because of sexual orientation or gender identity with discrimination because of sex, the Court's decision will be cited as a ground for subjecting all three forms of discrimination to the same exacting standard of review." He went on to cite pending litigation challenging discrimination based on gender identity in the realms of military service, access to bathrooms and competitive sports, among others. Justice Kavanaugh's dissent also touched on the issue in the course of arguing that sexual orientation discrimination is not the same thing as sex discrimination. He noted that none of the Court's major constitutional decisions on gay rights had employed constitutional principles of sex discrimination.

Revisit the issue of discrimination against gay, lesbian and transgender teachers addressed in Problem 4-6. Drawing on *Bostock*, what arguments could plaintiffs challenging that discrimination make in support of raising the level of scrutiny to intermediate? What arguments could the government make in response? Which, in your view, should prevail?

CHAPTER 5

PROTECTING FUNDAMENTAL RIGHTS

■ ■ ■

SECTION 1. SHOULD COURTS EVER ENFORCE UNENUMERATED RIGHTS?

Page 508. Insert after Note 5:

In the next case, the Court answered some of the questions posed in Note 5 about the scope of the Second Amendment going forward.

NEW YORK STATE RIFLE & PISTOL ASSOCIATION, INC. V. BRUEN
597 U.S. ___, 142 S.Ct. 2111, ___ L.Ed.2d ___ (2022)

JUSTICE THOMAS delivered the opinion of the Court.

In *District of Columbia v. Heller* (2008), and *McDonald v. Chicago* (2010), we recognized that the Second and Fourteenth Amendments protect the right of an ordinary, law-abiding citizen to possess a handgun in the home for self-defense. In this case, petitioners and respondents agree that ordinary, law-abiding citizens have a similar right to carry handguns publicly for their self-defense. We too agree, and now hold, consistent with *Heller* and *McDonald*, that the Second and Fourteenth Amendments protect an individual's right to carry a handgun for self-defense outside the home.

The parties nevertheless dispute whether New York's licensing regime respects the constitutional right to carry handguns publicly for self-defense. In 43 States, the government issues licenses to carry based on objective criteria. But in six States, including New York, the government further conditions issuance of a license to carry on a citizen's showing of some additional special need. Because the State of New York issues public-carry licenses only when an applicant demonstrates a special need for self-defense, we conclude that the State's licensing regime violates the Constitution.* * *

[New York's current] licensing scheme largely tracks that of the early 1900s. It is a crime in New York to possess "any firearm" without a license, whether inside or outside the home, punishable by up to four years in prison or a $5,000 fine for a felony offense, and one year in prison or a

$1,000 fine for a misdemeanor. Meanwhile, possessing a loaded firearm outside one's home or place of business without a license is a felony punishable by up to 15 years in prison.

A license applicant who wants to possess a firearm *at home* (or in his place of business) must convince a "licensing officer"—usually a judge or law enforcement officer—that, among other things, he is of good moral character, has no history of crime or mental illness, and that "no good cause exists for the denial of the license." If he wants to carry a firearm *outside* his home or place of business for self-defense, the applicant must obtain an unrestricted license to "have and carry" a concealed "pistol or revolver." To secure that license, the applicant must prove that "proper cause exists" to issue it. If an applicant cannot make that showing, he can receive only a "restricted" license for public carry, which allows him to carry a firearm for a limited purpose, such as hunting, target shooting, or employment.

No New York statute defines "proper cause." But New York courts have held that an applicant shows proper cause only if he can "demonstrate a special need for self-protection distinguishable from that of the general community." This "special need" standard is demanding. For example, living or working in an area " 'noted for criminal activity' " does not suffice. Rather, New York courts generally require evidence "of particular threats, attacks or other extraordinary danger to personal safety."

When a licensing officer denies an application, judicial review is limited. New York courts defer to an officer's application of the proper-cause standard unless it is "arbitrary and capricious."* * *

New York is not alone in requiring a permit to carry a handgun in public. But the vast majority of States—43 by our count—are "shall issue" jurisdictions, where authorities must issue concealed-carry licenses whenever applicants satisfy certain threshold requirements, without granting licensing officials discretion to deny licenses based on a perceived lack of need or suitability. Meanwhile, only six States and the District of Columbia have "may issue" licensing laws, under which authorities have discretion to deny concealed-carry licenses even when the applicant satisfies the statutory criteria, usually because the applicant has not demonstrated cause or suitability for the relevant license. Aside from New York, then, only California, the District of Columbia, Hawaii, Maryland, Massachusetts, and New Jersey have analogues to the "proper cause" standard. All of these "proper cause" analogues have been upheld by the Courts of Appeals, save for the District of Columbia's, which has been permanently enjoined since 2017.

[Petitioners Brandon Koch and Robert Nash are "law-abiding, adult citizens,". . .and petitioner New York State Rifle & Pistol Association, Inc., is a public-interest group organized to defend the Second Amendment rights of New Yorkers. Both Koch and Nash are members. Koch and Nash each separately requested an unrestricted license to carry a handgun in public. The State denied both applications. It granted each a restricted license that allowed them to carry a weapon outside the home, but limited its use to hunting and target practice. Nash subsequently asked a licensing officer to remove the restrictions, citing a string of recent robberies in his neighborhood, but he was denied. Koch also sought to remove the restrictions on his license, citing his extensive experience in safely handling firearms, but he was also unsuccessful. Petitioners challenged the constitutionality of the New York law.]

II

In *Heller* and *McDonald*, we held that the Second and Fourteenth Amendments protect an individual right to keep and bear arms for self-defense. In doing so, we held unconstitutional two laws that prohibited the possession and use of handguns in the home. In the years since, the Courts of Appeals have coalesced around a "two-step" framework for analyzing Second Amendment challenges that combines history with means-end scrutiny.

Today, we decline to adopt that two-part approach. In keeping with *Heller*, we hold that when the Second Amendment's plain text covers an individual's conduct, the Constitution presumptively protects that conduct. To justify its regulation, the government may not simply posit that the regulation promotes an important interest. Rather, the government must demonstrate that the regulation is consistent with this Nation's historical tradition of firearm regulation. Only if a firearm regulation is consistent with this Nation's historical tradition may a court conclude that the individual's conduct falls outside the Second Amendment's "unqualified command."

Since *Heller* and *McDonald*, the two-step test that Courts of Appeals have developed to assess Second Amendment claims proceeds as follows. At the first step, the government may justify its regulation by "establish[ing] that the challenged law regulates activity falling outside the scope of the right as originally understood." The Courts of Appeals then ascertains the original scope of the right based on its historical meaning. If the government can prove that the regulated conduct falls beyond the Amendment's original scope, "then the analysis can stop there; the regulated activity is categorically unprotected." But if the historical evidence at this step is "inconclusive or suggests that the regulated activity is *not* categorically unprotected," the courts generally proceed to step two.

At the second step, courts often analyze "how close the law comes to the core of the Second Amendment right and the severity of the law's burden on that right." The Courts of Appeals generally maintain "that the core Second Amendment right is limited to self-defense *in the home*." If a "core" Second Amendment right is burdened, courts apply "strict scrutiny" and ask whether the Government can prove that the law is "narrowly tailored to achieve a compelling governmental interest." Otherwise, they apply intermediate scrutiny and consider whether the Government can show that the regulation is "substantially related to the achievement of an important governmental interest." Both respondents and the United States largely agree with this consensus, arguing that intermediate scrutiny is appropriate when text and history are unclear in attempting to delineate the scope of the right.

Despite the popularity of this two-step approach, it is one step too many. Step one of the predominant framework is broadly consistent with *Heller*, which demands a test rooted in the Second Amendment's text, as informed by history. But *Heller* and *McDonald* do not support applying means-end scrutiny in the Second Amendment context. Instead, the government must affirmatively prove that its firearms regulation is part of the historical tradition that delimits the outer bounds of the right to keep and bear arms.* * *

Heller's methodology centered on constitutional text and history. Whether it came to defining the character of the right (individual or militia dependent), suggesting the outer limits of the right, or assessing the constitutionality of a particular regulation, *Heller* relied on text and history. It did not invoke any means-end test such as strict or intermediate scrutiny.

Moreover, *Heller* and *McDonald* expressly rejected the application of any "judge-empowering 'interest-balancing inquiry' that 'asks whether the statute burdens a protected interest in a way or to an extent that is out of proportion to the statute's salutary effects upon other important governmental interests.'" We declined to engage in means-end scrutiny because "[t]he very enumeration of the right takes out of the hands of government—even the Third Branch of Government—the power to decide on a case-by-case basis whether the right is *really worth* insisting upon." We then concluded: "A constitutional guarantee subject to future judges' assessments of its usefulness is no constitutional guarantee at all."* * *

In sum, the Courts of Appeals' second step is inconsistent with *Heller*'s historical approach and its rejection of means-end scrutiny. We reiterate that the standard for applying the Second Amendment is as follows: When the Second Amendment's plain text covers an individual's conduct, the Constitution presumptively protects that conduct. The government must then justify its regulation by demonstrating that it is consistent with the Nation's historical tradition of firearm regulation. Only then may a court conclude that the individual's conduct falls outside the Second Amendment's "unqualified command."* * *

To be sure, "[h]istorical analysis can be difficult; it sometimes requires resolving threshold questions, and making nuanced judgments about which evidence to consult and how to interpret it." But reliance on history to inform the meaning of constitutional text—especially text meant to codify a *pre-existing* right—is, in our view, more legitimate, and more administrable, than asking judges to "make difficult empirical judgments" about "the costs and benefits of firearms restrictions," especially given their "lack [of] expertise" in the field.

If the last decade of Second Amendment litigation has taught this Court anything, it is that federal courts tasked with making such difficult empirical judgments regarding firearm regulations under the banner of "intermediate scrutiny" often defer to the determinations of legislatures. But while that judicial deference to legislative interest balancing is understandable—and, elsewhere, appropriate—it is not deference that the Constitution demands here. The Second Amendment "is the very *product* of an interest balancing by the people" and it "surely elevates above all other interests the right of law-abiding, responsible citizens to use arms" for self-defense. *Heller*. It is this balance—struck by the traditions of the American people—that demands our unqualified deference.

The [inquiry required by the historical test set forth in *Heller* will in some cases] be fairly straightforward. For instance, when a challenged regulation addresses a general societal problem that has persisted since the 18th century, the lack of a distinctly similar historical regulation addressing that problem is relevant evidence that the challenged regulation is inconsistent with the Second Amendment. Likewise, if earlier generations addressed the societal problem, but did so through materially different means, that also could be evidence that a modern regulation is unconstitutional. And if some jurisdictions actually attempted to enact analogous regulations during this timeframe, but those proposals were rejected on constitutional grounds, that rejection surely would provide some probative evidence of unconstitutionality.* * *

New York's proper-cause requirement concerns the same alleged societal problem addressed in *Heller*: "handgun violence," primarily in "urban area[s]." Following the course charted by *Heller*, we will consider whether "historical precedent" from before, during, and even after the founding evinces a comparable tradition of regulation. And, as we explain below, we find no such tradition in the historical materials that respondents and their *amici* have brought to bear on that question.

While the historical analogies here and in *Heller* are relatively simple to draw, other cases implicating unprecedented societal concerns or dramatic technological changes may require a more nuanced approach. The regulatory challenges posed by firearms today are not always the same as those that preoccupied the Founders in 1791 or the Reconstruction generation in 1868. Fortunately, the Founders created a Constitution—and a Second Amendment—"intended to endure for ages to come, and consequently, to be adapted to the various crises of human affairs." *McCulloch v. Maryland* (1819). Although its meaning is fixed according to the understandings of those who ratified it, the Constitution can, and must, apply to circumstances beyond those the Founders specifically anticipated.

We have already recognized in *Heller* at least one way in which the Second Amendment's historically fixed meaning applies to new circumstances: Its reference to "arms" does not apply "only [to] those arms in existence in the 18th century." "Just as the First Amendment protects modern forms of communications, and the Fourth Amendment applies to modern forms of search, the Second Amendment extends, prima facie, to all instruments that constitute bearable arms, even those that were not in existence at the time of the founding." Thus, even though the Second Amendment's definition of "arms" is fixed according to its historical understanding, that general definition covers modern instruments that facilitate armed self-defense.

Much like we use history to determine which modern "arms" are protected by the Second Amendment, so too does history guide our consideration of modern regulations that were unimaginable at the founding. When confronting such present-day firearm regulations, this historical inquiry that courts must conduct will often involve reasoning by analogy—a commonplace task for any lawyer or judge. Like all analogical reasoning, determining whether a historical regulation is a proper analogue for a distinctly modern firearm regulation requires a determination of whether the two regulations are "relevantly similar." C. Sunstein, On Analogical Reasoning, 106 Harv. L. Rev. 741, 773 (1993). And because "[e]verything is similar in infinite ways to everything else," *id.,* at 774, one needs "some metric enabling the analogizer to assess which similarities are important and which are not," F. Schauer & B. Spellman, Analogy, Expertise, and Experience, 84 U. Chi. L. Rev. 249, 254 (2017). For instance, a green truck and a green hat are relevantly similar if one's metric is "things that are green." See *ibid.* They are not relevantly similar if the applicable metric is "things you can wear."

While we do not now provide an exhaustive survey of the features that render regulations relevantly similar under the Second Amendment, we do think that *Heller* and *McDonald* point toward at least two metrics: how and why the regulations burden a law-abiding citizen's right to armed self-defense. As we stated in *Heller* and repeated in *McDonald,* "individual self-defense is 'the *central component*' of the Second Amendment right." Therefore, whether modern and historical regulations impose a comparable burden on the right of armed self-defense and whether that burden is comparably justified are " '*central*' " considerations when engaging in an analogical inquiry.

To be clear, analogical reasoning under the Second Amendment is neither a regulatory straightjacket nor a regulatory blank check.* * *[E]ven if a modern-day regulation is not a dead ringer for historical precursors, it still may be analogous enough to pass constitutional muster.

Consider, for example, *Heller*'s discussion of "longstanding" "laws forbidding the carrying of firearms in sensitive places such as schools and government buildings." Although the historical record yields relatively few 18th- and 19th-century "sensitive places" where weapons were altogether prohibited—*e.g.,* legislative assemblies, polling places, and courthouses—we are also aware of no disputes regarding the lawfulness of such prohibitions. We therefore can assume it settled that these locations were "sensitive places" where arms carrying could be prohibited consistent with the Second Amendment. And courts can use analogies to those historical regulations of "sensitive places" to determine that modern regulations prohibiting the carry of firearms in *new* and analogous sensitive places are constitutionally permissible.

Although we have no occasion to comprehensively define "sensitive places" in this case, we do think respondents err in their attempt to characterize New York's proper-cause requirement as a "sensitive-place" law. In their view, "sensitive places" where the government may lawfully disarm law-abiding citizens include all "places where people typically congregate and where law-enforcement and other public-safety professionals are presumptively available." Brief for Respondents 34. It is true that people sometimes congregate in "sensitive places," and it is likewise true that law enforcement professionals are usually presumptively available in those locations. But expanding the category of "sensitive places" simply to all places of public congregation that are not isolated from law enforcement defines the category of "sensitive places" far too broadly. Respondents' argument would in effect exempt cities from the Second Amendment and would eviscerate the general right to publicly carry arms for self-defense that we discuss in detail below. Put simply, there is no historical basis for New York to effectively declare the island of Manhattan a "sensitive place" simply because it is crowded and protected generally by the New York City Police Department.

[The Court then embarked on a lengthy historical discussion of "the Anglo-American history of public carry," ultimately concluding "that respondents have not met their burden to identify an American tradition justifying the State's proper-cause requirement. The Second Amendment guaranteed to 'all Americans' the right to bear commonly used arms in public subject to certain reasonable, well-defined restrictions. Those restrictions, for example, limited the intent for which one could carry arms, the manner by which one carried arms, or the exceptional circumstances under which one could not carry arms, such as before justices of the peace and other government officials. Apart from a few late-19th-century outlier jurisdictions, American governments simply have not broadly prohibited the public carry of commonly used firearms for personal defense. Nor, subject to a few late-in-time outliers, have American governments required law-abiding, responsible citizens to 'demonstrate a special need for self-protection distinguishable from that of the general community' in order to carry arms in public."]

[Concurring opinions by JUSTICE ALITO, JUSTICE KAVANAGH and JUSTICE BARRETT are omitted].

JUSTICE BREYER, with whom JUSTICE SOTOMAYOR and JUSTICE KAGAN join, dissenting.

In 2020, 45,222 Americans were killed by firearms. See Centers for Disease Control and Prevention, Fast Facts: Firearm Violence Prevention (last updated May 4, 2022) (CDC, Fast Facts), https://www.cdc.gov/ violenceprevention/firearms/fastfact.html. Since the start of this year (2022), there have been 277 reported mass shootings—an average of more than one per day. See Gun Violence Archive (last visited June 20, 2022), https://www.gunviolencearchive.org. Gun violence has now surpassed motor vehicle crashes as the leading cause of death among children and adolescents. J. Goldstick, R. Cunningham, & P. Carter, Current Causes of Death in Children and Adolescents in the United States, 386 New England J. Med. 1955 (May 19, 2022) (Goldstick).

Many States have tried to address some of the dangers of gun violence just described by passing laws that limit, in various ways, who may purchase, carry, or use firearms of different kinds. The Court today severely burdens States' efforts to do so. It invokes the Second Amendment to strike down a New York law regulating the public carriage of concealed handguns. In my view, that decision rests upon several serious mistakes.

First, the Court decides this case on the basis of the pleadings, without the benefit of discovery or an evidentiary record. As a result, it may well rest its decision on a mistaken understanding of how New York's law operates in practice. Second, the Court wrongly limits its analysis to focus nearly exclusively on history. It refuses to consider the government interests that justify a challenged gun regulation, regardless of how compelling those interests may be. The Constitution contains no such limitation, and neither do our precedents. Third, the Court itself demonstrates the practical problems with its history-only approach. In applying that approach to New York's law, the Court fails to correctly identify and analyze the relevant historical facts. Only by ignoring an abundance of historical evidence supporting regulations restricting the public carriage of firearms can the Court conclude that New York's law is not "consistent with the Nation's historical tradition of firearm regulation." See *ante*, at ___.

In my view, when courts interpret the Second Amendment, it is constitutionally proper, indeed often necessary, for them to consider the serious dangers and consequences of gun violence that lead States to regulate firearms. The Second Circuit has done so and has held that New York's law does not violate the Second Amendment. See *Kachalsky v. County of Westchester*, 701 F.3d 81, 97–99, 101 (2012).* * *

[The dissent then traced at length the rise and extent of gun violence in the United States and noted the uniqueness of America in this regard].

Justice ALITO asks why I have begun my opinion by reviewing some of the dangers and challenges posed by gun violence and what relevance that has to today's case. All of the above considerations illustrate that the question of firearm regulation presents a complex problem—one that should be solved by legislatures rather than courts. What kinds of firearm regulations should a State adopt? Different States might choose to answer that question differently. They may face different challenges because of their different geographic and demographic compositions. A State like New York, which must account for the roughly 8.5 million people living in the 303 square miles of New York City, might choose to adopt different (and stricter) firearms regulations than States like Montana or Wyoming, which do not contain any city remotely comparable in terms of population or density. See U.S. Census Bureau, Quick Facts: New York City (last updated July 1, 2021) (Quick Facts: New York City), https://www.census.gov/quickfacts/newyorkcitynewyork/; Brief for City of New York as *Amicus Curiae* 8, 22. For a variety of reasons, States may also be willing to tolerate different degrees of risk and therefore choose to balance the competing benefits and dangers of firearms differently.

The question presented in this case concerns the extent to which the Second Amendment restricts different States (and the Federal Government) from working out solutions to these problems through democratic processes. The primary difference between the Court's view and mine is that I believe the Amendment allows States to take account of the serious problems posed by gun violence that I have just described. I fear that the Court's interpretation ignores these significant dangers and leaves States without the ability to address them.* * *

The Court's near-exclusive reliance on history is not only unnecessary, it is deeply impractical. It imposes a task on the lower courts that judges cannot easily accomplish. Judges understand well how to weigh a law's objectives (its "ends") against the methods used to achieve those objectives (its "means"). Judges are far less accustomed to resolving difficult historical questions. Courts are, after all, staffed by lawyers, not historians. Legal experts typically have little experience answering contested historical questions or applying those answers to resolve contemporary problems.

The Court's insistence that judges and lawyers rely nearly exclusively on history to interpret the Second Amendment thus raises a host of troubling questions. Consider, for example, the following. Do lower courts have the research resources necessary to conduct exhaustive historical analyses in every Second Amendment case? What historical regulations and decisions qualify as representative analogues to modern laws? How will judges determine which historians have the better view of close historical questions? Will the meaning of the Second Amendment change if or when new historical evidence becomes available? And, most importantly, will the Court's approach permit judges to reach the outcomes they prefer and then cloak those outcomes in the language of history? See S. Cornell, *Heller*, New Originalism, and Law Office History: "Meet the New Boss, Same as the Old Boss," 56 UCLA L. Rev. 1095, 1098 (2009) (describing "law office history" as "a results oriented methodology in which evidence is selectively gathered and interpreted to produce a preordained conclusion").* * *

[After an extended critique of the idea that only historical sources should be relevant to Second Amendment questions, the dissent offered its own detailed history and reached the opposite conclusion to the majority.] The historical examples of regulations similar to New York's licensing regime are legion. Closely analogous English laws were enacted beginning in the 13th century, and similar American regulations were passed during the colonial period, the founding era, the 19th century, and the 20th century. Not all of these laws were identical to New York's, but that is inevitable in an analysis that demands examination of seven centuries of history. At a minimum, the laws I have recounted *resembled* New York's law, similarly restricting the right to publicly carry weapons and serving roughly similar purposes. That is all that the Court's test, which allows and even encourages "analogical reasoning," purports to require. See *ante,* at ___ (disclaiming the necessity of a "historical *twin*").

In each instance, the Court finds a reason to discount the historical evidence's persuasive force. Some of the laws New York has identified are too old. But others are too recent. Still others did not last long enough. Some applied to too few people. Some were enacted for the wrong reasons. Some may have been based on a constitutional rationale that is now impossible to identify. Some arose in historically unique circumstances. And some are not sufficiently analogous to the licensing regime at issue here. But if the examples discussed above, taken together, do not show a tradition and history of regulation that supports the validity of New York's law, what could? Sadly, I do not know the answer to that question. What is worse, the Court appears to have no answer either.

We are bound by *Heller* insofar as *Heller* interpreted the Second Amendment to protect an individual right to possess a firearm for self-defense. But *Heller* recognized that that right was not without limits and could appropriately be subject to government regulation. *Heller* therefore does not require holding that New York's law violates the Second Amendment. In so holding, the Court goes beyond *Heller*.

It bases its decision to strike down New York's law almost exclusively on its application of what it calls historical "analogical reasoning." As I have admitted above, I am not a historian, and neither is the Court. But the history, as it appears to me, seems to establish a robust tradition of regulations restricting the public carriage of concealed firearms. To the extent that any uncertainty remains between the Court's view of the history and mine, that uncertainty counsels against relying on history alone. In my view, it is appropriate in such circumstances to look beyond the history and engage in what the Court calls means-end scrutiny. Courts must be permitted to consider the State's interest in preventing gun violence, the effectiveness of the contested law in achieving that interest, the degree to which the law burdens the Second Amendment right, and, if appropriate, any less restrictive alternatives.* * *

New York's Legislature considered the empirical evidence about gun violence and adopted a reasonable licensing law to regulate the concealed carriage of handguns in order to keep the people of New York safe. The Court today strikes down that law based only on the pleadings. It gives the State no opportunity to present evidence justifying its reasons for adopting the law or showing how the law actually operates in practice, and it does not so much as acknowledge these important considerations. Because I cannot agree with the Court's decision to strike New York's law down without allowing for discovery or the development of any evidentiary record, without considering the State's compelling interest in preventing gun violence and protecting the safety of its citizens, and without considering the potentially deadly consequences of its decision, I respectfully dissent.

NOTES

1.   *Jettisoning Means-End Scrutiny?* Given the ubiquity of means-end scrutiny in post-*Heller* and post-*McDonald* cases in the lower courts, is it surprising that *Bruen* categorically rejected that approach? Is Justice Breyer correct that judges are better suited to that sort of analysis than to the historical inquiry *Bruen* prescribes? Is he correct that means-end scrutiny is especially appropriate to assess gun regulation?

2.   *Implications for Other Fourteenth Amendment Doctrines.* Might the rejection of means-end scrutiny spread to other areas? Justice Thomas, for example, has long been critical of the tiers of scrutiny in equal protection. Might we see the Court eschew that doctrine in favor a purely historical approach to the equal protection clause? How would you assess such a possibility?

3. *Permissible State Regulation of Guns.* Justice Thomas distinguishes between "may issue" laws like New York's (also in place in a handful of other states) and "shall issue" laws (in place in 43 states), reasoning that the former give too much discretion to governmental decisionmakers. In a concurrence joined by the Chief Justice, Justice Kavanaugh placed special emphasis on the permissibility of "shall issue" regulation. His opinion also repeated language from *Heller* and *McDonald* affirming the continued viability of "longstanding prohibitions on the possession of firearms by felons and the mentally ill, or laws forbidding the carrying of firearms in sensitive places such as schools and government buildings, or laws imposing conditions and qualifications on the commercial sale of arms." What will qualify as a "sensitive place?" Is it clear that the historical methodology laid out by Justice Thomas will necessarily result in a favorable ruling on the constitutionality of such "longstanding" laws, some of which might post-date the Second or Fourteenth Amendment? Is it clear under *Bruen* whether the relevant date for the inquiry would be 1791 (when the former was adopted) or 1868 (when the latter was)?

SECTION 3. EQUAL PROTECTION AND "FUNDAMENTAL INTERESTS"

A. VOTING

Page 538. Add at the end of the Note on Political Gerrymandering:

In its opinion in Rucho v. Common Cause, 139 S.Ct. 2484 (2019) (covered in Chapter 9 of this Supplement), the Court ended the years of uncertainty and ruled that partisan gerrymandering claims are non-justiciable political questions.

C. THE RIGHT TO TRAVEL

Page 567. Insert after Note 2:

3. One consequence of the Court's decision in *Dobbs v. Jackson Women's Health Org.* (excerpted below) may be renewed attention to the right to travel in connection with interstate variability in access to abortion. In that case, Justice Kavanaugh said in his concurrence that he thought the "right to interstate travel" would bar a state from enacting a law barring "a resident of that State from traveling to another State to obtain an abortion." As you will see, the dissent was less sure this would be the case, and stressed the potential complexity of the issue. Indeed, a state law preventing interstate travel for the purpose of obtaining an abortion could potentially involve not only the right to travel, but questions about the extraterritorial reach of a state's criminal laws. For an analysis of the range of issues that would be posed by state anti-abortion laws of this kind, see David Cohen, Greer Donley & Rachel Rebouché, *The New Abortion Battleground*, 123 COLUM. L. REV. (forthcoming 2023), https://papers.ssrn.com/sol3/papers.cfm?abstract_id=4032931.

SECTION 4. FUNDAMENTAL PRIVACY RIGHTS

B. ABORTION

Page 639. Add after the Notes on Whole Woman's Health v. Hellerstedt:

June Medical Services v. Russo

140 S.Ct. 2103 (2020)

In 2014, Louisiana passed Act 620, which required physicians performing abortions to secure admitting privileges at a hospital within 30 miles of the clinic at which abortions are performed. Violations of the Act subjected physicians and clinics to various penalties. The Louisiana requirement bore obvious similarities to the Texas admitting privileges requirement struck down in *Whole Woman's Health v. Hellerstedt*. Indeed, in a plurality opinion striking down the Louisiana law, Justice Breyer characterized it as "almost word-for-word identical" to the Texas law.

In striking down the law, the plurality employed the balancing approach adopted in *Whole Woman's Health* and relied on extensive factual findings made by the District Court supporting the conclusion that the law imposed substantial burdens while offering no benefits to women. The Fifth Circuit had attempted to distinguish the Louisiana law from its Texas counterpart, arguing that it provided some "minimal benefit" to women through a credentialing function; and that the burdens of the law were not substantial because the affected doctors could have done more to secure privileges and any clinic closures that might result would not cause the capacity problems at issue in Texas.

Justice Breyer's plurality opinion was a fairly straightforward application of *Whole Woman's Health*. And the dissenting justices rehearsed familiar objections to abortion doctrine. Perhaps most surprising was the vote of Chief Justice Roberts. The Chief Justice had never before voted to strike down a restriction on abortion. Indeed, he noted that he had "joined the dissent in *Whole Woman's Health* and continue[d] to believe that the case was wrongly decided." Nevertheless, he said, the question in *June Medical* "is not whether *Whole Woman's Health* was right or wrong, but whether to adhere to it in deciding the present case." His concurring opinion offered an extended ode to *stare decisis*, arguing that "fidelity to precedent" is necessary to " 'keep the scale of justice even and steady, and not liable to waver with every new judge's opinion,' " and is an important part of what "distinguishes the judicial 'method and philosophy from those of the political and legislative process.' " (quoting Jackson, *Decisional Law and Stare Decisis*, 30 A. B. A. J. 334 (1944)).

Although the Chief Justice vigorously underscored the importance of precedent, much of his concurrence went on, paradoxically, to challenge key parts of the very decision to which he professed the duty of fealty. Roberts expressly rejected the idea that application of *Casey* requires judges to balance benefits against burdens. He argued that "nothing about *Casey* suggested that a weighing of costs and benefits of an abortion regulation was a job for the courts," and that, properly understood, *Casey* instead focuses on "the existence of a substantial obstacle, the sort of inquiry familiar to judges across a variety of contexts."

Two years after *June Medical*, the Court radically altered the constitutional law of abortion with the following decision, which seems destined to become one of the most controversial in the Court's history.

DOBBS V. JACKSON WOMEN'S HEALTH ORG.
___ U.S. ___, 142 S.Ct. 2228, ___ L.Ed.2d ___ (2022)

JUSTICE ALITO delivered the opinion of the Court.

Abortion presents a profound moral issue on which Americans hold sharply conflicting views. Some believe fervently that a human person comes into being at conception and that abortion ends an innocent life. Others feel just as strongly that any regulation of abortion invades a woman's right to control her own body and prevents women from achieving full equality. Still others in a third group think that abortion should be allowed under some but not all circumstances, and those within this group hold a variety of views about the particular restrictions that should be imposed.

For the first 185 years after the adoption of the Constitution, each State was permitted to address this issue in accordance with the views of its citizens. Then, in 1973, this Court decided *Roe v. Wade*. Even though the Constitution makes no mention of abortion, the Court held that it confers a broad right to obtain one.* * *

Eventually, in *Planned Parenthood of Southeastern Pa. v. Casey*, the Court revisited *Roe*, but the Members of the Court split three ways. Two Justices expressed no desire to change *Roe* in any way. Four others wanted to overrule the decision in its entirety. And the three remaining Justices, who jointly signed the controlling opinion, took a third position. Their opinion did not endorse *Roe*'s reasoning, and it even hinted that one or more of its authors might have "reservations" about whether the Constitution protects a right to abortion. But the opinion concluded that *stare decisis*, which calls for prior decisions to be followed in most instances, required adherence to what it called *Roe*'s "central holding"—that a State may not constitutionally protect fetal life before "viability"—even if that holding was wrong. Anything less, the opinion claimed, would undermine respect for this Court and the rule of law.

Paradoxically, the judgment in *Casey* did a fair amount of overruling. Several important abortion decisions were overruled *in toto*, and *Roe* itself was overruled in part. *Casey* threw out *Roe*'s trimester scheme and substituted a new rule of uncertain origin under which States were forbidden to adopt any regulation that imposed an "undue burden" on a woman's right to have an abortion. The decision provided no clear guidance about the difference between a "due" and an "undue" burden. But the three Justices who authored the controlling opinion "call[ed] the contending sides of a national controversy to end their national division" by treating the Court's decision as the final settlement of the question of the constitutional right to abortion.

As has become increasingly apparent in the intervening years, *Casey* did not achieve that goal. Americans continue to hold passionate and widely divergent views on abortion, and state legislatures have acted accordingly. Some have recently enacted laws allowing abortion, with few restrictions, at all stages of pregnancy. Others have tightly restricted abortion beginning well before viability. And in this case, 26 States have expressly asked this Court to overrule *Roe* and *Casey* and allow the States to regulate or prohibit pre-viability abortions.* * *

We hold that *Roe* and *Casey* must be overruled. The Constitution makes no reference to abortion, and no such right is implicitly protected by any constitutional provision, including the one on which the defenders of *Roe* and *Casey* now chiefly rely—the Due Process Clause of the Fourteenth Amendment.* * *

I

The law at issue in this case, Mississippi's Gestational Age Act, see Miss. Code Ann. § 41–41–191 (2018), contains this central provision: "Except in a medical emergency or in the case of a severe fetal abnormality, a person shall not intentionally or knowingly perform . . . or induce an abortion of an unborn human being if the probable gestational age of the unborn human being has been determined to be greater than fifteen (15) weeks." § 4(b).

To support this Act, the legislature made a series of factual findings. It began by noting that, at the time of enactment, only six countries besides the United States "permit[ted] nontherapeutic or elective abortion-on-demand after the twentieth week of gestation." § 2(a). The legislature then found that at 5 or 6 weeks' gestational age an "unborn human being's heart begins beating"; at 8 weeks the "unborn human being begins to move about in the womb"; at 9 weeks "all basic physiological functions are present"; at 10 weeks "vital organs begin to function," and "[h]air, fingernails, and toenails . . . begin to form"; at 11 weeks "an unborn human being's diaphragm is developing," and he or she may "move about freely in the womb"; and at 12 weeks the "unborn human being" has "taken on 'the human form' in all relevant respects." § 2(b)(i) (quoting *Gonzales v. Carhart*). It found that most abortions after 15 weeks employ "dilation and evacuation procedures which involve the use of surgical instruments to crush and tear the unborn child," and it concluded that the "intentional commitment of such acts for nontherapeutic or elective reasons is a barbaric practice, dangerous for the maternal patient, and demeaning to the medical profession." § 2(b)(i)(8).

Respondents are an abortion clinic, Jackson Women's Health Organization, and one of its doctors. On the day the Gestational Age Act was enacted, respondents filed suit in Federal District Court against various Mississippi officials, alleging that the Act violated this Court's precedents establishing a constitutional right to abortion. The District Court granted summary judgment in favor of respondents and permanently enjoined enforcement of the Act, reasoning that "viability marks the earliest point at which the State's interest in fetal life is constitutionally adequate to justify a legislative ban on nontherapeutic abortions" and that 15 weeks' gestational age is "prior to viability." The Fifth Circuit affirmed. 945 F. 3d 265 (2019).

We granted certiorari, to resolve the question whether "all pre-viability prohibitions on elective abortions are unconstitutional," Petitioners' primary defense of the Mississippi Gestational Age Act is that *Roe* and *Casey* were wrongly decided and that "the Act is constitutional because it satisfies rational-basis review." Respondents answer that allowing Mississippi to ban pre-viability abortions "would be no different than overruling *Casey* and *Roe* entirely." They tell us that "no half-measures" are available: We must either reaffirm or overrule *Roe* and *Casey*.

II

* * *

Constitutional analysis must begin with "the language of the instrument," *Gibbons v. Ogden*, which offers a "fixed standard" for ascertaining what our founding document means, 1 J. Story, Commentaries on the Constitution of the United States § 399, p. 383 (1833). The Constitution makes no express reference to a right to obtain an abortion, and therefore those who claim that it protects such a right must show that the right is somehow implicit in the constitutional text.

Roe, however, was remarkably loose in its treatment of the constitutional text. It held that the abortion right, which is not mentioned in the Constitution, is part of a right to privacy, which is also not mentioned. And that privacy right, *Roe* observed, had been found to spring from no fewer than five different constitutional provisions—the First, Fourth, Fifth, Ninth, and Fourteenth Amendments.

The Court's discussion left open at least three ways in which some combination of these provisions could protect the abortion right. One possibility was that the right was "founded . . . in the Ninth Amendment's reservation of rights to the people." Another was that the right was rooted in the First, Fourth, or Fifth Amendment, or in some combination of those provisions, and that this right had been "incorporated" into the Due Process Clause of the Fourteenth Amendment just as many other Bill of Rights provisions had by then been incorporated. And a third path was that the First, Fourth, and Fifth Amendments played no role and that the right was simply a component of the "liberty" protected by the Fourteenth Amendment's Due Process Clause. *Roe.* *Roe* expressed the "feel[ing]" that the Fourteenth Amendment was the provision that did the work, but its message seemed to be that the abortion right could be found *somewhere* in the Constitution and that specifying its exact location was not of paramount importance. The *Casey* Court did not defend this unfocused analysis and instead grounded its decision solely on the theory that the right to obtain an abortion is part of the "liberty" protected by the Fourteenth Amendment's Due Process Clause.

We discuss this theory in depth below, but before doing so, we briefly address one additional constitutional provision that some of respondents' *amici* have now offered as yet another potential home for the abortion right: the Fourteenth Amendment's Equal Protection Clause. Neither *Roe* nor *Casey* saw fit to invoke this theory, and it is squarely foreclosed by our precedents, which establish that a State's regulation of abortion is not a sex-based classification and is thus not subject to the "heightened scrutiny" that applies to such classifications. The regulation of a medical procedure that only one sex can undergo does not trigger heightened constitutional scrutiny unless the regulation is a "mere pretex[t] designed to effect an invidious discrimination against members of one sex or the other." *Geduldig v. Aiello.* And as the Court has stated, the "goal of preventing abortion" does not constitute "invidiously discriminatory animus" against women. *Bray v. Alexandria Women's Health Clinic.* Accordingly, laws regulating or prohibiting abortion are not subject to heightened scrutiny. Rather, they are governed by the same standard of review as other health and safety measures.* * *

The underlying theory on which this argument rests—that the Fourteenth Amendment's Due Process Clause provides substantive, as well as procedural, protection for "liberty"—has long been controversial. But our decisions have held that the Due Process Clause protects two categories of substantive rights.

The first consists of rights guaranteed by the first eight Amendments. * * *The second category—which is the one in question here—comprises a select list of fundamental rights that are not mentioned anywhere in the Constitution.

In deciding whether a right falls into either of these categories, the Court has long asked whether the right is "deeply rooted in [our] history and tradition" and whether it is essential to our Nation's "scheme of ordered liberty." And in conducting this inquiry, we have engaged in a careful analysis of the history of the right at issue. [The court summarized the historical analysis used in recent decisions incorporating the excessive fines clause of the Eighth Amendment in *Timbs* and the Second Amendment in *McDonald*].

Timbs and *McDonald* concerned the question whether the Fourteenth Amendment protects rights that are expressly set out in the *Bill of Rights*, and it would be anomalous if similar historical support were not required when a putative right is not mentioned anywhere in the Constitution. Thus, in *Glucksberg*, which held that the Due Process Clause does not confer a right to assisted suicide, the Court surveyed more than 700 years of "Anglo-American common law tradition," and made clear that a fundamental right must be "objectively, deeply rooted in this Nation's history and tradition."

Historical inquiries of this nature are essential whenever we are asked to recognize a new component of the "liberty" protected by the Due Process Clause because the term "liberty" alone provides little guidance. "Liberty" is a capacious term. As Lincoln once said: "We all declare for Liberty; but in using the same word we do not all mean the same thing." * * *

"Substantive due process has at times been a treacherous field for this Court," and it has sometimes led the Court to usurp authority that the Constitution entrusts to the people's elected representatives. As the Court cautioned in *Glucksberg*, "[w]e must . . . exercise the utmost care whenever we are asked to break new ground in this field, lest the liberty protected by the Due Process Clause be subtly transformed into the policy preferences of the Members of this Court."

On occasion, when the Court has ignored the "[a]ppropriate limits" imposed by " 'respect for the teachings of history,' " it has fallen into the freewheeling judicial policymaking that characterized discredited decisions such as *Lochner v. New York*. The Court must not fall prey to such an unprincipled approach. Instead, guided by the history and tradition that map the essential components of our Nation's concept of ordered liberty, we must ask what the Fourteenth Amendment means by the term "liberty." When we engage in that inquiry in the present case, the clear answer is that the Fourteenth Amendment does not protect the right to an abortion.

Until the latter part of the 20th century, there was no support in American law for a constitutional right to obtain an abortion. No state constitutional provision had recognized such a right. Until a few years before *Roe* was handed down, no federal or state court had recognized such a right. Nor had any scholarly treatise of which we are aware. And although law review articles are not reticent about advocating new rights, the earliest article proposing a constitutional right to abortion that has come to our attention was published only a few years before *Roe*.

Not only was there no support for such a constitutional right until shortly before *Roe*, but abortion had long been a *crime* in every single State. At common law, abortion was criminal in at least some stages of pregnancy and was regarded as unlawful and could have very serious consequences at all stages. American law followed the common law until a wave of statutory restrictions in the 1800s expanded criminal liability for abortions. By the time of the adoption of the Fourteenth Amendment, three-quarters of the States had made abortion a crime at any stage of pregnancy, and the remaining States would soon follow.

Roe either ignored or misstated this history, and *Casey* declined to reconsider *Roe*'s faulty historical analysis. It is therefore important to set the record straight.

We begin with the common law, under which abortion was a crime at least after "quickening"—*i.e.*, the first felt movement of the fetus in the womb, which usually occurs between the 16th and 18th week of pregnancy.

The "eminent common-law authorities (Blackstone, Coke, Hale, and the like)," *all* describe abortion after quickening as criminal. [The court discussed multiple treatises, as well as English common law].* * *

In sum, although common-law authorities differed on the severity of punishment for abortions committed at different points in pregnancy, none endorsed the practice. Moreover, we are aware of no common-law case or authority, and the parties have not pointed to any, that remotely suggests a positive *right* to procure an abortion at any stage of pregnancy.

In this country, the historical record is similar. [The court traced seventeenth- and eighteenth-century sources that regarded abortion as a crime].* * *

In this country during the 19th century, the vast majority of the States enacted statutes criminalizing abortion at all stages of pregnancy. [The court cited to an appendix that it attached to the majority opinion listing state statutory provisions in chronological order). By 1868, the year when the Fourteenth Amendment was ratified, three-quarters of the States, 28 out of 37, had enacted statutes making abortion a crime even if it was performed before quickening. Of the nine States that had not yet criminalized abortion at all stages, all but one did so by 1910.

[The court noted a similar trend in the Territories that would later become states].* * *

This overwhelming consensus endured until the day *Roe* was decided. At that time, also by the *Roe* Court's own count, a substantial majority—

30 States—still prohibited abortion at all stages except to save the life of the mother. And though *Roe* discerned a "trend toward liberalization" in about "one-third of the States," those States still criminalized some abortions and regulated them more stringently than *Roe* would allow. In short, the "Court's opinion in *Roe* itself convincingly refutes the notion that the abortion liberty is deeply rooted in the history or tradition of our people."

The inescapable conclusion is that a right to abortion is not deeply rooted in the Nation's history and traditions. On the contrary, an unbroken tradition of prohibiting abortion on pain of criminal punishment persisted from the earliest days of the common law until 1973.* * *

[The Solicitor General] suggests that history supports an abortion right because the common law's failure to criminalize abortion before quickening means that "at the Founding and for decades thereafter, women generally could terminate a pregnancy, at least in its early stages." But the insistence on quickening was not universal. . .When legislatures began to exercise that authority as the century wore on, no one, as far as we are aware, argued that the laws they enacted violated a fundamental right. That is not surprising since common-law authorities had repeatedly condemned abortion and described it as an "unlawful" act without regard to whether it occurred before or after quickening.* * *

Instead of seriously pressing the argument that the abortion right itself has deep roots, supporters of *Roe* and *Casey* contend that the abortion right is an integral part of a broader entrenched right. *Roe* termed this a right to privacy, and *Casey* described it as the freedom to make "intimate and personal choices" that are "central to personal dignity and autonomy." *Casey* elaborated: "At the heart of liberty is the right to define one's own concept of existence, of meaning, of the universe, and of the mystery of human life."

The Court did not claim that this broadly framed right is absolute, and no such claim would be plausible. While individuals are certainly free *to think* and *to say* what they wish about "existence," "meaning," the "universe," and "the mystery of human life," they are not always free *to act* in accordance with those thoughts. License to act on the basis of such beliefs may correspond to one of the many understandings of "liberty," but it is certainly not "ordered liberty."

Ordered liberty sets limits and defines the boundary between competing interests. *Roe* and *Casey* each struck a particular balance between the interests of a woman who wants an abortion and the interests of what they termed "potential life." But the people of the various States may evaluate those interests differently. In some States, voters may believe that the abortion right should be even more extensive than the right that *Roe* and *Casey* recognized. Voters in other States may wish to impose tight restrictions based on their belief that abortion destroys an "unborn human being." Miss. Code Ann. § 41–41–191(4)(b). Our Nation's historical understanding of ordered liberty does not prevent the people's elected representatives from deciding how abortion should be regulated.

Nor does the right to obtain an abortion have a sound basis in precedent. *Casey* relied on cases involving the right to marry a person of a different race, *Loving v. Virginia*; the right to marry while in prison, *Turner v. Safley*; the right to obtain contraceptives, *Griswold v. Connecticut*; *Eisenstadt v. Baird, Carey v. Population Services*; the right to reside with relatives, *Moore v. East Cleveland*; the right to make decisions about the education of one's children, *Pierce v. Society of Sisters*; *Meyer v. Nebraska*; the right not to be sterilized without consent, *Skinner v. Oklahoma ex rel. Williamson;* and the right in certain circumstances not to undergo involuntary surgery, forced administration of drugs, or other substantially similar procedures, *Winston v. Lee; Washington v. Harper; Rochin v. California*. Respondents and the Solicitor General also rely on post-*Casey* decisions like *Lawrence v. Texas* (right to engage in private, consensual sexual acts) and *Obergefell v. Hodges* (right to marry a person of the same sex).

These attempts to justify abortion through appeals to a broader right to autonomy and to define one's "concept of existence" prove too much. Those criteria, at a high level of generality, could license fundamental rights to illicit drug use, prostitution, and the like. None of these rights has any claim to being deeply rooted in history.

What sharply distinguishes the abortion right from the rights recognized in the cases on which *Roe* and *Casey* rely is something that both those decisions acknowledged: Abortion destroys what those decisions call "potential life" and what the law at issue in this case regards as the life of an "unborn human being." None of the other decisions cited by *Roe* and *Casey* involved the critical moral question posed by abortion. They are therefore inapposite. They do not support the right to obtain an abortion, and by the same token, our conclusion that the Constitution does not confer such a right does not undermine them in any way.* * *

Because the dissent cannot argue that the abortion right is rooted in this Nation's history and tradition, it contends that the "constitutional tradition" is "not captured whole at a single moment," and that its "meaning gains content from the long sweep of our history and from successive judicial precedents." This vague formulation imposes no clear restraints on what Justice White called the "exercise of raw judicial power," and while the dissent claims that its standard "does not mean anything goes," any real restraints are hard to discern.* * *

The most striking feature of the dissent is the absence of any serious discussion of the legitimacy of the States' interest in protecting fetal life.

This is evident in the analogy that the dissent draws between the abortion right and the rights recognized in *Griswold* (contraception), *Eisenstadt* (same), *Lawrence* (sexual conduct with member of the same sex), and *Obergefell* (same-sex marriage). Perhaps this is designed to stoke unfounded fear that our decision will imperil those other rights, but the dissent's analogy is objectionable for a more important reason: what it reveals about the dissent's views on the protection of what *Roe* called "potential life."* * *

That view is evident throughout the dissent. The dissent has much to say about the effects of pregnancy on women, the burdens of motherhood, and the difficulties faced by poor women. These are important concerns. However, the dissent evinces no similar regard for a State's interest in protecting prenatal life. The dissent repeatedly praises the "balance" that the viability line strikes between a woman's liberty interest and the State's interest in prenatal life. But for reasons we discuss later, and given in the opinion of THE CHIEF JUSTICE, the viability line makes no sense. It was not adequately justified in *Roe*, and the dissent does not even try to defend it today. Nor does it identify any other point in a pregnancy after which a State is permitted to prohibit the destruction of a fetus.

Our opinion is not based on any view about if and when prenatal life is entitled to any of the rights enjoyed after birth. The dissent, by contrast, would impose on the people a particular theory about when the rights of personhood begin. According to the dissent, the Constitution *requires* the States to regard a fetus as lacking even the most basic human right—to live—at least until an arbitrary point in a pregnancy has passed. Nothing in the Constitution or in our Nation's legal traditions authorizes the Court to adopt that " 'theory of life.' "

III

We next consider whether the doctrine of *stare decisis* counsels continued acceptance of *Roe* and *Casey*. *Stare decisis* plays an important role in our case law, and we have explained that it serves many valuable ends. It protects the interests of those who have taken action in reliance on a past decision. It "reduces incentives for challenging settled precedents, saving parties and courts the expense of endless relitigation." It fosters "evenhanded" decisionmaking by requiring that like cases be decided in a like manner. It "contributes to the actual and perceived integrity of the judicial process." And it restrains judicial hubris and reminds us to respect the judgment of those who have grappled with important questions in the past.* * *

We have long recognized, however, that *stare decisis* is "not an inexorable command," and it "is at its weakest when we interpret the Constitution." * * *[W]hen one of our constitutional decisions goes astray, the country is usually stuck with the bad decision unless we correct our own mistake. An erroneous constitutional decision can be fixed by amending the Constitution, but our Constitution is notoriously hard to amend. See Art. V. Therefore, in appropriate circumstances we must be willing to reconsider and, if necessary, overrule constitutional decisions.

Some of our most important constitutional decisions have overruled prior precedents. We mention three. In *Brown v. Board of Education,* the Court repudiated the "separate but equal" doctrine, which had allowed States to maintain racially segregated schools and other facilities. In so doing, the Court overruled the infamous decision in *Plessy v. Ferguson* (1896), along with six other Supreme Court precedents that had applied the separate-but-equal rule.

In *West Coast Hotel Co. v. Parrish* (1937), the Court overruled *Adkins v. Children's Hosp.* (1923), which had held that a law setting minimum wages for women violated the "liberty" protected by the Fifth Amendment's Due Process Clause. *West Coast Hotel* signaled the demise of an entire line of important precedents that had protected an individual liberty right against state and federal health and welfare legislation. See *Lochner v. New York.*

Finally, in *West Virginia Bd. of Ed. v. Barnette* (1943), after the lapse of only three years, the Court overruled *Minersville School Dist. v. Gobitis,* (1940), and held that public school students could not be compelled to salute the flag in violation of their sincere beliefs. *Barnette* stands out because nothing had changed during the intervening period other than the Court's belated recognition that its earlier decision had been seriously wrong.

On many other occasions, this Court has overruled important constitutional decisions. [The Court included a long list in a footnote]. Without these decisions, American constitutional law as we know it would be unrecognizable, and this would be a different country.* * *

In this case, five factors weigh strongly in favor of overruling *Roe* and *Casey*: the nature of their error, the quality of their reasoning, the "workability" of the rules they imposed on the country, their disruptive effect on other areas of the law, and the absence of concrete reliance.

The nature of the Court's error. An erroneous interpretation of the Constitution is always important, but some are more damaging than others.

The infamous decision in *Plessy v. Ferguson,* was one such decision. It betrayed our commitment to "equality before the law." It was "egregiously wrong" on the day it was decided.* * *

Roe was also egregiously wrong and deeply damaging. For reasons already explained, *Roe*'s constitutional analysis was far outside the bounds of any reasonable interpretation of the various constitutional provisions to which it vaguely pointed.* * *

The quality of the reasoning. Under our precedents, the quality of the reasoning in a prior case has an important bearing on whether it should be reconsidered.* * *

Roe found that the Constitution implicitly conferred a right to obtain an abortion, but it failed to ground its decision in text, history, or precedent. It relied on an erroneous historical narrative; it devoted great attention to and presumably relied on matters that have no bearing on the meaning of the Constitution; it disregarded the fundamental difference between the precedents on which it relied and the question before the Court; it concocted an elaborate set of rules, with different restrictions for each trimester of pregnancy, but it did not explain how this veritable code could be teased out of anything in the Constitution, the history of abortion laws, prior precedent, or any other cited source; and its most important rule (that States cannot protect fetal life prior to "viability") was never raised by any party and has never been plausibly explained. *Roe*'s reasoning quickly drew scathing scholarly criticism, even from supporters of broad access to abortion.* * *

Dividing pregnancy into three trimesters, the Court imposed special rules for each.* * *

Not only did this scheme resemble the work of a legislature, but the Court made little effort to explain how these rules could be deduced from any of the sources on which constitutional decisions are usually based.* * *

When *Casey* revisited *Roe* almost 20 years later, very little of *Roe*'s reasoning was defended or preserved.* * *

Workability. Our precedents counsel that another important consideration in deciding whether a precedent should be overruled is whether the rule it imposes is workable—that is, whether it can be understood and applied in a consistent and predictable manner. *Casey*'s "undue burden" test has scored poorly on the workability scale. [The Court proceeded to criticize multiple aspects of the undue burden test as indeterminate or uncertain, and argued that it had produced many Circuit conflicts].* * *

Effect on other areas of law. Roe and *Casey* have led to the distortion of many important but unrelated legal doctrines, and that effect provides further support for overruling those decisions.

Members of this Court have repeatedly lamented that "no legal rule or doctrine is safe from ad hoc nullification by this Court when an occasion for its application arises in a case involving state regulation of abortion."* * *

The Court's abortion cases have diluted the strict standard for facial constitutional challenges. They have ignored the Court's third-party standing doctrine. They have disregarded standard *res judicata* principles. They have flouted the ordinary rules on the severability of unconstitutional provisions, as well as the rule that statutes should be read where possible to avoid unconstitutionality. And they have distorted First Amendment doctrines.* * *

Reliance interests. We last consider whether overruling *Roe* and *Casey* will upend substantial reliance interests.

Traditional reliance interests arise "where advance planning of great precision is most obviously a necessity." In *Casey*, the controlling opinion conceded that those traditional reliance interests were not implicated because getting an abortion is generally "unplanned activity," and "reproductive planning could take virtually immediate account of any sudden restoration of state authority to ban abortions."* * *

Unable to find reliance in the conventional sense, the controlling opinion in *Casey* perceived a more intangible form of reliance. It wrote that "people [had] organized intimate relationships and made choices that define their views of themselves and their places in society . . . in reliance on the availability of abortion in the event that contraception should fail" and that "[t]he ability of women to participate equally in the economic and social life of the Nation has been facilitated by their ability to control their reproductive lives." But this Court is ill-equipped to assess "generalized assertions about the national psyche." *Casey*'s notion of reliance thus finds little support in our cases, which instead emphasize very concrete reliance interests, like those that develop in "cases involving property and contract rights."* * *

Our decision returns the issue of abortion to. . . legislative bodies, and it allows women on both sides of the abortion issue to seek to affect the legislative process by influencing public opinion, lobbying legislators, voting, and running for office. Women are not without electoral or political power. It is noteworthy that the percentage of women who register to vote and cast ballots is consistently higher than the percentage of men who do so. In the last election in November 2020, women, who make up around 51.5 percent of the population of Mississippi, constituted 55.5 percent of the voters who cast ballots.

Unable to show concrete reliance on *Roe* and *Casey* themselves, the Solicitor General suggests that overruling those decisions would "threaten the Court's precedents holding that the Due Process Clause protects other rights." That is not correct for reasons we have already discussed. As even the *Casey* plurality recognized, "[a]bortion is a unique act" because it terminates "life or potential life." And to ensure that our decision is not misunderstood or mischaracterized, we emphasize that our decision concerns the constitutional right to abortion and no other right. Nothing in this opinion should be understood to cast doubt on precedents that do not concern abortion.

IV

Having shown that traditional *stare decisis* factors do not weigh in favor of retaining *Roe* or *Casey*, we must address one final argument that featured prominently in the *Casey* plurality opinion.

The argument was cast in different terms, but stated simply, it was essentially as follows. The American people's belief in the rule of law would be shaken if they lost respect for this Court as an institution that decides important cases based on principle, not "social and political pressures." There is a special danger that the public will perceive a decision as having been made for unprincipled reasons when the Court overrules a controversial "watershed" decision, such as *Casey*. A decision overruling *Roe* would be perceived as having been made "under fire" and as a "surrender to political pressure," and therefore the preservation of public approval of the Court weighs heavily in favor of retaining *Roe*.

This analysis starts out on the right foot but ultimately veers off course. The *Casey* plurality was certainly right that it is important for the public to perceive that our decisions are based on principle, and we should make every effort to achieve that objective by issuing opinions that carefully show how a proper understanding of the law leads to the results we reach. But we cannot exceed the scope of our authority under the Constitution, and we cannot allow our decisions to be affected by any extraneous influences such as concern about the public's reaction to our work.* * *

The *Casey* plurality. . .claimed the authority to impose a permanent settlement of the issue of a constitutional abortion right simply by saying that the matter was closed. That unprecedented claim exceeded the power vested in us by the Constitution. As Alexander Hamilton famously put it, the Constitution gives the judiciary "neither Force nor Will." The Federalist No. 78, p. 523 (J. Cooke ed. 1961). Our sole authority is to exercise "judgment"—which is to say, the authority to judge what the law means and how it should apply to the case at hand.* * *

The *Casey* plurality also misjudged the practical limits of this Court's influence. *Roe* certainly did not succeed in ending division on the issue of abortion. On the contrary, *Roe* "inflamed" a national issue that has remained bitterly divisive for the past half century.* * *

Neither decision has ended debate over the issue of a constitutional right to obtain an abortion. Indeed, in this case, 26 States expressly ask us to overrule *Roe* and *Casey* and to return the issue of abortion to the people and their elected representatives. This Court's inability to end debate on the issue should not have been surprising. This Court cannot bring about the permanent resolution of a rancorous national controversy simply by dictating a settlement and telling the people to move on.* * *

V.

[The Court then responded in detail to the dissent, making many of the same points made above].

We now turn to the concurrence in the judgment, which reproves us for deciding whether *Roe* and *Casey* should be retained or overruled. That opinion (which for convenience we will call simply "the concurrence") recommends a "more measured course," which it defends based on what it claims is "a straightforward *stare decisis* analysis." (opinion of ROBERTS, C. J.). The concurrence would "leave for another day whether to reject any right to an abortion at all," *post*, at 7, and would hold only that if the Constitution protects any such right, the right ends once women have had "a reasonable opportunity" to obtain an abortion. The concurrence does not specify what period of time is sufficient to provide such an opportunity, but it would hold that 15 weeks, the period allowed under Mississippi's law, is enough—at least "absent rare circumstances." * * *

The concurrence's most fundamental defect is its failure to offer any principled basis for its approach. The concurrence would "discar[d]" "the rule from *Roe* and *Casey* that a woman's right to terminate her pregnancy extends up to the point that the fetus is regarded as 'viable' outside the womb." But this rule was a critical component of the holdings in *Roe* and *Casey*, and *stare decisis* is "a doctrine of preservation, not transformation," Therefore, a new rule that discards the viability rule cannot be defended on *stare decisis* grounds.* * *

When the Court reconsidered *Roe* in *Casey*, it left no doubt about the importance of the viability rule. It described the rule as *Roe*'s "central holding," and repeatedly stated that the right it reaffirmed was "the right of the woman to choose to have an abortion *before viability*." * * *

[S]tare decisis cannot justify the new "reasonable opportunity" rule propounded by the concurrence. If that rule is to become the law of the land, it must stand on its own, but the concurrence makes no attempt to show that this rule represents a correct interpretation of the Constitution. The concurrence does not claim that the right to a reasonable opportunity to obtain an abortion is " 'deeply rooted in this Nation's history and tradition' " and " 'implicit in the concept of ordered liberty.' " Nor does it propound any other theory that could show that the Constitution supports its new rule. And if the Constitution protects a woman's right to obtain an abortion, the opinion does not explain why that right should end after the point at which all "reasonable" women will have decided whether to seek an abortion. While the concurrence is moved by a desire for judicial

minimalism, "we cannot embrace a narrow ground of decision simply because it is narrow; it must also be right."* * *

The concurrence would "leave for another day whether to reject any right to an abortion at all," *post*, at 7, but "another day" would not be long in coming. Some States have set deadlines for obtaining an abortion that are shorter than Mississippi's.* * *

VI.

We must now decide what standard will govern if state abortion regulations undergo constitutional challenge and whether the law before us satisfies the appropriate standard.

Under our precedents, rational-basis review is the appropriate standard for such challenges. As we have explained, procuring an abortion is not a fundamental constitutional right because such a right has no basis in the Constitution's text or in our Nation's history.

It follows that the States may regulate abortion for legitimate reasons, and when such regulations are challenged under the Constitution, courts cannot "substitute their social and economic beliefs for the judgment of legislative bodies."* * *

A law regulating abortion, like other health and welfare laws, is entitled to a "strong presumption of validity." *Heller v. Doe* (1993). It must be sustained if there is a rational basis on which the legislature could have thought that it would serve legitimate state interests. *Id.*, at 320; *FCC v. Beach Communications, Inc.* (1993); *New Orleans v. Dukes,* 427 U.S. 297 (1976) (*per curiam*); *Williamson v. Lee Optical of Okla., Inc.,* 348 U.S. 483 (1955). These legitimate interests include respect for and preservation of prenatal life at all stages of development, *Gonzales*; the protection of maternal health and safety; the elimination of particularly gruesome or barbaric medical procedures; the preservation of the integrity of the medical profession; the mitigation of fetal pain; and the prevention of discrimination on the basis of race, sex, or disability

These legitimate interests justify Mississippi's Gestational Age Act.* * *The Mississippi Legislature's findings recount the stages of "human prenatal development" and assert the State's interest in "protecting the life of the unborn." The legislature also found that abortions performed after 15 weeks typically use the dilation and evacuation procedure, and the legislature found the use of this procedure "for nontherapeutic or elective reasons [to be] a barbaric practice, dangerous for the maternal patient, and demeaning to the medical profession." see also *Gonzales,* 550 U.S., at 135–143 (describing such procedures). These legitimate interests provide a rational basis for the Gestational Age Act, and it follows that respondents' constitutional challenge must fail.

VII.

We end this opinion where we began. Abortion presents a profound moral question. The Constitution does not prohibit the citizens of each State from regulating or prohibiting abortion. *Roe* and *Casey* arrogated that authority. We now overrule those decisions and return that authority to the people and their elected representatives.

The judgment of the Fifth Circuit is reversed, and the case is remanded for further proceedings consistent with this opinion.

[The opinion included appendices of state and territorial statutes criminalizing abortion, most dating to the nineteenth century].

JUSTICE THOMAS, concurring.

I join the opinion of the Court because it correctly holds that there is no constitutional right to abortion. Respondents invoke one source for that right: the Fourteenth Amendment's guarantee that no State shall "deprive any person of life, liberty, or property without due process of law." The Court well explains why, under our substantive due process precedents, the purported right to abortion is not a form of "liberty" protected by the Due Process Clause.* * *

I write separately to emphasize a second, more fundamental reason why there is no abortion guarantee lurking in the Due Process Clause. Considerable historical evidence indicates that "due process of law" merely required executive and judicial actors to comply with legislative enactments and the common law when depriving a person of life, liberty, or property.* * *

As I have previously explained, "substantive due process" is an oxymoron that "lack[s] any basis in the Constitution."* * *

The Court today declines to disturb substantive due process jurisprudence generally or the doctrine's application in other, specific contexts. Cases like *Griswold v. Connecticut; Lawrence v. Texas*; and *Obergefell v. Hodges* (right to same-sex marriage), are not at issue. The Court's abortion cases are unique, and no party has asked us to decide "whether our entire Fourteenth Amendment jurisprudence must be preserved or revised." Thus, I agree that "[n]othing in [the Court's] opinion should be understood to cast doubt on precedents that do not concern abortion."

[I]n future cases, we should reconsider all of this Court's substantive due process precedents, including *Griswold, Lawrence*, and *Obergefell*. Because any substantive due process decision is "demonstrably erroneous," we have a duty to "correct the error" established in those precedents. After overruling these demonstrably erroneous decisions, the question would remain whether other constitutional provisions guarantee the myriad rights that our substantive due process cases have generated. For example, we could consider whether any of the rights announced in this Court's substantive due process cases are "privileges or immunities of citizens of the United States" protected by the Fourteenth Amendment. To answer that question, we would need to decide important antecedent questions, including whether the Privileges or Immunities Clause protects *any* rights that are not enumerated in the Constitution and, if so, how to identify those rights. That said, even if the Clause does protect unenumerated rights, the Court conclusively demonstrates that abortion is not one of them under any plausible interpretive approach.* * *

[S]ubstantive due process is often wielded to "disastrous ends." For instance, in *Dred Scott v. Sandford* (1857), the Court invoked a species of substantive due process to announce that Congress was powerless to emancipate slaves brought into the federal territories. While *Dred Scott* "was overruled on the battlefields of the Civil War and by constitutional amendment after Appomattox," *Obergefell* (Roberts, C. J., dissenting), that overruling was "[p]urchased at the price of immeasurable human suffering," Now today, the Court rightly overrules *Roe* and *Casey*—two of this Court's "most notoriously incorrect" substantive due process decisions,—after more than 63 million abortions have been performed, see National Right to Life Committee, Abortion Statistics (Jan. 2022), https:// www.nrlc.org/uploads/factsheets/FS01AbortionintheUS.pdf. The harm caused by this Court's forays into substantive due process remains immeasurable.

* * *

JUSTICE KAVANAUGH, concurring.

I write separately to explain my additional views about why *Roe* was wrongly decided, why *Roe* should be overruled at this time, and the future implications of today's decision.

Abortion is a profoundly difficult and contentious issue because it presents an irreconcilable conflict between the interests of a pregnant woman who seeks an abortion and the interests in protecting fetal life. The interests on both sides of the abortion issue are extraordinarily weighty.* * *

When it comes to abortion, one interest must prevail over the other at any given point in a pregnancy. Many Americans of good faith would prioritize the interests of the pregnant woman. Many other Americans of good faith instead would prioritize the interests in protecting fetal life—at least unless, for example, an abortion is necessary to save the life of the mother. Of course, many Americans are conflicted or have nuanced views that may vary depending on the particular time in pregnancy, or the particular circumstances of a pregnancy.

The issue before this Court, however, is not the policy or morality of abortion. The issue before this Court is what the Constitution says about abortion. The Constitution does not take sides on the issue of abortion. The text of the Constitution does not refer to or encompass abortion. To be sure, this Court has held that the Constitution protects unenumerated rights that are deeply rooted in this Nation's history and tradition, and implicit in the concept of ordered liberty. But a right to abortion is not deeply rooted in American history and tradition, as the Court today thoroughly explains.

On the question of abortion, the Constitution is therefore neither pro-life nor pro-choice. The Constitution is neutral and leaves the issue for the people and their elected representatives to resolve through the democratic process in the States or Congress—like the numerous other difficult questions of American social and economic policy that the Constitution does not address.

Because the Constitution is neutral on the issue of abortion, this Court also must be scrupulously neutral. The nine unelected Members of this Court do not possess the constitutional authority to override the democratic process and to decree either a pro-life or a pro-choice abortion policy for all 330 million people in the United States.* * *

Some *amicus* briefs argue that the Court today should not only overrule *Roe* and return to a position of judicial neutrality on abortion, but should go further and hold that the Constitution *outlaws* abortion throughout the United States. No Justice of this Court has ever advanced that position. I respect those who advocate for that position, just as I respect those who argue that this Court should hold that the Constitution legalizes pre-viability abortion throughout the United States. But both positions are wrong as a constitutional matter, in my view. The Constitution neither outlaws abortion nor legalizes abortion.* * *

Today's decision therefore does not prevent the numerous States that readily allow abortion from continuing to readily allow abortion. That includes, if they choose, the *amici* States supporting the plaintiff in this Court: New York, California, Illinois, Maine, Massachusetts, Rhode Island, Vermont, Connecticut, New Jersey, Pennsylvania, Delaware, Maryland, Michigan, Wisconsin, Minnesota, New Mexico, Colorado, Nevada, Oregon, Washington, and Hawaii. By contrast, other States may maintain laws that more strictly limit abortion. After today's decision, all of the States may evaluate the competing interests and decide how to address this consequential issue.

In arguing for a *constitutional* right to abortion that would override the people's choices in the democratic process, the plaintiff Jackson Women's Health Organization and its *amici* emphasize that the Constitution does not freeze the American people's rights as of 1791 or 1868. I fully agree. To begin, I agree that constitutional rights apply to situations that were unforeseen in 1791 or 1868—such as applying the First Amendment to the Internet or the Fourth Amendment to cars. Moreover, the Constitution authorizes the creation of new rights—state and federal, statutory and constitutional. But when it comes to creating new rights, the Constitution directs the people to the various processes of democratic self-government contemplated by the Constitution—state legislation, state constitutional amendments, federal legislation, and federal constitutional amendments.

The Constitution does not grant the nine unelected Members of this Court the unilateral authority to rewrite the Constitution to create new rights and liberties based on our own moral or policy views.* * *

The more difficult question in this case is *stare decisis*—that is, whether to overrule the *Roe* decision.* * *

Adherence to precedent is the norm, and *stare decisis* imposes a high bar before this Court may overrule a precedent. This Court's history shows, however, that *stare decisis* is not absolute, and indeed cannot be absolute. Otherwise, as the Court today explains, many long-since-overruled cases. . .would never have been overruled and would still be the law.* * *

But that history alone does not answer the critical question: When precisely should the Court overrule an erroneous constitutional precedent? The history of *stare decisis* in this Court establishes that a constitutional precedent may be overruled only when (i) the prior decision is not just wrong, but is egregiously wrong, (ii) the prior decision has caused significant negative jurisprudential or real-world consequences, and (iii) overruling the prior decision would not unduly upset legitimate reliance interests.

Applying those factors, I agree with the Court today that *Roe* should be overruled.* * *

But the *stare decisis* analysis here is somewhat more complicated because of *Casey*. In 1992, 19 years after *Roe*, *Casey* acknowledged the continuing dispute over *Roe*. The Court sought to find common ground that would resolve the abortion debate and end the national controversy. After careful and thoughtful consideration, the *Casey* plurality reaffirmed a right to abortion through viability (about 24 weeks), while also allowing somewhat more regulation of abortion than *Roe* had allowed.

I have deep and unyielding respect for the Justices who wrote the *Casey* plurality opinion. And I respect the *Casey* plurality's good-faith effort to locate some middle ground or compromise that could resolve this controversy for America.

But as has become increasingly evident over time, *Casey*'s well-intentioned effort did not resolve the abortion debate. The national division has not ended.* * *

After today's decision, the nine Members of this Court will no longer decide the basic legality of pre-viability abortion for all 330 million Americans. That issue will be resolved by the people and their representatives in the democratic process in the States or Congress. But the parties' arguments have raised other related questions, and I address some of them here.

First is the question of how this decision will affect other precedents involving issues such as contraception and marriage—in particular, the decisions in *Griswold v. Connecticut* (1965); *Eisenstadt v. Baird* (1972); *Loving v. Virginia* (1967); and *Obergefell v. Hodges* (2015). I emphasize what the Court today states: Overruling *Roe* does *not* mean the overruling of those precedents, and does *not* threaten or cast doubt on those precedents.

Second, as I see it, some of the other abortion-related legal questions raised by today's decision are not especially difficult as a constitutional matter. For example, may a State bar a resident of that State from traveling to another State to obtain an abortion? In my view, the answer is no based on the constitutional right to interstate travel. May a State retroactively impose liability or punishment for an abortion that occurred before today's decision takes effect? In my view, the answer is no based on the Due Process Clause or the Ex Post Facto Clause.* * *

Since 1973, more than 20 Justices of this Court have now grappled with the divisive issue of abortion. I greatly respect all of the Justices, past and present, who have done so. Amidst extraordinary controversy and challenges, all of them have addressed the abortion issue in good faith after careful deliberation, and based on their sincere understandings of the Constitution and of precedent. I have endeavored to do the same.

CHIEF JUSTICE ROBERTS, concurring in the judgment.

We granted certiorari to decide one question: "Whether all pre-viability prohibitions on elective abortions are unconstitutional." Pet. for Cert. i. That question is directly implicated here: Mississippi's Gestational Age Act, Miss. Code Ann. § 41–41–191 (2018), generally prohibits abortion after the fifteenth week of pregnancy—several weeks before a fetus is regarded as "viable" outside the womb. In urging our review, Mississippi stated that its case was "an ideal vehicle" to "reconsider the bright-line viability rule," and that a judgment in its favor would "not require the Court to overturn" *Roe v. Wade* and *Planned Parenthood of Southeastern Pa. v. Casey*.

Today, the Court nonetheless rules for Mississippi by doing just that. I would take a more measured course. I agree with the Court that the viability line established by *Roe* and *Casey* should be discarded under a straightforward *stare decisis* analysis. That line never made any sense. Our abortion precedents describe the right at issue as a woman's right to choose to terminate her pregnancy. That right should therefore extend far enough to ensure a reasonable opportunity to choose, but need not extend any further—certainly not all the way to viability. Mississippi's law allows a woman three months to obtain an abortion, well beyond the point at which it is considered "late" to discover a pregnancy. I see no sound basis for questioning the adequacy of that opportunity.

But that is all I would say, out of adherence to a simple yet fundamental principle of judicial restraint: If it is not necessary to decide more to dispose of a case, then it is necessary *not* to decide more. Perhaps we are not always perfect in following that command, and certainly there are cases that warrant an exception. But this is not one of them. Surely we should adhere closely to principles of judicial restraint here, where the broader path the Court chooses entails repudiating a constitutional right we have not only previously recognized, but also expressly reaffirmed applying the doctrine of *stare decisis*. The Court's opinion is thoughtful and thorough, but those virtues cannot compensate for the fact that its dramatic and consequential ruling is unnecessary to decide the case before us.* * *

[T]he viability rule was created outside the ordinary course of litigation, is and always has been completely unreasoned, and fails to take account of state interests since recognized as legitimate. It is indeed "telling that other countries almost uniformly eschew" a viability line. *Ante*, at 53 (opinion of the Court). Only a handful of countries, among them China and North Korea, permit elective abortions after twenty weeks; the rest have coalesced around a 12-week line.* * *

When the State petitioned for our review, its basic request was straightforward: "clarify whether abortion prohibitions before viability are always unconstitutional." Pet. for Cert. 14.* * *

After we granted certiorari, however, Mississippi changed course. In its principal brief, the State bluntly announced that the Court should overrule *Roe* and *Casey*. The Constitution does not protect a right to an abortion, it argued, and a State should be able to prohibit elective abortions if a rational basis supports doing so.

The Court now rewards that gambit.* * *

In support of its holding, the Court cites three seminal constitutional decisions that involved overruling prior precedents: *Brown v. Board of Education* (1954), *West Virginia Bd. of Ed. v. Barnette* (1943), and *West Coast Hotel Co. v. Parrish*, (1937). The opinion in *Brown* was unanimous and eleven pages long; this one is neither. *Barnette* was decided only three years after the decision it overruled, three Justices having had second thoughts. And *West Coast Hotel* was issued against a backdrop of unprecedented economic despair that focused attention on the fundamental flaws of existing precedent. It also was part of a sea change in this Court's interpretation of the Constitution, "signal[ing] the demise of an entire line of important precedents,"—a feature the Court expressly disclaims in today's decision. None of these leading cases, in short, provides a template for what the Court does today.* * *

Both the Court's opinion and the dissent display a relentless freedom from doubt on the legal issue that I cannot share. I am not sure, for example, that a ban on terminating a pregnancy from the moment of conception must be treated the same under the Constitution as a ban after fifteen weeks. A thoughtful Member of this Court once counseled that the difficulty of a question "admonishes us to observe the wise limitations on our function and to confine ourselves to deciding only what is necessary to the disposition of the immediate case." *Whitehouse v. Illinois Central R. Co.* (Frankfurter, J., for the Court). I would decide the question we granted review to answer—whether the previously recognized abortion right bars all abortion restrictions prior to viability, such that a ban on abortions after fifteen weeks of pregnancy is necessarily unlawful. The answer to that question is no, and there is no need to go further to decide this case.

I therefore concur only in the judgment.

JUSTICE BREYER, JUSTICE SOTOMAYOR, and JUSTICE KAGAN, dissenting.

For half a century, *Roe v. Wade* and *Planned Parenthood of Southeastern Pa. v. Casey* have protected the liberty and equality of women. *Roe* held, and *Casey* reaffirmed, that the Constitution safeguards a woman's right to decide for herself whether to bear a child. *Roe* held, and *Casey* reaffirmed, that in the first stages of pregnancy, the government could not make that choice for women. The government could not control a woman's body or the course of a woman's life: It could not determine what the woman's future would be. Respecting a woman as an autonomous being, and granting her full equality, meant giving her substantial choice over this most personal and most consequential of all life decisions.

Roe and *Casey* well understood the difficulty and divisiveness of the abortion issue. The Court knew that Americans hold profoundly different views about the "moral[ity]" of "terminating a pregnancy, even in its earliest stage." *Casey* And the Court recognized that "the State has legitimate interests from the outset of the pregnancy in protecting" the "life of the fetus that may become a child." So the Court struck a balance, as it often does when values and goals compete. It held that the State could prohibit abortions after fetal viability, so long as the ban contained exceptions to safeguard a woman's life or health. It held that even before viability, the State could regulate the abortion procedure in multiple and meaningful ways. But until the viability line was crossed, the Court held, a State could not impose a "substantial obstacle" on a woman's "right to elect the procedure" as she (not the government) thought proper, in light of all the circumstances and complexities of her own life.

Today, the Court discards that balance. It says that from the very moment of fertilization, a woman has no rights to speak of. A State can force her to bring a pregnancy to term, even at the steepest personal and familial costs. An abortion restriction, the majority holds, is permissible whenever rational, the lowest level of scrutiny known to the law. And because, as the Court has often stated, protecting fetal life is rational, States will feel free to enact all manner of restrictions. The Mississippi law at issue here bars abortions after the 15th week of pregnancy. Under the majority's ruling, though, another State's law could do so after ten weeks, or five or three or one—or, again, from the moment of fertilization. States have already passed such laws, in anticipation of today's ruling. More will follow. Some States have enacted laws extending to all forms of abortion procedure, including taking medication in one's own home. They have passed laws without any exceptions for when the woman is the victim of rape or incest. Under those laws, a woman will have to bear her rapist's child or a young girl her father's—no matter if doing so will destroy her life. So too, after today's ruling, some States may compel women to carry to term a fetus with severe physical anomalies—for example, one afflicted with Tay-Sachs disease, sure to die within a few years of birth. States may even argue that a prohibition on abortion need make no provision for protecting a woman from risk of death or physical harm. Across a vast array of circumstances, a State will be able to impose its moral choice on a woman and coerce her to give birth to a child.

Enforcement of all these draconian restrictions will also be left largely to the States' devices. A State can of course impose criminal penalties on abortion providers, including lengthy prison sentences. But some States will not stop there. Perhaps, in the wake of today's decision, a state law will criminalize the woman's conduct too, incarcerating or fining her for daring to seek or obtain an abortion. And as Texas has recently shown, a State can turn neighbor against neighbor, enlisting fellow citizens in the effort to root out anyone who tries to get an abortion, or to assist another in doing so.

The majority tries to hide the geographically expansive effects of its holding. Today's decision, the majority says, permits "each State" to address abortion as it pleases. That is cold comfort, of course, for the poor woman who cannot get the money to fly to a distant State for a procedure. Above all others, women lacking financial resources will suffer from today's decision. In any event, interstate restrictions will also soon be in the offing. After this decision, some States may block women from traveling out of State to obtain abortions, or even from receiving abortion medications from out of State. Some may criminalize efforts, including the provision of information or funding, to help women gain access to other States' abortion services. Most threatening of all, no language in today's decision stops the Federal Government from prohibiting abortions nationwide, once again from the moment of conception and without exceptions for rape or incest. If that happens, "the views of [an individual State's] citizens" will not matter. The challenge for a woman will be to finance a trip not to "New York [or] California" but to Toronto. *Ante*, at 4 (KAVANAUGH, J., concurring).

Whatever the exact scope of the coming laws, one result of today's decision is certain: the curtailment of women's rights, and of their status as free and equal citizens. Yesterday, the Constitution guaranteed that a woman confronted with an unplanned pregnancy could (within reasonable limits) make her own decision about whether to bear a child, with all the life-transforming consequences that act involves.* * * The Constitution will [now], today's majority holds, provide no shield, despite its guarantees of liberty and equality for all.

And no one should be confident that this majority is done with its work. The right *Roe* and *Casey* recognized does not stand alone. To the contrary, the Court has linked it for decades to other settled freedoms involving bodily integrity, familial relationships, and procreation. Most obviously, the right to terminate a pregnancy arose straight out of the right to purchase and use contraception. See *Griswold v. Connecticut*; *Eisenstadt v. Baird*. In turn, those rights led, more recently, to rights of same-sex intimacy and marriage. See *Lawrence v. Texas*; *Obergefell v. Hodges*. They are all part of the same constitutional fabric, protecting autonomous decisionmaking over the most personal of life decisions. The majority (or to be more accurate, most of it) is eager to tell us today that nothing it does "cast[s] doubt on precedents that do not concern abortion." Cf. (THOMAS, J., concurring) (advocating the overruling of *Griswold, Lawrence,* and *Obergefell*). But how could that be? The lone rationale for what the majority does today is that the right to elect an abortion is not "deeply rooted in history." Not until *Roe*, the majority argues, did people think abortion fell within the Constitution's guarantee of liberty. The same could be said, though, of most of the rights the majority claims it is not tampering with. The majority could write just as long an opinion showing, for example, that until the mid-20th century, "there was no support in American law for a constitutional right to obtain [contraceptives]." So one of two things must be true. Either the majority does not really believe in its own reasoning. Or if it does, all rights that have no history stretching back to the mid-19th century are insecure. Either the mass of the majority's opinion is hypocrisy, or additional constitutional rights are under threat. It is one or the other.

One piece of evidence on that score seems especially salient: The majority's cavalier approach to overturning this Court's precedents.* * * The majority has no good reason for the upheaval in law and society it sets off. *Roe* and *Casey* have been the law of the land for decades, shaping women's expectations of their choices when an unplanned pregnancy occurs. Women have relied on the availability of abortion both in structuring their relationships and in planning their lives. The legal framework *Roe* and *Casey* developed to balance the competing interests in this sphere has proved workable in courts across the country. No recent developments, in either law or fact, have eroded or cast doubt on those precedents. Nothing, in short, has changed. Indeed, the Court in *Casey* already found all of that to be true. *Casey* is a precedent about precedent. It reviewed the same arguments made here in support of overruling *Roe*, and it found that doing so was not warranted. The Court reverses course today for one reason and one reason only: because the composition of this Court has changed. *Stare decisis*, this Court has often said, "contributes to the actual and perceived integrity of the judicial process" by ensuring that decisions are "founded in the law rather than in the proclivities of individuals." Today, the proclivities of individuals rule. The Court departs from its obligation to faithfully and impartially apply the law. We dissent.

We start with *Roe* and *Casey*, and with their deep connections to a broad swath of this Court's precedents. To hear the majority tell the tale, *Roe* and *Casey* are aberrations: They came from nowhere, went nowhere—and so are easy to excise from this Nation's constitutional law.* * *[But] *Roe* and *Casey* were from the beginning, and are even more now, embedded in core constitutional concepts of individual freedom, and of the equal rights of citizens to decide on the shape of their lives. Those legal concepts, one might even say, have gone far toward defining what it means to be an American. For in this Nation, we do not believe that a government controlling all private choices is compatible with a free people. So we do not (as the majority insists today) place everything within "the reach of majorities and [government] officials." *West Virginia Bd. of Ed. v. Barnette.* We believe in a Constitution that puts some issues off limits to majority rule. Even in the face of public opposition, we uphold the right of individuals—yes, including women—to make their own choices and chart their own futures. Or at least, we did once.* * *

The majority makes this change based on a single question: Did the reproductive right recognized in *Roe* and *Casey* exist in "1868, the year when the Fourteenth Amendment was ratified"? The majority says (and with this much we agree) that the answer to this question is no: In 1868, there was no nationwide right to end a pregnancy, and no thought that the Fourteenth Amendment provided one.

Of course, the majority opinion refers as well to some later and earlier history. On the one side of 1868, it goes back as far as the 13th (the 13th!) century. But that turns out to be wheel-spinning. First, it is not clear what relevance such early history should have, even to the majority. See *New York State Rifle & Pistol Assn., Inc. v. Bruen*, 597 U.S. ___, ___ (2022) (slip op., at 26) ("Historical evidence that long predates [ratification] may not illuminate the scope of the right"). If the early history obviously supported abortion rights, the majority would no doubt say that only the views of the Fourteenth Amendment's ratifiers are germane. See *ibid.* (It is "better not to go too far back into antiquity," except if olden "law survived to become our Founders' law"). Second—and embarrassingly for the majority—early law in fact does provide some support for abortion rights. Common-law authorities did not treat abortion as a crime before "quickening"—the point when the fetus moved in the womb. And early American law followed the common-law rule. So the criminal law of that early time might be taken as roughly consonant with *Roe*'s and *Casey*'s different treatment of early and late abortions. Better, then, to move forward in time. On the other side of 1868, the majority occasionally notes that many States barred abortion up to the time of *Roe*. See *ante*, at 24, 36. That is convenient for the majority, but it is window dressing. As the same majority (plus one) just informed us, "post-ratification adoption or acceptance of laws that are *inconsistent* with the original meaning of the constitutional text obviously cannot overcome or alter that text." *New York State Rifle & Pistol Assn., Inc.*, 597 U.S., at ___–___ (slip op., at 27–28). Had the pre-*Roe* liberalization of abortion laws occurred more quickly and more widely in the 20th century, the majority would say (once again) that only the ratifiers' views are germane.

The majority's core legal postulate, then, is that we in the 21st century must read the Fourteenth Amendment just as its ratifiers did. And that is indeed what the majority emphasizes over and over again. If the ratifiers did not understand something as central to freedom, then neither can we. Or said more particularly: If those people did not understand reproductive rights as part of the guarantee of liberty conferred in the Fourteenth Amendment, then those rights do not exist.

As an initial matter, note a mistake in the just preceding sentence. We referred there to the "people" who ratified the Fourteenth Amendment: What rights did those "people" have in their heads at the time? But, of course, "people" did not ratify the Fourteenth Amendment. Men did. So it is perhaps not so surprising that the ratifiers were not perfectly attuned to the importance of reproductive rights for women's liberty, or for their capacity to participate as equal members of our Nation. Indeed, the ratifiers—both in 1868 and when the original Constitution was approved in 1788—did not understand women as full members of the community embraced by the phrase "We the People." In 1868, the first wave of American feminists were explicitly told—of course by men—that it was not their time to seek constitutional protections. (Women would not get even the vote for another half-century.) To be sure, most women in 1868 also had a foreshortened view of their rights: If most men could not then imagine giving women control over their bodies, most women could not imagine having that kind of autonomy. But that takes away nothing from the core point. Those responsible for the original Constitution, including the Fourteenth Amendment, did not perceive women as equals, and did not recognize women's rights. When the majority says that we must read our foundational charter as viewed at the time of ratification (except that we may also check it against the Dark Ages), it consigns women to second-class citizenship.* * *

So how is it that, as *Casey* said, our Constitution, read now, grants rights to women, though it did not in 1868? How is it that our Constitution subjects discrimination against them to heightened judicial scrutiny? How is it that our Constitution, through the Fourteenth Amendment's liberty clause, guarantees access to contraception (also not legally protected in 1868) so that women can decide for themselves whether and when to bear a child? How is it that until today, that same constitutional clause protected a woman's right, in the event contraception failed, to end a pregnancy in its earlier stages?

The answer is that this Court has rejected the majority's pinched view of how to read our Constitution. "The Founders," we recently wrote, "knew they were writing a document designed to apply to ever-changing circumstances over centuries." *NLRB v. Noel Canning*. Or in the words of the great Chief Justice John Marshall, our Constitution is "intended to endure for ages to come," and must adapt itself to a future "seen dimly," if at all. *McCulloch v. Maryland*. That is indeed why our Constitution is written as it is. The Framers (both in 1788 and 1868) understood that the world changes. So they did not define rights by reference to the specific practices existing at the time. Instead, the Framers defined rights in general terms, to permit future evolution in their scope and meaning. And over the course of our history, this Court has taken up the Framers' invitation. It has kept true to the Framers' principles by applying them in new ways, responsive to new societal understandings and conditions.* * *

The Constitution does not freeze for all time the original view of what those rights guarantee, or how they apply.

That does not mean anything goes. The majority wishes people to think there are but two alternatives: (1) accept the original applications of the Fourteenth Amendment and no others, or (2) surrender to judges' "own ardent views," ungrounded in law, about the "liberty that Americans should enjoy." At least, that idea is what the majority *sometimes* tries to convey. At other times, the majority (or, rather, most of it) tries to assure the public that it has no designs on rights (for example, to contraception) that arose only in the back half of the 20th century—in other words, that it is happy to pick and choose, in accord with individual preferences. . .For now, our point is different: It is that applications of liberty and equality can evolve while remaining grounded in constitutional principles, constitutional history, and constitutional precedents. The second Justice

Harlan discussed how to strike the right balance when he explained why he would have invalidated a State's ban on contraceptive use. Judges, he said, are not "free to roam where unguided speculation might take them." *Poe v. Ullman* (dissenting opinion). Yet they also must recognize that the constitutional "tradition" of this country is not captured whole at a single moment. Rather, its meaning gains content from the long sweep of our history and from successive judicial precedents—each looking to the last and each seeking to apply the Constitution's most fundamental commitments to new conditions. That is why Americans, to go back to *Obergefell*'s example, have a right to marry across racial lines. And it is why, to go back to Justice Harlan's case, Americans have a right to use contraceptives so they can choose for themselves whether to have children.* * *

It was settled at the time of *Roe*, settled at the time of *Casey*, and settled yesterday that the Constitution places limits on a State's power to assert control over an individual's body and most personal decisionmaking. A multitude of decisions supporting that principle led to *Roe*'s recognition and *Casey*'s reaffirmation of the right to choose; and *Roe* and *Casey* in turn supported additional protections for intimate and familial relations. The majority has embarrassingly little to say about those precedents. It (literally) rattles them off in a single paragraph; and it implies that they have nothing to do with each other, or with the right to terminate an early pregnancy.* * * But that is flat wrong. The Court's precedents about bodily autonomy, sexual and familial relations, and procreation are all interwoven—all part of the fabric of our constitutional law, and because that is so, of our lives. Especially women's lives, where they safeguard a right to self-determination.

And eliminating that right, we need to say before further describing our precedents, is not taking a "neutral" position, as JUSTICE KAVANAUGH tries to argue. His idea is that neutrality lies in giving the abortion issue to the States, where some can go one way and some another. But would he say that the Court is being "scrupulously neutral" if it allowed New York and California to ban all the guns they want? If the Court allowed some States to use unanimous juries and others not? If the Court told the States: Decide for yourselves whether to put restrictions on church attendance? We could go on—and in fact we will. Suppose JUSTICE KAVANAUGH were to say (in line with the majority opinion) that the rights we just listed are more textually or historically grounded than the right to choose. What, then, of the right to contraception or same-sex marriage? Would it be "scrupulously neutral" for the Court to eliminate those rights too? The point of all these examples is that when it comes to rights, the Court does not act "neutrally" when it leaves everything up to the States. Rather, the Court acts neutrally when it protects the right against all comers. And to apply that point to the case here: When the Court decimates a right women have held for 50 years, the Court is not being "scrupulously neutral." It is instead taking sides: against women who wish to exercise the right, and for States (like Mississippi) that want to bar them from doing so. JUSTICE KAVANAUGH cannot obscure that point by appropriating the rhetoric of even-handedness. His position just is what it is: A brook-no-compromise refusal to recognize a woman's right to choose, from the first day of a pregnancy. And that position, as we will now show, cannot be squared with this Court's longstanding view that women indeed have rights (whatever the state of the world in 1868) to make the most personal and consequential decisions about their bodies and their lives.* * *

Nor does it even help just to take the majority at its word. Assume the majority is sincere in saying, for whatever reason, that it will go so far and no further. Scout's honor. Still, the future significance of today's opinion will be decided in the future. And law often has a way of evolving without regard to original intentions—a way of actually following where logic leads, rather than tolerating hard-to-explain lines. Rights can expand in that way. Dissenting in *Lawrence*, Justice Scalia explained why he took no comfort in the Court's statement that a decision recognizing the right to same-sex intimacy did "not involve" same-sex marriage. That could be true, he wrote, "only if one entertains the belief that principle and logic have nothing to do with the decisions of this Court." Score one for the dissent, as a matter of prophecy. And logic and principle are not one-way ratchets. Rights can contract in the same way and for the same reason—because whatever today's majority might say, one thing really does lead to another. We fervently hope that does not happen because of today's decision. We hope that we will not join Justice Scalia in the book of prophets. But we cannot understand how anyone can be confident that today's opinion will be the last of its kind.* * *

Anyway, today's decision, taken on its own, is catastrophic enough. As a matter of constitutional method, the majority's commitment to replicate in 2022 every view about the meaning of liberty held in 1868 has precious little to recommend it.* * *

By overruling *Roe, Casey,* and more than 20 cases reaffirming or applying the constitutional right to abortion, the majority abandons *stare decisis,* a principle central to the rule of law.* * *

The majority has overruled *Roe* and *Casey* for one and only one reason: because it has always despised them, and now it has the votes to discard them. The majority thereby substitutes a rule by judges for the rule of law.

Contrary to the majority's view, there is nothing unworkable about *Casey*'s "undue burden" standard.* * *

General standards, like the undue burden standard, are ubiquitous in the law, and particularly in constitutional adjudication. When called on to give effect to the Constitution's broad principles, this Court often crafts flexible standards that can be applied case-by-case to a myriad of unforeseeable circumstances.* * *

Anyone concerned about workability should consider the majority's substitute standard. The majority says a law regulating or banning abortion "must be sustained if there is a rational basis on which the legislature could have thought that it would serve legitimate state interests." And the majority lists interests like "respect for and preservation of prenatal life," "protection of maternal health," elimination of certain "medical procedures," "mitigation of fetal pain," and others. This Court will surely face critical questions about how that test applies. Must a state law allow abortions when necessary to protect a woman's life and health? And if so, exactly when? How much risk to a woman's life can a State force her to incur, before the Fourteenth Amendment's protection of life kicks in? Suppose a patient with pulmonary hypertension has a 30-to-50 percent risk of dying with ongoing pregnancy; is that enough? And short of death, how much illness or injury can the State require her to accept, consistent with the Amendment's protection of liberty and equality? Further, the Court may face questions about the application of abortion regulations to medical care most people view as quite different from abortion. What about the morning-after pill? IUDs? In vitro fertilization? And how about the use of dilation and evacuation or medication for miscarriage management? * * *

Finally, the majority's ruling today invites a host of questions about interstate conflicts. Can a State bar women from traveling to another State to obtain an abortion? Can a State prohibit advertising out-of-state abortions or helping women get to out-of-state providers? Can a State interfere with the mailing of drugs used for medication abortions? The Constitution protects travel and speech and interstate commerce, so today's ruling will give rise to a host of new constitutional questions. Far from removing the Court from the abortion issue, the majority puts the Court at the center of the coming "interjurisdictional abortion wars."* * *

Mississippi's own record illustrates how little facts on the ground have changed since *Roe* and *Casey,* notwithstanding the majority's supposed "modern developments." Sixty-two percent of pregnancies in Mississippi are unplanned, yet Mississippi does not require insurance to cover contraceptives and prohibits educators from demonstrating proper contraceptive use. The State neither bans pregnancy discrimination nor requires provision of paid parental leave. It has strict eligibility requirements for Medicaid and nutrition assistance, leaving many women and families without basic medical care or enough food. Although 86 percent of pregnancy-related deaths in the State are due to postpartum complications, Mississippi rejected federal funding to provide a year's worth of Medicaid coverage to women after giving birth. Perhaps unsurprisingly, health outcomes in Mississippi are abysmal for both women and children. Mississippi has the highest infant mortality rate in the country, and some of the highest rates for preterm birth, low birthweight, cesarean section, and maternal death. It is approximately 75 times more dangerous for a woman in the State to carry a pregnancy to term than to have an abortion. We do not say that every State is Mississippi, and we are sure some have made gains since *Roe* and *Casey* in providing support for women and children. But a state-by-state analysis by public health professionals shows that States with the most restrictive abortion policies also continue to invest the least in women's and children's health.

The only notable change we can see since *Roe* and *Casey* cuts in favor of adhering to precedent: It is that American abortion law has become more and more aligned with other nations. The majority, like the Mississippi Legislature, claims that the United States is an extreme outlier when it comes to abortion regulation. The global trend, however, has been toward increased provision of legal and safe abortion care. A number of countries, including New Zealand, the Netherlands, and Iceland, permit abortions up to a roughly similar time as *Roe* and *Casey* set. Canada has decriminalized abortion at any point in a pregnancy. Most Western European countries impose restrictions on abortion after 12 to 14 weeks, but they often have liberal exceptions to those time limits, including to prevent harm to a woman's physical or mental health. They also typically make access to early abortion easier, for example, by helping cover its cost. Perhaps most notable, more than 50 countries around the world—in Asia, Latin America, Africa, and Europe—have expanded access to abortion in the past 25 years. In light of that worldwide liberalization of abortion laws, it is American States that will become international outliers after today.* * *

In sum, the majority can point to neither legal nor factual developments in support of its decision.* * *

In support of its holding, the majority invokes two watershed cases overruling prior constitutional precedents: *West Coast Hotel Co.* v. *Parrish* and *Brown* v. *Board of Education*. But those decisions, unlike today's, responded to changed law and to changed facts and attitudes that had taken hold throughout society.* * *

Casey itself addressed both *West Coast Hotel* and *Brown*, and found that neither supported *Roe*'s overruling. In *West Coast Hotel*, *Casey* explained, "the facts of economic life" had proved "different from those previously assumed." And even though "*Plessy* was wrong the day it was decided," the passage of time had made that ever more clear to ever more citizens: "Society's understanding of the facts" in 1954 was "fundamentally different" than in 1896. So the Court needed to reverse course. "In constitutional adjudication as elsewhere in life, changed circumstances may impose new obligations." And because such dramatic change had occurred, the public could understand why the Court was acting. "[T]he Nation could accept each decision" as a "response to the Court's constitutional duty." But that would not be true of a reversal of *Roe*— "[b]ecause neither the factual underpinnings of *Roe*'s central holding nor our understanding of it has changed."* * *

The disruption of overturning *Roe* and *Casey* will therefore be profound. Abortion is a common medical procedure and a familiar experience in women's lives. About 18 percent of pregnancies in this country end in abortion, and about one quarter of American women will have an abortion before the age of 45. Those numbers reflect the predictable and life-changing effects of carrying a pregnancy, giving birth, and becoming a parent. As *Casey* understood, people today rely on their ability to control and time pregnancies when making countless life decisions: where to live, whether and how to invest in education or careers, how to allocate financial resources, and how to approach intimate and family relationships. Women may count on abortion access for when contraception fails. They may count on abortion access for when contraception cannot be used, for example, if they were raped. They may count on abortion for when something changes in the midst of a pregnancy, whether it involves family or financial circumstances, unanticipated medical complications, or heartbreaking fetal diagnoses. Taking away the right to abortion, as the majority does today, destroys all those individual plans and expectations. In so doing, it diminishes women's opportunities to participate fully and equally in the Nation's political, social, and economic life.* * *

The majority's response to these obvious points exists far from the reality American women actually live. The majority proclaims that " 'reproductive planning could take virtually immediate account of any sudden restoration of state authority to ban abortions.' " . . .The facts are: 45 percent of pregnancies in the United States are unplanned. Even the most effective contraceptives fail, and effective contraceptives are not universally accessible. Not all sexual activity is consensual and not all contraceptive choices are made by the party who risks pregnancy. The Mississippi law at issue here, for example, has no exception for rape or incest, even for underage women. Finally, the majority ignores, as explained above, that some women decide to have an abortion because their circumstances change during a pregnancy. Human bodies care little for hopes and plans. Events can occur after conception, from unexpected medical risks to changes in family circumstances, which profoundly alter what it means to carry a pregnancy to term. In all these situations, women have expected that they will get to decide, perhaps in consultation with their families or doctors but free from state interference, whether to continue a pregnancy. For those who will now have to undergo that pregnancy, the loss of *Roe* and *Casey* could be disastrous.

That is especially so for women without money.* * * These are the women most likely to seek abortion care in the first place. Women living below the federal poverty line experience unintended pregnancies at rates five times higher than higher income women do, and nearly half of women who seek abortion care live in households below the poverty line.* * *

After today, young women will come of age with fewer rights than their mothers and grandmothers had. The majority accomplishes that result without so much as considering how women have relied on the right to choose or what it means to take that right away. The majority's refusal even to consider the life-altering consequences of reversing *Roe* and *Casey* is a stunning indictment of its decision.

One last consideration counsels against the majority's ruling: the very controversy surrounding *Roe* and *Casey*.* * *

"Power, not reason, is the new currency of this Court's decisionmaking." *Roe* has stood for fifty years. *Casey*, a precedent about precedent specifically confirming *Roe*, has stood for thirty. And the doctrine of *stare decisis*—a critical element of the rule of law—stands foursquare behind their continued existence. The right those decisions established and preserved is embedded in our constitutional law, both originating in and leading to other rights protecting bodily integrity, personal autonomy, and family relationships. The abortion right is also embedded in the lives of women—shaping their expectations, influencing their choices about relationships and work, supporting (as all reproductive rights do) their social and economic equality. Since the right's recognition (and affirmation), nothing has changed to support what the majority does today. Neither law nor facts nor attitudes have provided any new reasons to reach a different result than *Roe* and *Casey* did. All that has changed is this Court.

Mississippi—and other States too—knew exactly what they were doing in ginning up new legal challenges to *Roe* and *Casey*. The 15-week ban at issue here was enacted in 2018. Other States quickly followed: Between 2019 and 2021, eight States banned abortion procedures after six to eight weeks of pregnancy, and three States enacted all-out bans. Mississippi itself decided in 2019 that it had not gone far enough: The year after enacting the law under review, the State passed a 6-week restriction. A state senator who championed both Mississippi laws said the obvious out loud. "[A] lot of people thought," he explained, that "finally, we have" a conservative Court "and so now would be a good time to start testing the limits of *Roe*." In its petition for certiorari, the State had exercised a smidgen of restraint. It had urged the Court merely to roll back *Roe* and *Casey*, specifically assuring the Court that "the questions presented in this petition do not require the Court to overturn" those precedents. But as Mississippi grew ever more confident in its prospects, it resolved to go all in. It urged the Court to overrule *Roe* and *Casey*. Nothing but everything would be enough.

Earlier this Term, this Court signaled that Mississippi's stratagem would succeed. Texas was one of the fistful of States to have recently banned abortions after six weeks of pregnancy. It added to that "flagrantly unconstitutional" restriction an unprecedented scheme to "evade judicial scrutiny." And five Justices acceded to that cynical maneuver. They let Texas defy this Court's constitutional rulings, nullifying *Roe* and *Casey* ahead of schedule in the Nation's second largest State.

And now the other shoe drops, courtesy of that same five-person majority. (We believe that THE CHIEF JUSTICE's opinion is wrong too, but no one should think that there is not a large difference between upholding a 15-week ban on the grounds he does and allowing States to prohibit abortion from the time of conception.) Now a new and bare majority of this Court—acting at practically the first moment possible—overrules *Roe* and *Casey*. It converts a series of dissenting opinions expressing antipathy toward *Roe* and *Casey* into a decision greenlighting even total abortion bans. It eliminates a 50-year-old constitutional right that safeguards women's freedom and equal station. It breaches a core rule-of-law principle, designed to promote constancy in the law. In doing all of that, it places in jeopardy other rights, from contraception to same-sex intimacy and marriage. And finally, it undermines the Court's legitimacy.* * *

Quoting Justice Stewart, *Casey* explained that to [reverse prior law] "upon a ground no firmer than a change in [the Court's] membership"— would invite the view that "this institution is little different from the two political branches of the Government." No view, *Casey* thought, could do "more lasting injury to this Court and to the system of law which it is our abiding mission to serve." For overruling *Roe*, *Casey* concluded, the Court would pay a "terrible price."

The Justices who wrote those words—O'Connor, Kennedy, and Souter—they were judges of wisdom. They would not have won any contests for the kind of ideological purity some court watchers want Justices to deliver. But if there were awards for Justices who left this Court better than they found it? And who for that reason left this country better? And the rule of law stronger? Sign those Justices up.

They knew that "the legitimacy of the Court [is] earned over time." They also would have recognized that it can be destroyed much more quickly. They worked hard to avert that outcome in *Casey*. The American public, they thought, should never conclude that its constitutional protections hung by a thread—that a new majority, adhering to a new "doctrinal school," could "by dint of numbers" alone expunge their rights. It is hard—no, it is impossible—to conclude that anything else has happened here. One of us once said that "[i]t is not often in the law that so few have so quickly changed so much." S. Breyer, Breaking the Promise of *Brown*: The Resegregation of America's Schools 30 (2022). For all of us, in our time on this Court, that has never been more true than today. In overruling *Roe* and *Casey*, this Court betrays its guiding principles.

With sorrow—for this Court, but more, for the many millions of American women who have today lost a fundamental constitutional protection—we dissent.

[The dissenters included an appendix that analyzed the 28 cases cited by the majority in support of overruling *Roe* and *Casey*, *stare decisis* notwithstanding.]

NOTES

1. *Approach to Stare Decisis?* How do the majority and dissent differ in their approach to *stare decisis*? Should it matter that *Casey* reaffirmed *Roe* two decades later? Did that reaffirmation create a double dose of *stare decisis* that was entitled to greater weight than the majority gave it?

2. *Judicial Legitimacy.* At several points in the opinion, the majority quoted Justice Byron White, a staunch opponent of *Roe*, as calling *Roe* an exercise of "raw judicial power." The dissent, in turn, asserted that "power, not reason, is the new currency of this Court's decisionmaking." How do you evaluate these competing claims? Along similar lines, how do the majority, the concurrence in the judgment by the Chief Justice, and the dissent differ in the way they understand judicial legitimacy? Which account do you find more persuasive? How can legitimacy be measured? Is it something the justices should take into account? Is it relevant that the Supreme Court's public approval has dropped sharply over the last year? Jeffrey M. Jones, *Confidence un U.S. Supreme Court Sinks to Historic Law*, Gallup News, June 23, 2022, https://news.gallup.com/poll/394103/confidence-supreme-court-sinks-historic-low.aspx. How might the controversial leak of the draft *Dobbs* opinion in May, 2022 bear on the issue of legitimacy? See Adam Liptak, *A Leaky Supreme Court Starts to Resemble the Other Branches*, N.Y. TIMES, May 12, 2022, at A16.

3. *Effect on Other Substantive Due Process Cases.* Both the majority and Justice Kavanaugh in his separate concurrence repeatedly assert that precedents like *Griswold*, *Lawrence* and *Obergefell* are not jeopardized by *Dobbs*. But the reasoning and use of history in *Dobbs* would seem to point clearly in the opposite direction. What do you make of this contradiction? And what light, if any, is shed on the question by Justice Thomas' explicit proposal to reconsider all these precedents, readiness to jettison substantive due process entirely, and interest in revitalizing the Fourteenth Amendment's privileges or immunities clause? When you read *Lawrence* and *Obergefell* later in this chapter, return to *Dobbs* and reconsider this question.

4. *Equal Protection Alternative.* Note that the majority quickly dispenses with the idea that the equal protection clause could provide an alternative basis for abortion rights. Is the opinion's one-paragraph rejection

of this idea sufficient? Does the opinion place too much weight on *Geduldig v. Aiello* (Casebook, p. 420)? Recall that Congress overruled the result of that 1974 decision, and the case has been heavily criticized as misunderstanding the role of pregnancy discrimination in perpetuating gender inequality.

5. *National Legislation?* Both the majority opinion and concurrence by Justice Kavanaugh refer repeatedly to allowing *states* to determine abortion policy. But the majority's repeated references to "the people's elected representatives" is capacious enough to include Congress, and Justice Kavanaugh twice specifically mentions Congress as an appropriate decisionmaker. In connection with the materials in chapter 7, consider what source of congressional power might support federal legislation on this issue.

6. *Federalism.* The emphasis the majority places on federalism and the virtues of allowing states to pursue different abortion policies contrasts sharply with the *Bruen* case excerpted earlier in this chapter. That case, striking down New York's law on gun permits, was decided the day before *Dobbs*. Why did the justices forming the majority in both cases not worry more about nine justices setting gun policy for the entire nation? Does the textual difference between gun and abortion rights offer a sufficient basis for distinguishing the two cases on that score?

7. *Potential Life?* The dissent asserts that, under the majority opinion, "from the very moment of fertilization, a woman has no rights to speak of." Does that conclusion necessarily follow from the majority? Pregnancy is commonly understood to begin when the fertilized egg implants in the uterine wall, which calls into question the dissent's claim. For an early analysis of this question, see Einer Elhauge, *Where Exactly is the New Constitutional Line Between Abortion and Contraception*, https://blog.petrieflom.law.harvard.edu/ 2022/06/27/where-exactly-is-the-new-constitutional-line-between-abortion-and-contraception.

Keep that issue in mind as you consider the following problem.

Page 640. Replace Problem 5-2 with the following:

PROBLEM 5-2:
A BAN ON CERTAIN CONTRACEPTIVES

Suppose that, in the wake of *Dobbs*, a state enacts a ban on two contraceptives. First, the new law bans emergency contraceptive pills (sometimes called "morning-after" pills, although they can be taken up to five days after intercourse to prevent pregnancy). Second, the law bans ordinary birth control pills (hormones taken on a regular basis by women who wish to avoid pregnancy).

In support of its ban on emergency contraceptives, the bill characterizes morning-after pills as abortifacients. The bill's legislative sponsors noted that in *Hobby Lobby v. Burwell* (Casebook, p. 844), the Supreme Court ruled that the Religious Freedom Restoration Act barred the federal government from requiring closely-held corporations to provide insurance coverage for certain forms of birth control that employers believed were abortifacients. In that case, Hobby Lobby, one of the employers who challenged the requirement, objected to paying for morning-after pills because it believed them to cause an abortion by preventing a fertilized egg from implanting in the uterine wall.

The view that morning-after pills are abortifacients is inconsistent with the prevailing views of the medical community. According to an analysis by the *New York Times*:

> Studies have not established that emergency contraceptive pills prevent fertilized eggs from implanting in the womb, leading scientists say. Rather, the pills delay ovulation, the release of eggs from ovaries that occurs before eggs are fertilized, and some pills also thicken cervical mucus so sperm have trouble swimming.

Pam Belluck, *Abortion Qualms on Morning-After Pills May be Unfounded*, N.Y. TIMES, June 6, 2012, at A1.

In characterizing morning-after pills as abortifacients, the legislative findings accompanying the bill cite to a group of physicians who dissent from the consensus view. The bill also includes a finding that taking multiple ordinary birth control pills within a few days of intercourse can sometimes function similarly to morning-after pills.

(1) Would the ban on morning-after pills be constitutional under *Dobbs*? Under *Griswold*?

(2) In answering question (1), how much would turn on whether morning-after pills do, in fact, prevent a fertilized egg from implanting in the womb, given that pregnancy is often deemed to begin at the point of implantation? Is it relevant to this question that studies estimate that, without any use of morning-after pills, one-third to one-half of fertilized eggs never implant, and that many that do implant lead to miscarriages?

(3) How would *Dobbs* and *Griswold* apply to the ban of ordinary birth control pills? As to this ban, would it matter if, instead of a legislative finding that taking multiple pills could function like a morning-after pill, the legislature simply said that "any drug whose purpose is to prevent or impair pregnancy supports the destructive and immoral idea that the function of sexual intercourse is anything other than to conceive babies."

(4) As part of your analysis, consider what level of scrutiny a court would apply to these scenarios.

As you think about the problem, set aside the question of whether approval by the Food & Drug Administration would have any impact on the outcome, as well as any religious liberty dimension to the issue. Focus only on applying *Dobbs*, *Griswold* and any other Fourteenth Amendment precedent that you deem relevant.

D. THE RIGHT TO MARRY

Page 670. Insert after Note 10:

11. Recall the extended debate among the justices in *Dobbs* about the effect of that decision on precedents like *Lawrence* and *Obergefell*. Can the results in those two cases be squared with the reason and interpretive approach employed in *Dobbs*? Are those precedents in jeopardy, notwithstanding the assertions by Justices Alito and Kavanaugh that *Dobbs* poses no threat to them?

12. It would appear that, at a minimum, *Obergefell*'s language limiting *Glucksberg* to the end-of-life context was nullified by *Dobbs*. Once you have read *Glucksberg*, consider how *Dobbs'* enthusiastic embrace of its approach might affect substantive due process cases going forward. Consider, as well, whether the attention on whether *Dobbs* will lead cases like *Lawrence* and *Obergefell* to be overruled obscures the potential of future cases to meaningfully *limit* those cases rather than to cast them aside entirely. On this point, review how Chief Justice Roberts emphasized the virtues of *stare decisis* in his *June Medical* opinion (page 21 above), while applying an interpretation of the case that significantly weakened its force.

CHAPTER 6

THE FIRST AMENDMENT

■ ■ ■

SECTION 1. FREE SPEECH AND COMPETING VALUES

Page 716. Replace the final paragraph of the Notes on *Reed* with the following:

The Court itself narrowed *Reed* in City of Austin v. Reagan National Advertising, ___ U.S. ___, 142 S.Ct. 1464 (2022). *City of Austin* was another signage case. An Austin city ordinance regulating signs gave some preferential treatment to signs advertising on-premises services. Companies advertising off-premises services sued, contending that this distinction constituted content discrimination under *Reed*. After all, without reading a sign, it is impossible to know whether the sign refers to activities in that location or not. Justice Sotomayor's opinion for the Court rejected this argument. It explained that:

> Unlike the sign code at issue in *Reed*, however, the City's provisions at issue here do not single out any topic or subject matter for differential treatment. A sign's substantive message itself is irrelevant to the application of the provisions; there are no content-discriminatory classifications for political messages, ideological messages, or directional messages concerning specific events, including those sponsored by religious and nonprofit organizations.

Instead, the Court said, the ordinance was more akin to a time, place, and manner restriction:

> Rather, the City's provisions distinguish based on location: A given sign is treated differently based solely on whether it is located on the same premises as the thing being discussed or not. The message on the sign matters only to the extent that it informs the sign's relative location. The on-/off-premises distinction is therefore similar to ordinary time, place, or manner restrictions. *Reed* does not require the application of strict scrutiny to this kind of location-based regulation.

The Supreme Court has continued to make aggressive use of the doctrine of content neutrality in other cases, brushing aside arguable exceptions to the doctrine. Consider the following case.

SECTION 3. CULTURAL DISCOURSE AND INTERGROUP RELATIONS

B. FIGHTING WORDS, CAPTIVE AUDIENCES, AND HATE SPEECH

Page 772. Insert after Note 2:

3.   *From "Fuck the Draft" to "Fuck Cheer."* The use of offensive language to criticize authority may take on a different valence in the setting of students in public schools. In a case involving a peaceful protest against the Vietnam War, *Tinker v. Des Moines Independent Community School Dist.*, 393 U.S. 503 (1969), the Court held that student speech in school is protected by the First Amendment but may be restricted if it substantially disrupts school activities or the rights of others. The extent to which school disciplinary authority extends beyond the school building is less clear. In *Mahanoy Area School District v. B.L.*, 141 S.Ct. 2038 (2021), the Court considered the application of *Tinker* to student use of social media. The plaintiff was a high school freshman who failed to make the varsity cheerleading squad. She posted two images on Snapchat, a phone app that allows users to share posts temporarily with friends. As the Court describes it, one of the images "showed B. L. and a friend with middle fingers raised; it bore the caption: 'Fuck school fuck softball fuck cheer fuck everything.'" One of the recipients took a picture of the image with a separate phone and shared it with members of the cheerleading squad. Several upset recipients approached the cheerleading coaches and even raised the subject in an algebra class taught by a coach. As a result, B.L. was suspended from the junior varsity cheerleading squad despite having apologized for the posts.

The Court was reluctant to impose categorical rules on the ability of schools to discipline students for misconduct. It refused to entirely bar schools for imposing discipline for activities taking place outside of the school itself. The Court held, however, that the school's interests were diminished. Given that B.L.'s statement was made privately when she was not in the school or participating in any school activity, and that she did not attack any individual student or school official, her discipline violated the First Amendment. Justice Thomas dissented on the ground that schools historically have had the power to punish student speech that undermined school authority, whether the speech took place in school or out.

SECTION 4. SPEECH WITH A GOVERNMENT NEXUS

A. PUBLIC FORUM DOCTRINE

Page 792. Insert before *McCullen*:

Justice Scalia's critique of *Hill* ultimately seems to have carried the day. In *Dobbs v. Jackson Women's Health Org.*, 142 S.Ct. 2228 (2022), Justice Alito cited *Hill* as a case where First Amendment doctrine had been "distorted" due to constitutional protection of abortion. Does this dictum mean that *Hill* has been overruled and that lower courts are now free to ignore it? Note that the issue can still arise since abortion remains legal in some states, so further picketing of clinics remains a possibility.

Page 805. Insert after Note 3:

4. *Extending* Matal. In *Iancu v. Brunetti*, 139 S.Ct. 2294 (2019), the Court struck down another provision of the Lanham Act, which prohibited registration of "immoral" or "scandalous" matter. In an opinion by Justice Kagan, the Court concluded that the provision was viewpoint-based:

> The meanings of "immoral" and "scandalous" are not mysterious, but resort to some dictionaries still helps to lay bare the problem. When is expressive material "immoral"? According to a standard definition, when it is "inconsistent with rectitude, purity, or good morals"; "wicked"; or "vicious . . . And when is such material "scandalous"? Says a typical definition, when it "giv[es] offense to the conscience or moral feelings"; "excite[s] reprobation"; or "call[s] out condemnation."
> . . . . Put the pair of overlapping terms together and the statute, on its face, distinguishes between two opposed sets of ideas: those aligned with conventional moral standards and those hostile to them; those inducing societal nods of approval and those provoking offense and condemnation.

Returning to the problem of hate speech, is it possible to draft restrictions on hate speech that would avoid being categorized as viewpoint-based?

B. GOVERNMENT-SUPPORTED SPEECH

Page 816. Insert after Note 3:

4. *Round Two of* AID. In 2020, the Supreme Court ruled in *AID II* that it was constitutional to apply the same funding restriction on the plaintiff's foreign affiliates. *Agency for International Development v. Alliance for Open Society Int'l, Inc.*, 140 S.Ct. 2082, 207 L.Ed.2d 654 (2020). The Court rested that conclusion on two "bedrock principles" of U.S. law: "foreign citizens outside U.S. territory do not possess rights under the U.S. Constitution," and "separately incorporated organizations are separate legal units with distinct

legal rights and obligations." The dissent argued that it was really the constitutional rights of the U.S. parent group that were at stake. The foreign affiliates existed only as arms of its activities, and often they were separately incorporated only because the host country required it.

SECTION 5. FREEDOM OF ASSOCIATION

Page 824. Insert before *Rotary International*:

If all members of associations could be penalized because of the misconduct of some of the members or the organization's leaders, there would be a powerful chilling effect on willingness to join organizations. *Claiborne Hardware* rests in part on the need to prevent that kind of chilling effect. In the following case, the Court imposed sweeping restrictions on disclosure requirements in order to prevent such a chilling effect, going well beyond earlier cases such as *NAACP v. Alabama ex rel. Patterson* in that respect.

Americans for Prosperity Foundation (APF) v. Bonta

141 S.Ct. 2373 (2021)

A California law required charitable foundations to disclose their major donors to the state government, as part of a state effort to prevent fraud. The state only began serious efforts to enforce this requirement in 2010. The disclosures were confidential, although there had been some leaks in the past. APF sued to enjoin enforcement of the disclosure requirement. The vote to strike down the disclosure requirement was 6–3, but the majority was divided about the standard of review and remedy. Chief Justice Roberts, joined by Justices Barrett and Justice Kavanaugh, concluded that the standard was "exacting scrutiny," which requires narrow tailoring but not the selection of the least restrictive means. Justice Alito, joined by Justice Gorsuch, questioned the use of this standard of review. Alito suggested arguments why the standard should be strict scrutiny but concluded it was unnecessary to decide the issue in this case. Meanwhile, Justice Thomas argued the striking down statutes "on their face" goes beyond a court's Article III powers, because the plaintiff only has the right to challenge the law as applied to itself. All six of these Justices, however, joined the portion of the Roberts opinion holding that the disclosure requirement was not sufficiently tailored to the state's goal of preventing fraud. In dissent, Justice Sotomayor, joined by Justices Breyer and Kagan, argued that heightened scrutiny for disclosure requirements was only warranted when an organization could demonstrate a substantial chilling effect. Sotomayor accused the majority of "recklessly hold[ing] a state regulation facially invalid despite petitioners' failure to show that a substantial proportion of those affected would prefer anonymity, much less that they are objectively burdened by the loss of it."

SECTION 6. THE RELIGION CLAUSES

Page 846. Insert after Note 3:

4. *The Scope of the Ministerial Exemption.* In *Our Lady of Guadalupe School v. Morrissey-Berru*, 140 S.Ct. 2049, 207 L.Ed.2d 870 (2020), the Court held that the ministerial exemption extends beyond the formally designated and trained teachers involved in *Hosanna-Tabor*. The lower court held that the ministerial exception did not apply because the teachers in question lacked ministerial training, credentials, and ministerial background, all of which were present in *Hosanna-Tabor*. The Court disagreed:

> Educating and forming students in the Catholic faith lay at the core of the mission of the schools where they taught, and their employment agreements and faculty handbooks specified in no uncertain terms that they were expected to help the schools carry out this mission and that their work would be evaluated to ensure that they were fulfilling that responsibility. As elementary school teachers responsible for providing instruction in all subjects, including religion, they were the members of the school staff who were entrusted most directly with the responsibility of educating their students in the faith. And not only were they obligated to provide instruction about the Catholic faith, but they were also expected to guide their students, by word and deed, toward the goal of living their lives in accordance with the faith. They prayed with their students, attended Mass with the students, and prepared the children for their participation in other religious activities.

The Court indicated that a church's description of the nature of a position was "important," but it did not adopt the approach taken by Justices Thomas and Gorsuch, under which courts must "defer to religious organizations' good-faith claims that a certain employee's position is 'ministerial.'"

CARSON v. MAKIN
___ U.S. ___, 142 S.Ct. 1987, ___ L.Ed.2d ___ (2022)

CHIEF JUSTICE ROBERTS delivered the opinion of the Court.

[Given Maine's rural character, 143 of its 260 school administrative units do not operate a secondary school. To help students in those districts attend secondary school, the state has paid for students to attend either another public school or a private school of their choice. Until 1982 that had included religious schools—but in that year the Maine Legislature adopted a statute excluding religiously affiliated schools that had a sectarian curriculum. Religiously affiliated schools with a secular curriculum were still eligible for the state tuition payments.

[The Carson family and two others who wanted to send their children to Christian schools with a faith-based curriculum sued for invalidation of the 1982 state law. Writing for a First Circuit panel that included retired Justice David Souter, Chief Judge David Barron ruled in favor of the state. The Supreme Court reversed.]

The Free Exercise Clause of the First Amendment protects against "indirect coercion or penalties on the free exercise of religion, not just outright prohibitions." In particular, we have repeatedly held that a State violates the Free Exercise Clause when it excludes religious observers from otherwise available public benefits.

We have recently applied these principles in the context of two state efforts to withhold otherwise available public benefits from religious organizations. In *Trinity Lutheran Church of Columbia, Inc. v. Comer*, 582 U.S. ___ (2017), we considered a Missouri program that offered grants to qualifying nonprofit organizations that installed cushioning playground surfaces made from recycled rubber tires. The Missouri Department of Natural Resources maintained an express policy of denying such grants to any applicant owned or controlled by a church, sect, or other religious entity. The Trinity Lutheran Church Child Learning Center applied for a grant to resurface its gravel playground, but the Department denied funding on the ground that the Center was operated by the Church.

We deemed it "unremarkable in light of our prior decisions" to conclude that the Free Exercise Clause did not permit Missouri to "expressly discriminate[ ] against otherwise eligible recipients by disqualifying them from a public benefit solely because of their religious character." While it was true that Trinity Lutheran remained "free to continue operating as a church," it could enjoy that freedom only "at the cost of automatic and absolute exclusion from the benefits of a public program for which the Center [was] otherwise fully qualified." Such discrimination, we said, was "odious to our Constitution" and could not stand.

Two Terms ago, in *Espinoza [v. Montana Dep't of Revenue,* 591 U.S. ___ (2021)], we reached the same conclusion as to a Montana program that provided tax credits to donors who sponsored scholarships for private school tuition. The Montana Supreme Court held that the program, to the extent it included religious schools, violated a provision of the Montana Constitution that barred government aid to any school controlled in whole or in part by a church, sect, or denomination. As a result of that holding, the State terminated the scholarship program, preventing the petitioners from accessing scholarship funds they otherwise would have used to fund their children's educations at religious schools.

We again held that the Free Exercise Clause forbade the State's action. The application of the Montana Constitution's no-aid provision, we explained, required strict scrutiny because it "bar[red] religious schools from public benefits solely because of the religious character of the schools." "A State need not subsidize private education," we concluded, "[b]ut once a

State decides to do so, it cannot disqualify some private schools solely because they are religious."

[The Court held that the Maine program was essentially indistinguishable from the Montana program invalidated in *Espinoza*: both programs discriminated against schools because of their religious affiliation, and neither program satisfied strict scrutiny because they were not narrowly tailored to the compelling public interest in uniform educational standards.]

The Court of Appeals also attempted to distinguish this case from *Trinity Lutheran* and *Espinoza* on the ground that the funding restrictions in those cases were "solely status-based religious discrimination," while the challenged provision here "imposes a use-based restriction."

In *Trinity Lutheran*, the Missouri Constitution banned the use of public funds in aid of "any church, sect or denomination of religion." We noted that the case involved "express discrimination based on religious identity," which was sufficient unto the day in deciding it, and that our opinion did "not address religious uses of funding."

So too in *Espinoza*, the discrimination at issue was described by the Montana Supreme Court as a prohibition on aiding "schools controlled by churches," and we analyzed the issue in terms of "religious status and not religious use." Foreshadowing Maine's argument here, Montana argued that its case was different from Trinity Lutheran's because it involved not playground resurfacing, but general funds that "could be used for religious ends by some recipients, particularly schools that believe faith should *permeate*[ ]' everything they do." We explained, however, that the strict scrutiny triggered by status-based discrimination could not be avoided by arguing that "one of its goals or effects [was] preventing religious organizations from putting aid to religious *uses*." And we noted that nothing in our analysis was "meant to suggest that we agree[d] with [Montana] that some lesser degree of scrutiny applies to discrimination against religious uses of government aid."

Maine's argument, however, * * * is premised on precisely such a distinction. That premise, however, misreads our precedents. In *Trinity Lutheran* and *Espinoza*, we held that the Free Exercise Clause forbids discrimination on the basis of religious status. But those decisions never suggested that use-based discrimination is any less offensive to the Free Exercise Clause. This case illustrates why. "[E]ducating young people in their faith, inculcating its teachings, and training them to live their faith are responsibilities that lie at the very core of the mission of a private religious school."

Any attempt to give effect to such a distinction by scrutinizing whether and how a religious school pursues its educational mission would also raise serious concerns about state entanglement with religion and denominational favoritism. Indeed, Maine concedes that the Department barely engages in any such scrutiny when enforcing the "nonsectarian" requirement. See Brief for Respondent 5 (asserting that there will be no need to probe private schools' uses of tuition assistance funds because "schools self-identify as nonsectarian" under the program and the need for any further questioning is "extremely rare"). That suggests that any status-use distinction lacks a meaningful application not only in theory, but in practice as well. In short, the prohibition on status-based discrimination under the Free Exercise Clause is not a permission to engage in use-based discrimination. * * *

JUSTICE BREYER [joined by JUSTICE KAGAN & JUSTICE SOTOMAYOR (except for Part I.B)] dissenting.

The First Amendment's two Religion Clauses together provide that the government "shall make no law respecting an establishment of religion, or prohibiting the free exercise thereof." Each Clause, linguistically speaking, is "cast in absolute terms." *Walz* v. *Tax Comm'n of City of New York*, 397 U.S. 664, 668 (1970). The first Clause, the Establishment Clause, seems to bar all government "sponsorship, financial support, [or] active involvement . . . in religious activity," while the second Clause, the Free Exercise Clause, seems to bar all "governmental restraint on religious practice." The apparently absolutist nature of these two prohibitions means that either Clause, "if expanded to a logical extreme, would tend to clash with the other." Because of this, we have said, the two Clauses "are frequently in tension," *Locke* v. *Davey*, 540 U.S. 712, 718 (2004), and "often exert conflicting pressures" on government action,

The Free Exercise Clause " 'protect[s] religious observers against unequal treatment.' " [*Trinity Lutheran*]. We have said that, in the education context, this means that States generally cannot "ba[r] religious schools from public benefits solely because of the religious character of the schools."

On the other hand, the Establishment Clause "commands a separation of church and state." A State cannot act to "aid one religion, aid all religions, or prefer one religion over another." *Everson* v. *Board of Ed. of Ewing*, 330 U.S. 1, 15 (1947). This means that a State cannot use "its public school system to aid any or all religious faiths or sects in the dissemination of their doctrines and ideals." Nor may a State "adopt programs or practices in its public schools . . . which 'aid or oppose' any religion "This prohibition," we have cautioned, "is absolute."

Although the Religion Clauses are, in practice, often in tension, they nonetheless "express complementary values." Together they attempt to chart a "course of constitutional neutrality" with respect to government and religion. They were written to help create an American Nation free of the religious conflict that had long plagued European nations with "governmentally established religion[s]." Through the Clauses, the Framers sought to avoid the "anguish, hardship and bitter strife" that resulted from the "union of Church and State" in those countries.

The Religion Clauses thus created a compromise in the form of religious freedom. They aspired to create a "benevolent neutrality"—one which would "permit religious exercise to exist without sponsorship and without interference." "[T]he basic purpose of these provisions" was "to insure that no religion be sponsored or favored, none commanded, and none inhibited." This religious freedom in effect meant that people "were entitled to worship God in their own way and to teach their children" in that way. We have historically interpreted the Religion Clauses with these basic principles in mind.

And in applying these Clauses, we have often said that "there is room for play in the joints" between them. This doctrine reflects the fact that it may be difficult to determine in any particular case whether the Free Exercise Clause *requires* a State to fund the activities of a religious institution, or whether the Establishment Clause *prohibits* the State from doing so. Rather than attempting to draw a highly reticulated and complex free-exercise/establishment line that varies based on the specific circumstances of each state-funded program, we have provided general interpretive principles that apply uniformly in all Religion Clause cases. At the same time, we have made clear that States enjoy a degree of freedom to navigate the Clauses' competing prohibitions. This includes choosing not to fund certain religious activity where States have strong, establishment-related reasons for not doing so. And, States have freedom to make this choice even when the Establishment Clause does not itself prohibit the State from funding that activity. The Court today nowhere mentions, and I fear effectively abandons, this longstanding doctrine.

I have previously discussed my views of the relationship between the Religion Clauses and how I believe these Clauses should be interpreted to advance their goal of avoiding religious strife. Here I simply note the increased risk of religiously based social conflict when government promotes religion in its public school system. "[T]he prescription of prayer and Bible reading in the public schools, during and as part of the curricular day, involving young impressionable children whose school attendance is statutorily compelled," can "give rise to those very divisive influences and inhibitions of freedom which both religion clauses of the First Amendment" sought to prevent.

This potential for religious strife is still with us. We are today a Nation with well over 100 different religious groups, from Free Will Baptist to African Methodist, Buddhist to Humanist. People in our country adhere to a vast array of beliefs, ideals, and philosophies. And with greater religious diversity comes greater risk of religiously based strife, conflict, and social division. The Religion Clauses were written in part to help avoid that disunion. As Thomas Jefferson, one of the leading drafters and proponents of those Clauses, wrote, " 'to compel a man to furnish contributions of money for the propagation of opinions which he disbelieves, is sinful and tyrannical.' " And as James Madison, another drafter and proponent, said, compelled taxpayer sponsorship of religion "is itself a signal of persecution," which "will destroy that moderation and harmony which the forbearance of our laws to intermeddle with Religion, has produced amongst its several sects." To interpret the Clauses with these concerns in mind may help to further their original purpose of avoiding religious-based division.

I have also previously explained why I believe that a "rigid, bright-line" approach to the Religion Clauses—an approach without any leeway or "play in the joints"—will too often work against the Clauses' underlying purposes. Not all state-funded programs that have religious restrictions carry the same risk of creating social division and conflict. In my view, that risk can best be understood by considering the particular benefit at issue, along with the reasons for the particular religious restriction at issue. Recognition that States enjoy a degree of constitutional leeway allows States to enact laws sensitive to local circumstances while also allowing this Court to consider those circumstances in light of the basic values underlying the Religion Clauses.

In a word, to interpret the two Clauses as if they were joined at the hip will work against their basic purpose: to allow for an American society with practitioners of over 100 different religions, and those who do not practice religion at all, to live together without serious risk of religion-based social divisions. [In Part II, of his dissenting opinion, Justice Breyer argued that the balanced approach directed by constitutional text and original meaning *Espinoza* should be limited along the lines suggested by Maine and the First Circuit.]

NOTES ON CARSON

1.   *Play in the Joints?* Justice Breyer invokes the idea that there is an area of state discretion regarding the treatment of religion. The majority invoked a similar idea in *Smith* to suggest that some religious accommodations do not violate the Establishment Clause, even though those accommodations are not required by the Free Exercise Clause. The majority opinion seems to leave very little room for such leeway in the converse situation, where the Establishment Clause does not bar state assistance for a religious activity but a state may wish to do so. Is this asymmetrical treatment justified? Or would it be sounder to hold that there is no daylight between the two clauses. Under that view, any state support for religion would be limited to what the Free Exercise Clause requires, and any restriction on state aid is limited to what the Establishment Clause requires.

2. *Background on State Aid to Religious Schools.* The Court has sometimes found it significant when state aid is tied to a choice of school by parents rather than being directly given to the school in the forms of goods or service. This distinction was highlighted in *Zelman v. Simmons-Harris*, 536 U.S. 639 (2002), in which the Court upheld a school voucher program. The parties agreed that the program had a purely secular purpose; the local public schools were a disaster, and the legislature wanted to provide some viable alternatives for poor students. A scholarship program provided tuition aid for some students to attend private schools, as well as funding for suburban schools accepting those students and for new "charter" schools in the public system. It also provided some tutorial aid for eligible students who chose to remain enrolled in their usual public schools. The majority opinion by Chief Justice Rehnquist found this to be a program of "true private choice," in which a neutral government program provides aid directly to a broad class of individuals, who in turn direct the aid to institutions of their own choosing. The majority was unimpressed by the fact that 96% of the participating students who attended private schools went to religious schools, or by the fact that none of the suburban public schools had agreed to participate. The four dissenters, led by Justice Stevens, protested that "the overwhelming proportion of large appropriations of voucher money must be spent on religious schools if it is to be spent at all, and will be spent in amounts that cover almost all of tuition."

3. *State Regulation of Religious Schools.* Given *Espinoza* and *Carson*, it is clear that school vouchers and similar programs must include religious schools. This raises the question of what conditions the state can apply to religious schools participating in these programs. In his dissent in *Zelman*, Justice Breyer emphasized that recipient schools in the voucher program were required to meet certain criteria. They were required to accept students of all religions. They were also forbidden to "advocate or foster unlawful behavior or teach hatred of any person or group on the basis of race, ethnicity, national origin, or religion." Do these restrictions violate free speech under unconstitutional conditions cases such as *Agency for International Development* [Casebook, p. 811]? If not, do they violate the free exercise rights of religions with contrary views about race or practitioners of other religions? What about state laws requiring that schools teach the theory of evolution, as applied to religious schools that favor creationism?

4. *The Amazing Shrinking Establishment Clause?* The Court has increasingly reduced the scope of the Establishment Clause as a corollary of its expansion of the Free Exercise Clause. We return to the Establishment Clause at the end of this chapter.

Page 855. Add at the end of Problem 6-3:

Masterpiece Cake and Problem 6-3 involve the problem of distinguishing discrimination against groups of people from discrimination against message. This issue may become less pressing in the future, because the following two cases have cut back on *Smith* to the point of raising questions about the doctrine's future viability. They may also subsume *Lukumi Babalu Aye* into a broader vision of free exercise.

TANDON V. NEWSOM

593 U.S. ___, 141 S.Ct. 1294, 209 L.Ed.2d 355 (2021)

[The facts are set forth in the lower court's opinion denying an injunction against a California public health rule. According to the trial court, the State considered eight objective risk criteria related to the spread of COVID-19: "(1) the ability to accommodate face covering wearing at all times; (2) the ability to physically distance between individuals of different households; (3) the ability to limit the number of people per square foot; (4) the ability to limit the duration of exposure; (5) the ability to limit the amount of mixing of people from different households; (6) the ability to limit the amount of physical interactions; (7) the ability to optimize ventilation; and (8) the ability to limit activities that are known to increase the possibility of viral spread, such as singing, shouting, and heavy breathing." In parts of the state presenting the highest level of COVID-19 risk, the state allowed no more than three households to gather for indoor home meetings, but allowed meetings of more than three households in a variety of commercial settings, ranging from stores to tattoo parlors (subject to social distancing requirements). The state also allowed indoor religious meetings, subject to precautions, in areas with lower levels of risk, as well as outdoor religious activities. The plaintiffs sought an injunction from the Supreme Court to prevent application of the rules to religious meetings in homes. By the time the case reached the Supreme Court, the disease rate had decreased and the restrictions against the plaintiffs' activities were no longer in effect.]

PER CURIAM:

* * * This Court's decisions have made the following points clear.

First, government regulations are not neutral and generally applicable, and therefore trigger strict scrutiny under the Free Exercise Clause, whenever they treat any comparable secular activity more favorably than religious exercise. It is no answer that a State treats some comparable secular businesses or other activities as poorly as or even less favorably than the religious exercise at issue.

Second, whether two activities are comparable for purposes of the Free Exercise Clause must be judged against the asserted government interest that justifies the regulation at issue. Comparability is concerned with the risks various activities pose, not the reasons why people gather.

Third, the government has the burden to establish that the challenged law satisfies strict scrutiny. To do so in this context, it must do more than assert that certain risk factors "are always present in worship, or always absent from the other secular activities" the government may allow. Instead, narrow tailoring requires the government to show that measures less restrictive of the First Amendment activity could not address its interest in reducing the spread of COVID. Where the government permits other activities to proceed with precautions, it must show that the religious exercise at issue is more dangerous than those activities even when the same precautions are applied. Otherwise, precautions that suffice for other activities suffice for religious exercise too.

Fourth, even if the government withdraws or modifies a COVID restriction in the course of litigation, that does not necessarily moot the case. And so long as a case is not moot, litigants otherwise entitled to emergency injunctive relief remain entitled to such relief where the applicants "remain under a constant threat" that government officials will use their power to reinstate the challenged restrictions.

These principles dictated the outcome in this case * * *. First, California treats some comparable secular activities more favorably than at-home religious exercise, permitting hair salons, retail stores, personal care services, movie theaters, private suites at sporting events and concerts, and indoor restaurants to bring together more than three households at a time. Second, the Ninth Circuit did not conclude that those activities pose a lesser risk of transmission than applicants' proposed religious exercise at home. The Ninth Circuit erroneously rejected these comparators simply because this Court's previous decisions involved public buildings as opposed to private buildings. Third, instead of requiring the State to explain why it could not safely permit at-home worshipers to gather in larger numbers while using precautions used in secular activities, the Ninth Circuit erroneously declared that such measures might not "translate readily" to the home. The State cannot "assume the worst when people go to worship but assume the best when people go to work." And fourth, although California officials changed the challenged policy shortly after this application was filed, the previous restrictions remain in place until April 15th, and officials with a track record of "moving the goalposts" retain authority to reinstate those heightened restrictions at any time.

Applicants are likely to succeed on the merits of their free exercise claim; they are irreparably harmed by the loss of free exercise rights "for even minimal periods of time"; and the State has not shown that "public health would be imperiled" by employing less restrictive measures. Accordingly, applicants are entitled to an injunction pending appeal.

This is the fifth time the Court has summarily rejected the Ninth Circuit's analysis of California's COVID restrictions on religious exercise. It is unsurprising that such litigants are entitled to relief. California's Blueprint System contains myriad exceptions and accommodations for comparable activities, thus requiring the application of strict scrutiny. And historically, strict scrutiny requires the State to further "interests of the highest order" by means "narrowly tailored in pursuit of those interests." That standard "is not watered down"; it "really means what it says."

[CHIEF JUSTICE ROBERTS voted to deny the injunction but did not provide an explanatory statement.]

JUSTICE KAGAN, with whom JUSTICE BREYER and JUSTICE SOTOMAYOR join, dissenting.

* * * The First Amendment requires that a State treat religious conduct as well as the State treats comparable secular conduct. Sometimes finding the right secular analogue may raise hard questions. But not today. California limits religious gatherings in homes to three households. If the State also limits all secular gatherings in homes to three households, it has complied with the First Amendment. And the State does exactly that: It has adopted a blanket restriction on at-home gatherings of all kinds, religious and secular alike. California need not, as the *per curiam* insists, treat at-home religious gatherings the same as hardware stores and hair salons—and thus unlike at-home secular gatherings, the obvious comparator here. As the *per curiam*'s reliance on separate opinions and unreasoned orders signals, the law does not require that the State equally treat apples and watermelons.

And even supposing a court should cast so expansive a comparative net, the *per curiam*'s analysis of this case defies the factual record. According to the *per curiam*, "the Ninth Circuit did not conclude that" activities like frequenting stores or salons "pose a lesser risk of transmission" than applicants' at-home religious activities. But Judges Milan Smith and Bade explained for the court that those activities do pose lesser risks for at least three reasons. First, "when people gather in social settings, their interactions are likely to be longer than they would be in a commercial setting," with participants "more likely to be involved in prolonged conversations." Second, "private houses are typically smaller and less ventilated than commercial establishments." And third, "social distancing and mask-wearing are less likely in private settings and enforcement is more difficult." These are not the mere musings of two appellate judges: The district court found each of these facts based on the uncontested testimony of California's public-health experts. No doubt this evidence is inconvenient for the *per curiam*'s preferred result. But the Court has no warrant to ignore the record in a case that (on its own view) turns on risk assessments.

In ordering California to weaken its restrictions on at-home gatherings, the majority yet again "insists on treating unlike cases, not like ones, equivalently."

NOTES ON TANDON V. NEWSOM

1.   *What Activities Are Comparable?* The majority assumes that religious gatherings in homes present similar health risks to people shopping in Big Box stores. State health authorities apparently thought the contrary. It may also be worth noting evidence about the danger of home gatherings. A careful study showed a 30% increase in COVID cases in families where a family member had recently had a birthday, presumably attributable to birthday parties. See Christopher M. Whaley & Anupam B. Jena, "Assessing the Association Between Social Gatherings and COVID-19 Risk Using Birthdays," *JAMA Intern Med.* (June 21, 2021), doi:10.1001/jamainternmed.2021.2915. This finding suggests that home gatherings are significantly more risky than the kinds of commercial activities the Court used as comparators.

Moreover, the majority says, the state must presume good faith compliance of religious actors, even in situations where monitoring is impossible. Are there other situations where the government is required to regulate on the "honor system" like this? Would it be constitutional for the government to use the same enforcement system for religious gatherings in private homes as it uses for commercial activities, such as administrative inspections during the gatherings?

2.   *Redefining Neutrality.* Note how the Court narrows the definition of neutrality to depend solely on comparable risk. Essentially, religious activities seem to have "most favored nation status." For instance, suppose that without health protective measures, prisons pose the same risk of disease transmission as churches. (In reality, the risk in prisons may be even higher.) Then, unless the government closes prisons, must it show that use of protective measures will be less effective in reducing risk in churches than in prisons? On the basis of this test, would any consideration of intent be necessary to strike down the application of an animal cruelty law to animal sacrifice, since secular slaughterhouses were already exempt in *Lukumi Babalu Aye*.

3.   *Free Speech Versus Free Exercise.* The analogy to *Tandon* would be a rule providing that a law is subject to strict scrutiny if any comparable non-expressive activity is treated more favorably than an expressive activity. That is definitely not the law. If the plaintiffs had wanted to conduct a political gathering in their home, the state's social distancing requirement would have been reviewed under the much less onerous *O'Brien* test. Has free speech become a second-class right compared to freedom of religion? Does the term "free exercise" connote coverage of a broader class of conduct than the terms "freedom of speech" or "freedom of the press"? Given that the planned religious activities included ordinary expressive acts, one might also ask whether it would be content discrimination to exempt religious expression but not other expressive activities from regulation.

4.   *Limits on* Tandon. Is there any justification for limiting *Tandon* based on its facts? Note that the government had explicitly dealt with religious activities as a separate category in parts of its regulation. Does that provide a basis for distinguishing cases in which a law makes no explicit reference to

religion? Would that distinguish the animal sacrifice case from *Tandon*? Alternatively, does it matter that *Tandon* involved religious worship and teaching, rather than conduct that is normally secular. For instance, under *Tandon*, would the baker in *Masterpiece Cake* be entitled to strict scrutiny if there are any exemptions from the discrimination law for any secular activities? To take another example, some states have eliminated religious exemptions from childhood vaccination mandates, but retained medical exemptions for people who are immune-impaired or allergic to vaccine ingredients. Is repeal of the exemption to religious objectors subject to strict scrutiny? What about a law that never included a religious exemption in the first place but did contain a medical exemption?

In the next case, the Court held that the free exercise clause requires a religious exemption from anti-discrimination law.

FULTON V. CITY OF PHILADELPHIA
593 U.S. ___, 141 S.Ct. 1868, 210 L.Ed.2d 137 (2021)

CHIEF JUSTICE ROBERTS delivered the opinion of the Court.

Catholic Social Services [CSS] is a foster care agency in Philadelphia. The City stopped referring children to CSS upon discovering that the agency would not certify same-sex couples to be foster parents due to its religious beliefs about marriage. The City will renew its foster care contract with CSS only if the agency agrees to certify same-sex couples. The question presented is whether the actions of Philadelphia violate the First Amendment. * * *

The Free Exercise Clause of the First Amendment, applicable to the States under the Fourteenth Amendment, provides that "Congress shall make no law . . . prohibiting the free exercise" of religion. As an initial matter, it is plain that the City's actions have burdened CSS's religious exercise by putting it to the choice of curtailing its mission or approving relationships inconsistent with its beliefs. The City disagrees. In its view, certification reflects only that foster parents satisfy the statutory criteria, not that the agency endorses their relationships. But CSS believes that certification is tantamount to endorsement. And "religious beliefs need not be acceptable, logical, consistent, or comprehensible to others in order to merit First Amendment protection." Our task is to decide whether the burden the City has placed on the religious exercise of CSS is constitutionally permissible.

Smith [*v. Employment Division*] held that laws incidentally burdening religion are ordinarily not subject to strict scrutiny under the Free Exercise Clause so long as they are neutral and generally applicable. CSS urges us to overrule *Smith*, and the concurrences in the judgment argue in favor of doing so. But we need not revisit that decision here. This case falls outside *Smith* because the City has burdened the religious exercise of CSS through policies that do not meet the requirement of being neutral and generally applicable.

Government fails to act neutrally when it proceeds in a manner intolerant of religious beliefs or restricts practices because of their religious nature [citing *Masterpiece Cake* and *Lukumi*]. CSS points to evidence in the record that it believes demonstrates that the City has transgressed this neutrality standard, but we find it more straightforward to resolve this case under the rubric of general applicability.

A law is not generally applicable if it "invite[s]" the government to consider the particular reasons for a person's conduct by providing " 'a mechanism for individualized exemptions.' " For example, in *Sherbert v. Verner*, 374 U.S. 398 (1963), a Seventh-day Adventist was fired because she would not work on Saturdays. Unable to find a job that would allow her to keep the Sabbath as her faith required, she applied for unemployment benefits. The State denied her application under a law prohibiting eligibility to claimants who had "failed, without good cause . . . to accept available suitable work." We held that the denial infringed her free exercise rights and could be justified only by a compelling interest.

Smith later explained that the unemployment benefits law in *Sherbert* was not generally applicable because the "good cause" standard permitted the government to grant exemptions based on the circumstances underlying each application. *Smith* went on to hold that "where the State has in place a system of individual exemptions, it may not refuse to extend that system to cases of 'religious hardship' without compelling reason."

A law also lacks general applicability if it prohibits religious conduct while permitting secular conduct that undermines the government's asserted interests in a similar way. In *Church of Lukumi Babalu Aye, Inc. v. Hialeah*, for instance, the City of Hialeah adopted several ordinances prohibiting animal sacrifice, a practice of the Santeria faith. The City claimed that the ordinances were necessary in part to protect public health, which was "threatened by the disposal of animal carcasses in open public places." But the ordinances did not regulate hunters' disposal of their kills or improper garbage disposal by restaurants, both of which posed a similar hazard. The Court concluded that this and other forms of under-inclusiveness meant that the ordinances were not generally applicable.

The City initially argued that CSS's practice violated section 3.21 of its standard foster care contract. We conclude, however, that this provision is not generally applicable as required by *Smith*. The current version of section 3.21 specifies in pertinent part:

> "Rejection of Referral [underlining in original]. Provider shall not reject a child or family including, but not limited to, . . . prospective foster or adoptive parents, for Services based upon . . . their . . . sexual orientation . . . unless an exception is granted by

the Commissioner or the Commissioner's designee, in his/her sole discretion."

This provision requires an agency to provide "Services," defined as "the work to be performed under this Contract," to prospective foster parents regardless of their sexual orientation.

Like the good cause provision in *Sherbert*, section 3.21 incorporates a system of individual exemptions, made available in this case at the "sole discretion" of the Commissioner. The City has made clear that the Commissioner "has no intention of granting an exception" to CSS. But the City "may not refuse to extend that [exemption] system to cases of 'religious hardship' without compelling reason."

The City and intervenor-respondents resist this conclusion on several grounds. They first argue that governments should enjoy greater leeway under the Free Exercise Clause when setting rules for contractors than when regulating the general public. The government, they observe, commands heightened powers when managing its internal operations. And when individuals enter into government employment or contracts, they accept certain restrictions on their freedom as part of the deal. Given this context, the City and intervenor-respondents contend, the government should have a freer hand when dealing with contractors like CSS.

These considerations cannot save the City here. As Philadelphia rightly acknowledges, "principles of neutrality and general applicability still constrain the government in its capacity as manager." We have never suggested that the government may discriminate against religion when acting in its managerial role. And *Smith* itself drew support for the neutral and generally applicable standard from cases involving internal government affairs. The City and intervenor-respondents accordingly ask only that courts apply a more deferential approach in determining whether a policy is neutral and generally applicable in the contracting context. We find no need to resolve that narrow issue in this case. No matter the level of deference we extend to the City, the inclusion of a formal system of entirely discretionary exceptions in section 3.21 renders the contractual non-discrimination requirement not generally applicable. * * *

Finally, the City and intervenor-respondents contend that the availability of exceptions under section 3.21 is irrelevant because the Commissioner has never granted one. That misapprehends the issue. The creation of a formal mechanism for granting exceptions renders a policy not generally applicable, regardless whether any exceptions have been given, because it "invite[s]" the government to decide which reasons for not complying with the policy are worthy of solicitude—here, at the Commissioner's "sole discretion." * * *

In addition to relying on the contract, the City argues that CSS's refusal to certify same-sex couples constitutes an "Unlawful Public

Accommodations Practice[ ]" in violation of the Fair Practices Ordinance. That ordinance forbids "deny[ing] or interfer[ing] with the public accommodations opportunities of an individual or otherwise discriminat[ing] based on his or her race, ethnicity, color, sex, sexual orientation, . . . disability, marital status, familial status," or several other protected categories. The City contends that foster care agencies are public accommodations and therefore forbidden from discriminating on the basis of sexual orientation when certifying foster parents. [The Court rejects this argument on the ground that "a public accommodation must 'provide a benefit to the general public allowing individual members of the general public to avail themselves of that benefit if they so desire,' " whereas foster family certification is open to relatively few applicants and only after careful screening.] * * *

The contractual non-discrimination requirement imposes a burden on CSS's religious exercise and does not qualify as generally applicable. The concurrence protests that the "Court granted certiorari to decide whether to overrule [*Smith*]," and chides the Court for seeking to "sidestep the question." But the Court also granted review to decide whether Philadelphia's actions were permissible under our precedents. CSS has demonstrated that the City's actions are subject to "the most rigorous of scrutiny" under those precedents. Because the City's actions are therefore examined under the strictest scrutiny regardless of *Smith*, we have no occasion to reconsider that decision here.

A government policy can survive strict scrutiny only if it advances "interests of the highest order" and is narrowly tailored to achieve those interests. Put another way, so long as the government can achieve its interests in a manner that does not burden religion, it must do so.

The City asserts that its non-discrimination policies serve three compelling interests: maximizing the number of foster parents, protecting the City from liability, and ensuring equal treatment of prospective foster parents and foster children. The City states these objectives at a high level of generality, but the First Amendment demands a more precise analysis. Rather than rely on "broadly formulated interests," courts must "scrutinize[ ] the asserted harm of granting specific exemptions to particular religious claimants." The question, then, is not whether the City has a compelling interest in enforcing its non-discrimination policies generally, but whether it has such an interest in denying an exception to CSS.

Once properly narrowed, the City's asserted interests are insufficient. Maximizing the number of foster families and minimizing liability are important goals, but the City fails to show that granting CSS an exception will put those goals at risk. If anything, including CSS in the program seems likely to increase, not reduce, the number of available foster parents.

As for liability, the City offers only speculation that it might be sued over CSS's certification practices. Such speculation is insufficient to satisfy strict scrutiny, particularly because the authority to certify foster families is delegated to agencies by the State, not the City.

That leaves the interest of the City in the equal treatment of prospective foster parents and foster children. We do not doubt that this interest is a weighty one, for "[o]ur society has come to the recognition that gay persons and gay couples cannot be treated as social outcasts or as inferior in dignity and worth." On the facts of this case, however, this interest cannot justify denying CSS an exception for its religious exercise. The creation of a system of exceptions under the contract undermines the City's contention that its non-discrimination policies can brook no departures. The City offers no compelling reason why it has a particular interest in denying an exception to CSS while making them available to others.* * *

As Philadelphia acknowledges, CSS has "long been a point of light in the City's foster-care system." CSS seeks only an accommodation that will allow it to continue serving the children of Philadelphia in a manner consistent with its religious beliefs; it does not seek to impose those beliefs on anyone else. The refusal of Philadelphia to contract with CSS for the provision of foster care services unless it agrees to certify same-sex couples as foster parents cannot survive strict scrutiny, and violates the First Amendment.

JUSTICE BARRETT, with whom **JUSTICE KAVANAUGH** joins, and with whom **JUSTICE BREYER** joins as to all but the first paragraph, concurring.

In *Smith*, this Court held that a neutral and generally applicable law typically does not violate the Free Exercise Clause—no matter how severely that law burdens religious exercise. Petitioners, their *amici*, scholars, and Justices of this Court have made serious arguments that *Smith* ought to be overruled. While history looms large in this debate, I find the historical record more silent than supportive on the question whether the founding generation understood the First Amendment to require religious exemptions from generally applicable laws in at least some circumstances. In my view, the textual and structural arguments against *Smith* are more compelling. As a matter of text and structure, it is difficult to see why the Free Exercise Clause—lone among the First Amendment freedoms—offers nothing more than protection from discrimination.

Yet what should replace *Smith*? The prevailing assumption seems to be that strict scrutiny would apply whenever a neutral and generally applicable law burdens religious exercise. But I am skeptical about swapping *Smith*'s categorical antidiscrimination approach for an equally categorical strict scrutiny regime, particularly when this Court's resolution of conflicts between generally applicable laws and other First Amendment rights—like speech and assembly—has been much more nuanced. There would be a number of issues to work through if *Smith* were overruled. To name a few: Should entities like Catholic Social Services—which is an arm of the Catholic Church—be treated differently than individuals? Should there be a distinction between indirect and direct burdens on religious exercise? What forms of scrutiny should apply? And if the answer is strict scrutiny, would pre-*Smith* cases rejecting free exercise challenges to garden-variety laws come out the same way?

We need not wrestle with these questions in this case, though, because the same standard applies regardless whether *Smith* stays or goes. A longstanding tenet of our free exercise jurisprudence—one that both pre-dates and survives *Smith*—is that a law burdening religious exercise must satisfy strict scrutiny if it gives government officials discretion to grant individualized exemptions. As the Court's opinion today explains, the government contract at issue provides for individualized exemptions from its nondiscrimination rule, thus triggering strict scrutiny. And all nine Justices agree that the City cannot satisfy strict scrutiny. I therefore see no reason to decide in this case whether *Smith* should be overruled, much less what should replace it. I join the Court's opinion in full.

JUSTICE ALITO, with whom JUSTICE THOMAS and JUSTICE GORSUCH join, concurring in the judgment.

This case presents an important constitutional question that urgently calls out for review: whether this Court's governing interpretation of a bedrock constitutional right, the right to the free exercise of religion, is fundamentally wrong and should be corrected. * * *

We should reconsider *Smith* without further delay. The correct interpretation of the Free Exercise Clause is a question of great importance, and *Smith*'s interpretation is hard to defend. It can't be squared with the ordinary meaning of the text of the Free Exercise Clause or with the prevalent understanding of the scope of the free-exercise right at the time of the First Amendment's adoption. It swept aside decades of established precedent, and it has not aged well. Its interpretation has been undermined by subsequent scholarship on the original meaning of the Free Exercise Clause. Contrary to what many initially expected, *Smith* has not provided a clear-cut rule that is easy to apply, and experience has disproved the *Smith* majority's fear that retention of the Court's prior free-exercise jurisprudence would lead to "anarchy." * * *

As interpreted in *Smith*, the Clause is essentially an anti-discrimination provision: It means that the Federal Government and the States cannot restrict conduct that constitutes a religious practice for some people unless it imposes the same restriction on everyone else who engages in the same conduct. *Smith* made no real attempt to square that equal-treatment interpretation with the ordinary meaning of the Free Exercise Clause's language, and it is hard to see how that could be done.

The key point for present purposes is that the text of the Free Exercise Clause gives a specific group of people (those who wish to engage in the "exercise of religion") the right to do so without hindrance. The language of the Clause does not tie this right to the treatment of persons not in this group. * * *

What was the free-exercise right understood to mean when the Bill of Rights was ratified? And in particular, was it clearly understood that the right simply required equal treatment for religious and secular conduct? When *Smith* was decided, scholars had not devoted much attention to the original meaning of the Free Exercise Clause, and the parties' briefs ignored this issue, as did the opinion of the Court. Since then, however, the historical record has been plumbed in detail, and we are now in a good position to examine how the free-exercise right was understood when the First Amendment was adopted. * * *

What was this right understood to protect? In seeking to discern that meaning, it is easy to get lost in the voluminous discussion of religious liberty that occurred during the long period from the first British settlements to the adoption of the Bill of Rights. Many different political figures, religious leaders, and others spoke and wrote about religious liberty and the relationship between the authority of civil governments and religious bodies. The works of a variety of thinkers were influential, and views on religious liberty were informed by religion, philosophy, historical experience, particular controversies and issues, and in no small measure by the practical task of uniting the Nation. The picture is complex.

For present purposes, we can narrow our focus and concentrate on the circumstances that relate most directly to the adoption of the Free Exercise Clause. As has often been recounted, critical state ratifying conventions approved the Constitution on the understanding that it would be amended to provide express protection for certain fundamental rights, and the right to religious liberty was unquestionably one of those rights. As noted, it was expressly protected in 12 of the 13 State Constitutions, and these state constitutional provisions provide the best evidence of the scope of the right embodied in the First Amendment.

When we look at these provisions, we see one predominant model. This model extends broad protection for religious liberty but expressly provides that the right does not protect conduct that would endanger "the public peace" or "safety." * * *

The model favored by Congress and the state legislatures—providing broad protection for the free exercise of religion except where public "peace" or "safety" would be endangered—is antithetical to *Smith*. If, as *Smith* held, the free-exercise right does not require any religious exemptions from generally applicable laws, it is not easy to imagine situations in which a public-peace-or-safety carveout would be necessary. Legislatures enact generally applicable laws to protect public peace and safety. If those laws are thought to be sufficient to address a particular type of conduct when engaged in for a secular purpose, why wouldn't they also be sufficient to address the same type of conduct when carried out for a religious reason?

Smith's defenders have no good answer. Their chief response is that the free-exercise provisions that included these carveouts were tantamount to the *Smith* rule because any conduct that is generally prohibited or generally required can be regarded as necessary to protect public peace or safety. * * *

That the free-exercise right included the right to certain religious exemptions is strongly supported by the practice of the Colonies and States. When there were important clashes between generally applicable laws and the religious practices of particular groups, colonial and state legislatures were willing to grant exemptions—even when the generally applicable laws served critical state interests. * * *

If *Smith* is overruled, what legal standard should be applied in this case? The answer that comes most readily to mind is the standard that *Smith* replaced: A law that imposes a substantial burden on religious exercise can be sustained only if it is narrowly tailored to serve a compelling government interest.

Whether this test should be rephrased or supplemented with specific rules is a question that need not be resolved here because Philadelphia's ouster of CSS from foster care work simply does not further any interest that can properly be protected in this case. As noted, CSS's policy has not hindered any same-sex couples from becoming foster parents, and there is no threat that it will do so in the future.

CSS's policy has only one effect: It expresses the idea that same-sex couples should not be foster parents because only a man and a woman should marry. Many people today find this idea not only objectionable but hurtful. Nevertheless, protecting against this form of harm is not an interest that can justify the abridgment of First Amendment rights.

We have covered this ground repeatedly in free speech cases. In an open, pluralistic, self-governing society, the expression of an idea cannot be suppressed simply because some find it offensive, insulting, or even wounding.

[In a separate opinion concurring in the judgment, **JUSTICE GORSUCH**, joined by **JUSTICE THOMAS**, and **JUSTICE ALITO**, argued that the majority had seriously misconstrued state law.]

NOTES ON FULTON V. PHILADELPHIA AND THE FRAGILITY OF PRECEDENT

1.   *Has* Obergefell *Been Overruled in Part?* The majority and concurring opinions give short shrift to the fact that the foster care program was a government program, and that CSS was acting as an agency of the government. *Obergefell* held, in part, that under the Fourteenth Amendment states cannot discriminate against married same-sex couples when they recognize valid out-of-state marriages. (Most of the plaintiff couples were validly married and were seeking recognition of their legal marriages by their home states.)

This stance does not necessarily require that *Obergefell's* main holding—the Fourteenth Amendment requires that states issue marriage licenses to qualified same-sex couples on the same terms as different-sex couples—be overruled. But it does require that the state allow its agents to discriminate against same-sex married couples in state programs like that in Philadelphia. Not a single Justice objected to this this violation of the neutrality the Equal Protection Clause demands of government programs: Why not? Some faith traditions still maintain that different-race marriages violate the Word of the Lord. Would the government be required to honor their policies in a foster care program run by the state? Policies against race discrimination could be a compelling state interest, but would the bar be narrowly tailored?

2.   *The Duty of Government Officials to Enforce Constitutional Rules That Burden Their Faith?* In the wake of *Obergefell*, Rowan County (Kentucky) Clerk Kim Davis refused to deliver marriage licenses to same-sex couples because it violated her faith; she was jailed for her refusal. Her office ultimately acquiesced and issued marriage licenses to same-sex couples, but without Davis's signature. She was defeated for reelection but has continued to litigate her constitutional right to refuse to enforce *Obergefell*.

The Supreme Court unanimously declined to take her case. *Davis v. Ermold,* 141 S.Ct. 3 (2020). But in a separate statement, Justices Thomas and Alito objected to *Obergefell's* effect on persons harboring religious objections to same-sex marriages. They opined that "the Court has created a problem," namely, persecution of "victims" like Davis, that "only it can fix." (statement of Thomas, J., joined by Alito, J.). *Fulton* may be a step in the direction of a Court "fix." Should they argue that Davis had a constitutional right to refuse to follow a constitutional mandate that imposed a burden on the free exercise of her faith? As the Rowan County Clerk, was she entitled to direct that no one in the clerk's office could follow the constitutional mandate?

3.   *Should* Smith *Be Overruled? Smith* has been a controversial test since the day it was decided. Justice Alito argues that it is contrary to the original understanding of "free exercise" and has proved hard to apply. His opinion is rather thin on the former question. Some scholarship supports his view that the "free exercise of religion" in 1791 would have assumed exemptions from civil laws burdening faith, e.g., Michael W. McConnell, *The Origins and Historical Understanding of Free Exercise of Religion,* 103 Harv.

L. Rev. 1409 (1990), while other scholarship does not. E.g., Philip A. Hamburger, *A Constitutional Right of Religious Exemption: An Historical Perspective,* 60 Geo. Wash. L. Rev. 915 (1992) (detailed response to McConnell). But even Professor McConnell's leading historical account does not identify a single instance where government officials or agents were allowed to impose their religious views upon a government program.

A Court majority (including Justice Scalia, the author of *Smith*) were aware of McConnell's and other critical accounts when they reaffirmed and applied *Smith* to invalidate the Religious Freedom Restoration Act of 1993, as applied to the states, in *City of Boerne v. Flores* (1997). After *Boerne, Masterpiece, Fulton,* and *Tandon,* there is an elaborate *Smith*-based jurisprudence. A major foundation for stare decisis is reliance: *Boerne* is classic reliance, and the other applications of *Smith* are also relevant.

Against the powerful arguments against overruling a landmark constitutional precedent, Justices Alito, Thomas, and Gorsuch set the feeling that religious minorities enjoy no protections and are "victims." But the Court has vigorously protected those minorities under the terms laid out in *Smith*—indeed, it has applied *Smith*'s neutrality rules much more aggressively than it has applied neutrality rules when the state adopts voting and other policies affecting racial and ethnic minorities, as illustrated by the Court's decision in *Brnovich v. Democratic National Comm.,* 141 S.Ct. 2321 (2021). This is ironic. The Reconstruction Amendments were overwhelmingly focused on racial minorities, yet the Equal Protection Clause and the Fifteenth Amendment have been tepidly applied to head off suppression of Black voters, while the Due Process Clause has been the basis for applying the Free Exercise Clause against the states with increasing vigor.

For some people, there is something disturbing about the idea that religious people are exempt from the rules of civil society except in the rare instances where the government can prove that an exemption would create an absolutely unavoidable impact on a compelling interest. Moreover, placing religions at a higher plane than secular activities may not violate the current Court's vision of the Establishment Clause, but it could lead to increasing backlash against religion in today's politically polarized society, given that religious views on social issues often bleed into politics. Will more muscular enforcement of the Free Exercise Clause lead to greater religious toleration or atomization of society into mutually hostile secular and religious groups?

4. *What Should Replace* Smith? There seem to be as many as five votes to overrule *Smith*, but no agreement on what should replace it. The complexity is indicated by Justice Alito's dissent itself. He goes to considerable lengths to show that caring for needy children is a traditional religious function going back centuries. The purpose seems to be to show that the ordinance is a restriction on an important religious activity, not merely an anti-discrimination provision applied to conduct that is not essentially itself religious. But it is not clear how to draw such lines. Nor is it clear how severe an impairment must be to qualify as a burden.

As regards Alito's suggestion that the Court should "return" to the pre-*Smith* approach, it is far from clear what that approach actually entailed—for many scholars that line of cases is much harder to apply than the *Smith* line of cases. Indeed, the pre-*Smith* cases suggest a milder review of claims that private religious views can dictate the administration of public programs. The Court in *Bowen v. Roy,* 476 U.S. 693 (1986), for example upheld the federal government's use of Social Security numbers within its own aid-distribution program and rejected a father's free exercise objections, which were assumed to be sincere. The *Sherbert/Yoder* test "is not appropriate in this setting." *Id.* at 707 (plurality opinion). "[T]he Free Exercise Clause simply cannot be understood to require the Government to conduct its own internal affairs in ways that comport with the religious beliefs of particular citizens." *Id.* at 699. Accord, *Lyng v. Northwest Indian Cemetery Protective Association,* 485 U.S. 439 (1988).

5.   *How Much Accommodation Is Required?* The University of California at San Francisco is a renowned medical school and research center. As part of its efforts to train students and provide medical services to the public, it entered into contracts with other health providers, one of which is a major Catholic hospital system. Catholic teachings are contrary to University of California policies with respect to access to reproductive services and the treatment of transsexuals. Is it constitutional for the University to cancel the contract if the Catholic health system does not agree to those terms? Can the university simply refuse to affiliate with hospitals that restrict reproductive services or services to transsexuals? Or would that violate *Fulton?* For the Catholic system's view of the dispute, see https://www.dignityhealth.org/uc partnerships. For the opposing view, see Michael Hiltzik, "UC Misses a Chance to Fix Its Anti-Abortion Deals with Catholic Hospitals," *LA Times* (Jan. 30, 2020),   https://www.latimes.com/business/story/2020-01-30/uc-catholic-hospitals.

6.   *Waiting for the Right Vehicle to Run over* Smith? On July 2, 2021, the Court denied review of *State v. Arlene's Flowers,* 441 P.3d 1203 (Wash. 2019), cert. denied, 2021 WL 2742795 (2021), where the state supreme court had applied a general anti-discrimination law to penalize a florist for refusing to provide flowers for a gay wedding. Because the florist was not participating in a state program, this case would appear to be a more attractive vehicle for overruling *Smith,* but only Justices Thomas, Alito, and Gorsuch voted to take the case. Why the delay? The issue is not going away. Consider the following problem.

PROBLEM 6-4:
FIRST AMENDMENT RIGHTS OF RELIGIOUS TRADITIONALISTS AFTER FULTON?

Assume the Supreme Court had taken review in *Arlene's Flowers.* The state anti-discrimination law, Wash. Rev. Code § 49.60.215, provides as follows:

> It shall be an unfair practice for any person or the person's agent or employee to commit an act which directly or indirectly results in any distinction, restriction, or discrimination, or the requiring of any person to pay a larger sum than the uniform rates charged other persons, or the refusing or withholding from any person the admission, patronage, custom, presence, frequenting, dwelling, staying, or lodging in any place of public resort, accommodation, assemblage, or amusement, except for conditions and limitations established by law and applicable to all persons, regardless of race, creed, color, national origin, citizenship or immigration status, sexual orientation, sex, honorably discharged veteran or military status, status as a mother breastfeeding her child, the presence of any sensory, mental, or physical disability, or the use of a trained dog guide or service animal by a person with a disability: PROVIDED, That this section shall not be construed to require structural changes, modifications, or additions to make any place accessible to a person with a disability except as otherwise required by law: PROVIDED, That behavior or actions constituting a risk to property or other persons can be grounds for refusal and shall not constitute an unfair practice.

Barronelle Stutzman is the religious owner of the flower enterprise. She has gay customers whom she treasures, including one of the plaintiffs. But she will not assist or participate, even indirectly, in a same-sex marriage ceremony. For that, she was sanctioned under the provision above.

If you represented Stutzman and Arlene's Flowers, what is your best argument before the Supreme Court? Do you have winning free exercise arguments under *Smith*? If you represent the state, what is your best response to those arguments? What arguments do you have under *Smith*? Is there any way you can persuade the putative *Fulton* majority not to overrule *Smith*? Can you win under the pre-*Smith* cases?

Note: The Supreme Court has granted cert. in 303 Creative v. Elenis (No. 21–476), which involves a related issue. The court did not agree to hear the free exercise issues raised by Elenis. The claim in *Elenis* is that it would violate freedom of speech to apply a state accommodation law to someone who designs websites for weddings but objects to doing so for same-sex weddings. Depending on when the Court decides the case, you may also want to consider whether Arlene's Flowers has a valid free speech claim.

PROBLEM 6-5:
RELIGIOUS FREEDOM VERSUS ABORTION BANS?

Generation to Generation, Inc. v. Florida (Leon County Florida, 2022), is a case filed by a Jewish congregation in state court after *Roe v. Wade* was overruled. https://www.documentcloud.org/documents/22060281-complaint-ldor-va-dor-vs-state-of-florida-final?responsive=1&title=1 Among other things, the complaint alleges that:

In Jewish law, abortion is required if necessary to protect the health, mental or physical well-being of the woman, or for many other reasons not permitted under the Act. . . . In Jewish law, abortion is required if necessary to protect the health, mental or physical well-being of the woman, or for many other reasons not permitted under the Act. As such, the Act prohibits Jewish women from practicing their faith free of government intrusion and thus violates their privacy rights and religious freedom. The most important institution in Jewish life is the family, which has withstood centuries of persecution and discrimination by clinging to values and ideals which are quintessential to the Jewish faith. By preventing Jews from making intimate, personal decisions about the size of their families, or when and under what circumstances to bring new life into the world, the Act not only threatens the lives, equality and dignity of Jewish women, the Act also threatens the integrity of the Jewish family and denies religious freedom to Jewish women and their families.

The Florida statute in question bans abortions after 15 weeks, with limited exceptions for saving the life of the mother, medical emergencies, and fatal fetal abnormalities. Assuming the allegations in the complaint represent the sincere religious beliefs of members of the congregation, how would you frame a free exercise argument under *Tandon* and *Fulton*? How might overruling *Smith* change the availability of a free exercise claim in this situation?

Assuming you were able to make a prima facie case, how would you respond if the state claims to have a compelling government interest in preserving fetal life? You may want to take another look at how the *Dobbs* opinion characterizes the state's possible interests in preventing abortions.

Page 861. Replace the Note on Establishment Clause Tests with the following:

In 1971, the Court attempted a synthesis of its case law in *Lemon v. Kurtzman,* 403 U.S. 602 (1971). *Lemon* struck down two state laws providing partial funding for teacher salaries at parochial schools. In an effort to make sense of the prior cases, the Court announced a three-part test: "First, the statute must have a secular legislative purpose; second, its principal or primary effect must be one that neither advances nor inhibits religion; finally, the statute must not foster 'an excessive government entanglement with religion.'" The salary supplements were unconstitutional because they involved excessive entanglement. In order to ensure that the money did not go for religious instruction, the state had to engage in intrusive supervision of parochial school activities. Moreover, the legislation also caused religious issues to become entangled in politics due to bitter disputes over this novel form of assistance to church-related activities. The *Lemon* test was overruled in the following case.

KENNEDY V. BREMERTON SCHOOL DISTRICT
___ U.S. ___, 142 S.Ct. 2407, ___ L.Ed.2d ___ (2022)

[The majority and dissent disagreed about the relevant facts. As the majority characterized it, the case involved a '[s]chool employee, who lost his job as a high school football coach after he knelt at midfield after games to offer a quiet personal prayer." The dissent emphasized that this incident took places after several others where he led the team out on the field for prayer." In omitted portions of the opinion, the Court concluded that he had shown infringements of his rights to free exercise and free speech. It then turned to whether the school board had a valid defense due to its desire to avoid being perceived as endorsing religious exercises.]

JUSTICE GORSUCH delivered the opinion of the Court.

Joseph Kennedy lost his job as a high school football coach because he knelt at midfield after games to offer a quiet prayer of thanks. Mr. Kennedy prayed during a period when school employees were free to speak with a friend, call for a reservation at a restaurant, check email, or attend to other personal matters. He offered his prayers quietly while his students were otherwise occupied. Still, the Bremerton School District disciplined him anyway. It did so because it thought anything less could lead a reasonable observer to conclude (mistakenly) that it endorsed Mr. Kennedy's religious beliefs. That reasoning was misguided. Both the Free Exercise and Free Speech Clauses of the First Amendment protect expressions like Mr. Kennedy's. Nor does a proper understanding of the Amendment's Establishment Clause require the government to single out private religious speech for special disfavor. The Constitution and the best of our traditions counsel mutual respect and tolerance, not censorship and suppression, for religious and nonreligious views alike.* * *

Whether one views the case through the lens of the Free Exercise or Free Speech Clause, at this point the burden shifts to the District. Under the Free Exercise Clause, a government entity normally must satisfy at least "strict scrutiny," showing that its restrictions on the plaintiff's protected rights serve a compelling interest and are narrowly tailored to that end. The District, however, asks us to apply to Mr. Kennedy's claims the more lenient second-step Pickering-Garcetti test, or alternatively intermediate scrutiny. Ultimately, however, it does not matter which standard we apply. The District cannot sustain its burden under any of them.

As we have seen, the District argues that its suspension of Mr. Kennedy was essential to avoid a violation of the Establishment Clause. On its account, Mr. Kennedy's prayers might have been protected by the Free Exercise and Free Speech Clauses. But his rights were in "direct tension" with the competing demands of the Establishment Clause. To resolve that clash, the District reasoned, Mr. Kennedy's rights had to "yield." * * *

But how could that be? It is true that this Court and others often refer to the "Establishment Clause," the "Free Exercise Clause," and the "Free Speech Clause" as separate units. But the three Clauses appear in the same sentence of the same Amendment: "Congress shall make no law respecting an establishment of religion, or prohibiting the free exercise thereof; or abridging the freedom of speech." A natural reading of that sentence would seem to suggest the Clauses have "complementary" purposes, not warring ones where one Clause is always sure to prevail over the others.

The District arrived at a different understanding this way. It began with the premise that the Establishment Clause is offended whenever a "reasonable observer" could conclude that the government has "endorse[d]" religion. The District then took the view that a "reasonable observer" could think it "endorsed Kennedy's religious activity by not stopping the practice." On the District's account, it did not matter whether the Free Exercise Clause protected Mr. Kennedy's prayer. It did not matter if his expression was private speech protected by the Free Speech Clause. It did not matter that the District never actually endorsed Mr. Kennedy's prayer, no one complained that it had, and a strong public reaction only followed after the District sought to ban Mr. Kennedy's prayer. Because a reasonable observer could (mistakenly) infer that by allowing the prayer the District endorsed Mr. Kennedy's message, the District felt it had to act, even if that meant suppressing otherwise protected First Amendment activities. In this way, the District effectively created its own "vise between the Establishment Clause on one side and the Free Speech and Free Exercise Clauses on the other," placed itself in the middle, and then chose its preferred way out of its self-imposed trap.

To defend its approach, the District relied on *Lemon v. Kurtzman*, 403 U.S. 602, 91 S.Ct. 2105, 29 L.Ed.2d 745 (1971), and its progeny. In upholding the District's actions, the Ninth Circuit followed the same course. And, to be sure, in *Lemon* this Court attempted a "grand unified theory" for assessing Establishment Clause claims. That approach called for an examination of a law's purposes, effects, and potential for entanglement with religion. In time, the approach also came to involve estimations about whether a "reasonable observer" would consider the government's challenged action an "endorsement" of religion.

What the District and the Ninth Circuit overlooked, however, is that the "shortcomings" associated with this "ambitiou[s]," abstract, and ahistorical approach to the Establishment Clause became so "apparent" that this Court long ago abandoned *Lemon* and its endorsement test offshoot. The Court has explained that these tests "invited chaos" in lower courts, led to "differing results" in materially identical cases, and created a "minefield" for legislators. This Court has since made plain, too, that the Establishment Clause does not include anything like a "modified heckler's veto, in which ... religious activity can be proscribed" based on " 'perceptions' " or " 'discomfort.' " In place of Lemon and the endorsement test, this Court has instructed that the Establishment Clause must be interpreted by " 'reference to historical practices and understandings.' " " '[T]he line' " that courts and governments "must draw between the permissible and the impermissible" has to " 'accor[d] with history and faithfully reflec[t] the understanding of the Founding Fathers.' " An analysis focused on original meaning and history, this Court has stressed, has long represented the rule rather than some " 'exception' " within the "Court's Establishment Clause jurisprudence." The District and the Ninth Circuit erred by failing to heed this guidance.

Perhaps sensing that the primary theory it pursued below rests on a mistaken understanding of the Establishment Clause, the District offers a backup argument in this Court. It still contends that its Establishment Clause concerns trump Mr. Kennedy's free exercise and free speech rights. But the District now seeks to supply different reasoning for that result. Now, it says, it was justified in suppressing Mr. Kennedy's religious activity because otherwise it would have been guilty of coercing students to pray. And, the District says, coercing worship amounts to an Establishment Clause violation on anyone's account of the Clause's original meaning.

As it turns out, however, there is a pretty obvious reason why the Ninth Circuit did not adopt this theory in proceedings below: The evidence cannot sustain it. To be sure, this Court has long held that government may not, consistent with a historically sensitive understanding of the Establishment Clause, "make a religious observance compulsory." Government "may not coerce anyone to attend church," nor may it force citizens to engage in "a formal religious exercise." No doubt, too, coercion along these lines was among the foremost hallmarks of religious establishments the framers sought to prohibit when they adopted the First Amendment. Members of this Court have sometimes disagreed on what exactly qualifies as impermissible coercion in light of the original meaning of the Establishment Clause.

But in this case Mr. Kennedy's private religious exercise did not come close to crossing any line one might imagine separating protected private expression from impermissible government coercion. Begin with the District's own contemporaneous description of the facts. In its correspondence with Mr. Kennedy, the District never raised coercion concerns. To the contrary, the District conceded in a public 2015 document that there was "no evidence that students [were] directly coerced to pray with Kennedy." This is consistent with Mr. Kennedy's account too. He has repeatedly stated that he "never coerced, required, or asked any student to pray," and that he never "told any student that it was important that they participate in any religious activity."

The absence of evidence of coercion in this record leaves the District to its final redoubt. Here, the District suggests that any visible religious conduct by a teacher or coach should be deemed—without more and as a matter of law—impermissibly coercive on students. In essence, the District asks us to adopt the view that the only acceptable government role models for students are those who eschew any visible religious expression. If the argument sounds familiar, it should. Really, it is just another way of repackaging the District's earlier submission that government may script everything a teacher or coach says in the workplace. The only added twist here is the District's suggestion not only that it may prohibit teachers from engaging in any demonstrative religious activity, but that it must do so in order to conform to the Constitution.

Such a rule would be a sure sign that our Establishment Clause jurisprudence had gone off the rails. In the name of protecting religious liberty, the District would have us suppress it. Rather than respect the First Amendment's double protection for religious expression, it would have us preference secular activity. Not only could schools fire teachers for praying quietly over their lunch, for wearing a yarmulke to school, or for offering a midday prayer during a break before practice. Under the District's rule, a school would be required to do so. It is a rule that would defy this Court's traditional understanding that permitting private speech is not the same thing as coercing others to participate in it. It is a rule, too, that would undermine a long constitutional tradition under which learning how to tolerate diverse expressive activities has always been "part of learning how to live in a pluralistic society." We are aware of no historically sound understanding of the Establishment Clause that begins to "mak[e] it necessary for government to be hostile to religion" in this way. * * *

In the end, the District's case hinges on the need to generate conflict between an individual's rights under the Free Exercise and Free Speech Clauses and its own Establishment Clause duties—and then develop some explanation why one of these Clauses in the First Amendment should " 'trum[p]' " the other two. But the project falters badly. Not only does the District fail to offer a sound reason to prefer one constitutional guarantee over another. It cannot even show that they are at odds. In truth, there is no conflict between the constitutional commands before us. There is only the "mere shadow" of a conflict, a false choice premised on a misconstruction of the Establishment Clause. And in no world may a government entity's concerns about phantom constitutional violations justify actual violations of an individual's First Amendment rights.

JUSTICE SOTOMAYOR, with whom **JUSTICE BREYER** and **JUSTICE KAGAN** join, dissenting.

Today's decision goes beyond merely misreading the record. The Court overrules *Lemon v. Kurtzman*, 403 U.S. 602, 91 S.Ct. 2105, 29 L.Ed.2d 745 (1971), and calls into question decades of subsequent precedents that it deems "offshoot[s]" of that decision. In the process, the Court rejects longstanding concerns surrounding government endorsement of religion and replaces the standard for reviewing such questions with a new "history and tradition" test. In addition, while the Court reaffirms that the Establishment Clause prohibits the government from coercing participation in religious exercise, it applies a nearly toothless version of the coercion analysis, failing to acknowledge the unique pressures faced by students when participating in school-sponsored activities. This decision does a disservice to schools and the young citizens they serve, as well as to our Nation's longstanding commitment to the separation of church and state. I respectfully dissent. * * *

Properly understood, this case is not about the limits on an individual's ability to engage in private prayer at work. This case is about whether a school district is required to allow one of its employees to incorporate a public, communicative display of the employee's personal religious beliefs into a school event, where that display is recognizable as part of a longstanding practice of the employee ministering religion to students as the public watched. A school district is not required to permit such conduct; in fact, the Establishment Clause prohibits it from doing so.

The Establishment Clause prohibits States from adopting laws "respecting an establishment of religion." The First Amendment's next Clause prohibits the government from making any law "prohibiting the free exercise thereof." Taken together, these two Clauses (the Religion Clauses) express the view, foundational to our constitutional system, "that religious beliefs and religious expression are too precious to be either proscribed or prescribed by the State." Instead, "preservation and transmission of religious beliefs and worship is a responsibility and a choice committed to the private sphere," which has the "freedom to pursue that mission."

The Establishment Clause protects this freedom by "command[ing] a separation of church and state." At its core, this means forbidding "sponsorship, financial support, and active involvement of the sovereign in religious activity." In the context of public schools, it means that a State cannot use "its public school system to aid any or all religious faiths or sects in the dissemination of their doctrines and ideals."

Indeed, "[t]he Court has been particularly vigilant in monitoring compliance with the Establishment Clause in elementary and secondary schools." The reasons motivating this vigilance inhere in the nature of schools themselves and the young people they serve. Two are relevant here.

First, government neutrality toward religion is particularly important in the public school context given the role public schools play in our society. " 'The public school is at once the symbol of our democracy and the most pervasive means for promoting our common destiny,' " meaning that " '[i]n no activity of the State is it more vital to keep out divisive forces than in its schools.' " Families "entrust public schools with the education of their children . . . on the understanding that the classroom will not purposely be used to advance religious views that may conflict with the private beliefs of the student and his or her family." Accordingly, the Establishment Clause "proscribes public schools from 'conveying or attempting to convey a message that religion or a particular religious belief is favored or preferred' " or otherwise endorsing religious beliefs.

Second, schools face a higher risk of unconstitutionally "coerc[ing] . . . support or participat[ion] in religion or its exercise" than other government entities. The State "exerts great authority and coercive power" in schools as a general matter "through mandatory attendance requirements." Moreover, the State exercises that great authority over children, who are uniquely susceptible to "subtle coercive pressure." Children are particularly vulnerable to coercion because of their "emulation of teachers as role models" and "susceptibility to peer pressure." Accordingly, this Court has emphasized that "the State may not, consistent with the Establishment Clause, place primary and secondary school children" in the dilemma of choosing between "participating, with all that implies, or protesting" a religious exercise in a public school.

Given the twin Establishment Clause concerns of endorsement and coercion, it is unsurprising that the Court has consistently held integrating prayer into public school activities to be unconstitutional, including when student participation is not a formal requirement or prayer is silent. The Court also has held that incorporating a nondenominational general benediction into a graduation ceremony is unconstitutional. Finally, this Court has held that including prayers in student football games is unconstitutional, even when delivered by students rather than staff and even when students themselves initiated the prayer.

Under these precedents, the Establishment Clause violation at hand is clear. This Court has held that a "[s]tate officia[l] direct[ing] the performance of a formal religious exercise" as a part of the "ceremon[y]" of a school event "conflicts with settled rules pertaining to prayer exercises for students." Kennedy was on the job as a school official "on government property" when he incorporated a public, demonstrative prayer into "government-sponsored school-related events" as a regularly scheduled feature of those events.

Kennedy's tradition of a 50-yard line prayer thus strikes at the heart of the Establishment Clause's concerns about endorsement. For students and community members at the game, Coach Kennedy was the face and the voice of the District during football games. The timing and location Kennedy selected for his prayers were "clothed in the traditional indicia of school sporting events." Kennedy spoke from the playing field, which was accessible only to students and school employees, not to the general public. Although the football game itself had ended, the football game events had not; Kennedy himself acknowledged that his responsibilities continued until the players went home. Kennedy's postgame responsibilities were what placed Kennedy on the 50-yard line in the first place; that was, after all, where he met the opposing team to shake hands after the game. Permitting a school coach to lead students and others he invited onto the field in prayer at a predictable time after each game could only be viewed as a postgame tradition occurring "with the approval of the school administration."

Kennedy's prayer practice also implicated the coercion concerns at the center of this Court's Establishment Clause jurisprudence. This Court has previously recognized a heightened potential for coercion where school officials are involved, as their "effort[s] to monitor prayer will be perceived by the students as inducing a participation they might otherwise reject." The reasons for fearing this pressure are self-evident. This Court has recognized that students face immense social pressure. Students look up to their teachers and coaches as role models and seek their approval. Students also depend on this approval for tangible benefits. Players recognize that gaining the coach's approval may pay dividends small and large, from extra playing time to a stronger letter of recommendation to additional support in college athletic recruiting. In addition to these pressures to please their coaches, this Court has recognized that players face "immense social pressure" from their peers in the "extracurricular event that is American high school football." * * *

The Free Exercise Clause and Establishment Clause are equally integral in protecting religious freedom in our society. The first serves as "a promise from our government," while the second erects a "backstop that disables our government from breaking it" and "start[ing] us down the path to the past, when [the right to free exercise] was routinely abridged."

Today, the Court once again weakens the backstop. It elevates one individual's interest in personal religious exercise, in the exact time and place of that individual's choosing, over society's interest in protecting the separation between church and state, eroding the protections for religious liberty for all. Today's decision is particularly misguided because it elevates the religious rights of a school official, who voluntarily accepted public employment and the limits that public employment entails, over those of his students, who are required to attend school and who this Court has long recognized are particularly vulnerable and deserving of protection. In doing so, the Court sets us further down a perilous path in forcing States to entangle themselves with religion, with all of our rights hanging in the balance. As much as the Court protests otherwise, today's decision is no victory for religious liberty. I respectfully dissent.

NOTES ON KENNEDY

1. *What Is the Test for Establishment Clause Violations?* The Court is clear in rejecting the *Lemon* test, but less clear on what is to replace it. Are the first two factors of the *Lemon* test (secular purpose and effect) still relevant at all, or can a law be constitutional even if its primary goal is to advance religion (or a specific religion)? The Court advises us to look at history and tradition. This may be a great opportunity for historians of the Founding Era to make money as consultants. It may be less helpful, however, in providing lawyers with a basis for advising government officials or private individuals who want to know their rights. Moreover, given the overwhelmingly Protestant nature of early American society, can the views of those in that more religiously homogenous society be extrapolated to today's more diverse country?

Another issue is who has the burden of proof: Must the government show historical precedent for its actions, or must the person making the Establishment Clause claim show that there were constitutional objections to a similar practice? What if both are true—a practice was not uncommon but was the subject of criticism? And finally, it is actually not clear that it is the Founding Era which ought to control a case like *Kennedy*. Kennedy had a claim only to the extent that the Fourteenth Amendment incorporates the Establishment Clause, so perhaps Civil War-era understandings ought to be controlling. Historians are specialized, so this would require a different consultant.

2. *Is the Establishment Clause Superfluous?* The only clear guidance from the opinion is that coercing religious activity violates the Establishment Clause? But wouldn't that violate the Free Exercise Clause anyway? What does the Establishment Clause add?

3. *What About Noncoercive Endorsements of Religion?* Suppose that a state adopted an official religion, placing religious texts on buildings and government documents but not otherwise taking any action to further the religion. Under *Lemon* and later cases, there would have been no question that this would have been unconstitutional. Does it remain true today? What would you have to know about Eighteenth and Nineteenth Century government practices in order to answer this question?

CHAPTER 7

FEDERALISM: CONGRESSIONAL POWER AND STATE AUTHORITY

■ ■ ■

SECTION 1. ENUMERATED FEDERAL POWER, RESERVED STATE AUTHORITY: INTRODUCTION

Page 880. Insert the following Note right after *Thornton*:

NOTE ON FISSION, FUSION, AND THE CONSTITUTION'S THEORY OF SOVEREIGNTY

In the Arkansas Term Limits Case, Justice Stevens asserts that the states retained their sovereign status under the Constitution, but the federal government owed its sovereign authority to We the People. Justice Thomas asserts that federal sovereignty is entirely derivative of authority granted by the states. Justice Kennedy says the Framers "split the atom of sovereignty." Two recent historical examinations suggest that Kennedy came closer to the "original public meaning" associated with the Constitution of 1789—but the implications of "popular sovereignty" were completely different in the early Republic than they are today.

Thus, Gregory Ablavsky argues in *Empire States: The Coming of Dual Federalism*, 128 Yale L.J. 1792 (2019), that the period of the American Revolution saw popular sovereignty triumph at all levels, just as Kennedy supposed. Unlike Kennedy, who saw fission, Ablavsky finds fusion: popular sovereignty had the effect of centralizing both national and state power. The new sovereignty was uniform within its domain. Hence, the immediate effects of dual federalism was to empower elected state governments against local centers of power (churches, municipalities, tribes). In the longer term, popular sovereignty justified empowerment of the national government, but in the 1790s and early 1800s the national government was modest and largely inactive.

In *The Imperial Treaty Power*, 168 U. Pa. L. Rev. 931 (2019), Brian Richardson develops another consequence of popular sovereignty. The Tenth Amendment says that the "powers not delegated to the United States by the Constitution, nor prohibited by it to the States, are reserved to the States respectively, or *to the people*" (emphasis added). As Richardson documents, a central debate in the nineteenth century concerned the authority of the state to acquire or cede property. Constitutionalists as distinguished as Daniel

Webster maintained that We the People retained "eminent dominion" over the lands as well as people within the nation and the states—and that neither the national nor the state governments could alienate that dominion without the consent of We the People.

Does the work of these two legal historians after your views about the "original meaning" of the Constitution, as applied to the Term Limits Case? *McCulloch*? Consider, too, the cases that follow.

SECTION 3. CONGRESSIONAL AUTHORITY TO PROMOTE CIVIL RIGHTS

B. CONGRESSIONAL POWER AND THE ELEVENTH AMENDMENT

Page 963. Add the following new Part B(4):

4.   State Structural Waiver of Immunity from Suit Through Consent to the Constitution of 1789

The previous cases involved Congress's authority to *abrogate* state immunity under constitutional authority to "enforce" the Reconstruction Amendments, but the Supreme Court had long held that states could *waive* their immunity, usually by consenting to or acquiescing in the exercise of federal jurisdiction. For example, if a state accepted federal funds in return for a waiver of immunity from suit by intended beneficiaries of those funds, the Eleventh Amendment was not implicated, because the state had consented to suit and had waived that immunity.

For more than a century, however, the Supreme Court has ruled that the states relinquished immunity defenses in certain kinds of lawsuits when they *consented* to the Constitution and joined the "United" States. E.g., *South Dakota* v. *North Carolina*, 192 U.S. 286, 24 S.Ct. 269 (1904) (structural waiver as to suits between states); *United States v. Texas*, 143 U.S. 621, 12 S.Ct. 488 (1892) (structural waiver as to suits by the United States against a state). The issue of structural consent has returned to the Court in a series of federal lawsuits against the states. These cases reflect the fact that state immunity from suit did not originate with the Eleventh Amendment and is not confined to the cases covered by that amendment. *Principality of Monaco v. Mississippi*, 292 U.S. 313 (1934), held that that Article III did not vest federal courts with authority to adjudicate lawsuits against unconsenting states even where the Eleventh Amendment did not provide immunity, and *Alden* held that unconsented state court lawsuits against the states violated the federalist structure of the Constitution. But if constitutional structure and original public meaning allow for broader state immunity from suit than that covered by the Eleventh Amendment, the same kind of analysis might allow broader congressional lawmaking that subjects states to suit notwithstanding the Eleventh Amendment, *Monaco,* or *Alden.*

Central Virginia Community College v. Katz

546 U.S. 356, 126 S.Ct. 990, 163 L.Ed.2d 145 (2006)

The Court held that states do not enjoy Eleventh Amendment immunity from orders entered in proceedings pursuant to the Bankruptcy Clause, which authorizes the establishment of "uniform Laws on the subject of Bankruptcies throughout the United States." Writing for a 5–4 Court, **Justice Stevens** reasoned that the Framers designed the Bankruptcy Clause to allow Congress to create a uniform, integrated national bankruptcy system to replace the inconsistent state approaches to the discharge of debts and to counteract the refusal of states to respect one another's discharge orders. Inherent in the constitutional plan was congressional authority to treat states as other creditors are treated. Unlike the Fourteenth Amendment cases, where the Court found constitutional authority for Congress to abrogate state Eleventh Amendment immunity, in this case the Court found that the states had waived that immunity by consenting to the Constitution of 1789.

"Insofar as orders ancillary to the bankruptcy courts' *in rem* jurisdiction, like orders directing turnover of preferential transfers, implicate States' sovereign immunity from suit, the States agreed in the plan of the Convention not to assert that immunity. So much is evidenced not only by the history of the Bankruptcy Clause, which shows that the Framers' primary goal was to prevent competing sovereigns' interference with the debtor's discharge, but also by legislation considered and enacted in the immediate wake of the Constitution's ratification.

"Congress considered proposed legislation establishing uniform federal bankruptcy laws in the first and each succeeding Congress until 1800, when the first Bankruptcy Act was passed. The Bankruptcy Act of 1800 was in many respects a copy of the English bankruptcy statute then in force. It was, like the English law, chiefly a measure designed to benefit creditors." But there was one significant difference, reflecting the layer-cake sovereignty of the United States: "The English statute gave a judge sitting on a court where the debtor had obtained his discharge the power to order a sheriff [et al.] to release the 'Bankrupt out of Custody' if he were arrested subsequent to the discharge. 5 Geo. 2, ch. 30, ¶ 13 (1732). The American version of this provision was worded differently; it specifically granted federal courts the authority to issue writs of habeas corpus effective to release debtors from state prisons. See § 38, 2 Stat. 32."

"This grant of habeas power is remarkable not least because it would be another 67 years, after Congress passed the Fourteenth Amendment, before the writ would be made generally available to state prisoners. Moreover, the provision of the 1800 Act granting that power was considered and adopted during a period when state sovereign immunity could hardly have been more prominent among the Nation's concerns. *Chisholm v. Georgia*, the case that had so "shock[ed]" the country in its lack of regard for state sovereign immunity, *Principality of Monaco v. Mississippi*, 292 U.S. 313, 325, 54 S.Ct. 745 (1934), was decided in 1793. The ensuing five years that culminated in adoption of the Eleventh Amendment were rife with discussion of States' sovereignty and their amenability to suit. Yet there appears to be no record of any objection to the bankruptcy legislation or its grant of habeas power to federal courts based on an infringement of sovereign immunity.

"This history strongly supports the view that the Bankruptcy Clause of Article I, the source of Congress' authority to effect this intrusion upon state sovereignty, simply did not contravene the norms this Court has understood the Eleventh Amendment to exemplify.' Based on this history, Justice Stevens concluded that the "States agreed in the plan of the Convention not to assert any sovereign immunity defense they might have had in proceedings brought pursuant to "Laws on the subject of Bankruptcies." See *Blatchford* (observing that a State is not 'subject to suit in federal court unless it has consented to suit, either expressly or in the "plan of the convention" '); *Alden v. Maine* (same). The scope of this consent was limited; the jurisdiction exercised in bankruptcy proceedings was chiefly *in rem*—a narrow jurisdiction that does not implicate state sovereignty to nearly the same degree as other kinds of jurisdiction. But while the principal focus of the bankruptcy proceedings is and was always the *res*, some exercises of bankruptcy courts' powers—issuance of writs of habeas corpus included—unquestionably involved more than mere adjudication of rights in a *res*. In ratifying the Bankruptcy Clause, the States acquiesced in a subordination of whatever sovereign immunity they might otherwise have asserted in proceedings necessary to effectuate the *in rem* jurisdiction of the bankruptcy courts

In dissent, **Justice Thomas**, joined by Chief Justice Roberts, Justice Scalia, and Justice Kennedy, argued that this holding was inconsistent with *Seminole Tribe* and earlier Eleventh Amendment decisions. "In contending that the States waived their immunity from suit by adopting the Bankruptcy Clause, the majority conflates two distinct attributes of sovereignty: the authority of a sovereign to enact legislation regulating its own citizens, and sovereign immunity against suit by private citizens. Nothing in the history of the Bankruptcy Clause suggests that, by including that clause in Article I, the founding generation intended to waive the latter aspect of sovereignty. These two attributes of sovereignty often do not run together—and for purposes of enacting a uniform law of bankruptcy, they need not run together.

"For example, Article I also empowers Congress to regulate interstate commerce and to protect copyrights and patents. These provisions, no less than the Bankruptcy Clause, were motivated by the Framers' desire for nationally uniform legislation. See James Madison, Preface to Debates in the Convention of 1787, reprinted in 3 M. Farrand, Records of the Federal Convention of 1787, pp. 539, 547–548 (1911) (noting lack of national regulation of commerce and uniform bankruptcy law as defects under the Articles of Confederation); M. Farrand, The Framing of the Constitution of the United States 48 (1913) (noting that the Articles of Confederation failed to provide for uniform national regulation of naturalization, bankruptcy, copyrights, and patents). Thus, we have recognized that '[t]he need for uniformity in the construction of patent law is undoubtedly important.' *Florida Prepaid*. Nonetheless, we have refused, in addressing patent law, to give the need for uniformity the weight the majority today assigns it in the context of bankruptcy, instead recognizing that this need 'is a factor which belongs to the Article I patent-power calculus, rather than to any determination of whether a state plea of sovereign immunity deprives a patentee of property without due process of law.' *Ibid.*

"Nor is the abrogation of state sovereign immunity from suit necessary to the enactment of nationally uniform bankruptcy laws. The sovereign immunity of the States against suit does not undermine the objective of a uniform national law of bankruptcy, any more than does any differential treatment between different categories of creditors."

PennEast Pipeline LLC v. New Jersey

594 U.S. ___, 141 S.Ct. 2244 (2021)

Under the Natural Gas Act of 1938 (NGA), a gas company needing to build an interstate pipeline must receive a certificate of public necessity and convenience from the Federal Energy Regulatory Commission (FERC). As amended in 1947, the Act authorizes holders of certificates to exercise the federal government's eminent domain authority to secure land needed for pipelines. PennEast exercised that delegated authority to secure land in which the state of New Jersey had a property interest. PennEast brought suit in federal court against New Jersey, which defended on grounds of immunity from suit.

Justice Gorsuch, joined by Justice Thomas, found this an easy case. By its terms, the Eleventh Amendment barred the case: "The Judicial Power of the United States," namely Article III, "shall not be construed to extend to any suit in law or equity, commenced or prosecuted against one of the United States," namely, New Jersey, "by Citizens of another State," namely, PennEast." As Gorsuch explained it, cases like *Monaco* were interpreting Article III directly, because those lawsuits fell outside the clear terms of the Eleventh Amendment. Cases like this one fell within the amendment's plan language, and Congress had no authority to abrogate that constitutional rule.

Justice Gorsuch did not speak for the Court, however. In his opinion for the Court, **Chief Justice Roberts** ruled in favor of PennEast, based upon the states' structural waiver of immunity when they ratified the Constitution. He started with the fact that the federal government has exercised its eminent domain authority since the founding. "When the Constitution and Bill of Rights were ratified, they did not include the words 'eminent domain.' The Takings Clause of the Fifth Amendment ('nor shall private property be taken for public use, without just compensation') nevertheless recognized the existence of such a power. Shortly after the founding, the Federal Government began exercising its eminent domain authority in areas subject to exclusive federal jurisdiction. See, *e.g.*, Act of Mar. 3, 1809, 2 Stat. 539 (authorizing construction of turnpike road in the District of Columbia); see also *Custiss v. Georgetown & Alexandria Turnpike Co.*, 6 Cranch 233, 3 L.Ed. 209 (1810) (suit by one of Martha Washington's grandsons to quash inquisition into value of land pursuant to Act).

"By the second half of the 19th century, however, this Court confirmed that federal eminent domain extended to property within state boundaries as well. In *Kohl v. United States*, 91 U.S. 367 (1876), we held that the United States could condemn land in Ohio to construct a federal building. We reasoned that '[t]he powers vested by the Constitution in the general government demand for their exercise the acquisition of lands in all the States.' *Id.*, at 371. And we noted that '[t]he right of eminent domain was one of those means well known when the Constitution was adopted, and employed to obtain lands for public uses.' *Id.*, at 372. The federal eminent domain power, we said, 'can neither be enlarged nor diminished by a State. Nor can any State prescribe the manner in which it must be exercised.' *Id.*, at 374. And to avoid any doubt, we added that '[t]he consent of a State can never be a condition precedent to [the] enjoyment' of federal eminent domain. Governments have long taken property for public use without the owner's consent. The United States is no different. While the Constitution and Bill of Rights did not use the term 'eminent domain,' the Takings Clause of the Fifth Amendment * * * presupposed the existence of such a power. Initially, the Federal Government exercised its eminent domain authority in areas subject to exclusive federal jurisdiction.

"While *Kohl* involved the condemnation of private land, we have since explained that federal eminent domain applies to state property interests as well. In *Oklahoma ex rel. Phillips v. Guy F. Atkinson Co.*, 313 U.S. 508, 61 S.Ct. 1050 (1941), we upheld an Act of Congress authorizing construction of a dam and a reservoir that would inundate thousands of acres of state-owned land. There, we made explicit a point that was implicit in *Kohl*'s reasoning: 'The fact that land is owned by a state is no barrier to its condemnation by the United States.'

"For as long as the eminent domain power has been exercised by the United States, it has also been delegated to private parties. It was commonplace before and after the founding for the Colonies and then the States to authorize the private condemnation of land for a variety of public works. The Federal Government was no different. As early as 1809, Congress authorized private parties to exercise the eminent domain power—including through the initiation of direct condemnation proceedings—within areas subject to federal jurisdiction. * * * Act of Mar. 2, 1831, 4 Stat. 477.

"In the years following *Kohl*, the Court confirmed that private delegatees can exercise the federal eminent domain power within the States as well. Our decision in *Luxton v. North River Bridge Co.*, 153 U.S. 525, 14 S.Ct. 891 (1894), is clear on this point. Congress authorized a corporation to build a bridge between New York and New Jersey, and to condemn property as necessary along the way. [S]ee Act of July 11, 1890, ch. 669, 26 Stat. 268. Luxton—who owned land in Hoboken against which the corporation had brought condemnation proceedings—objected on the ground that Congress had unconstitutionally delegated its eminent domain power to the corporation. We rejected Luxton's challenge, explaining that Congress 'may, at its discretion, use its sovereign powers, directly or through a corporation created for that object, to construct bridges for the accommodation of interstate commerce.' These powers, we noted, could be exercised 'with or without a concurrent act of the State in which the lands lie.' "

Given this common law background and the teaching of precedent, the Chief Justice had no problem rejecting New Jersey's Eleventh Amendment and sovereign immunity defenses.

Writing also for Justices Thomas, Kagan, and Gorsuch, **Justice Barrett** dissented. She argued that the majority opinion had framed the issue incorrectly. "[W]hile the Court casts the inquiry as one about the scope of the States' consent to the Federal Government's 'eminent-domain power,' that is the wrong way to think about the problem. Here is the right way: Title 15 U.S.C. § 717f(h) [the NGA provision authorizing the private eminent domain] is an exercise of Congress' power to regulate interstate commerce. Congress cannot authorize private suits against a nonconsenting State pursuant to its Commerce Clause power. *Seminole Tribe.* Nor does the Commerce Clause itself abrogate state sovereign immunity. Therefore, Congress cannot enable a private party like PennEast to institute a condemnation action against a nonconsenting State like New Jersey."

In response to the Court's research into past practice and precedent, Justice Barrett objected that "the question before us is not whether Congress can authorize a private party to exercise the right of eminent domain against another private party, which is the proposition this history supports. Nor is it whether Congress can authorize a private entity to take state property through means other than a condemnation suit. The question is whether Congress can authorize a private party to bring a condemnation suit against a State. And on that score, the Court comes up dry.

"The Court cannot muster even a *single* decision involving a private condemnation suit against a State, let alone any decision holding that the States lack immunity from such suits. It relies exclusively on suits brought by States, suits brought by the United States, suits brought by private parties against other private parties, and suits brought by Indian tribes against private parties—none of which implicate state sovereign immunity." At bottom, the Court's disposition rested upon raw "pragmatism" rather than binding precedent.

Query: Justice Barrett's dissenting opinion makes a powerful point: the Chief Justice was confusing state immunity from regulation (Article I and the Tenth Amendment) with state immunity from being sued in federal court (Article III and the Eleventh Amendment). Ditto Justice Gorsuch: Why was the Eleventh Amendment not conclusive? If directly addressed the issue—and it was adopted after the Constitution of 1789. Why would an uber-textualist Court override these obvious textual points? Notice that Justice Alito was in the majority, Justice Kagan in dissent.

TORRES V. TEXAS DEPARTMENT OF PUBLIC SAFETY
___ U.S. ___, 142 S.Ct. 2455, ___ L.Ed.2d ___ (2022)

JUSTICE BREYER delivered the opinion of the Court.

[Pursuant to its power "[t]o raise and support Armies" and "[t]o provide and maintain a Navy." U.S. Const. § 8, cls. 1, 12–13, Congress enacted the Uniformed Services Employment and Reemployment Rights Act of 1994 (USERRA), which gives returning servicemembers the right to reclaim their prior jobs with state employers and authorizes suit if those employers refuse to accommodate veterans' service-related disabilities. See 38 U.S.C. § 4301 *et seq.* Serving in the Army Reserves, Le Roy Torres was called to active duty and deployed to Iraq. There, he was exposed to toxic burn pits, a method of garbage disposal that sets open fire to all manner of trash, human waste, and military equipment.

[After he was discharged and returned home with constrictive bronchitis, a respiratory condition that narrowed his airways and made breathing difficult, Torres was unable to work his old job as a state trooper. He asked his former employer, the Texas Department of Public Safety, to accommodate his condition by reemploying him in a different role. When the department refused, Torres brought suit in state court to enforce his rights under USERRA. § 4313(a)(3). The Texas appellate courts ruled that the department enjoyed sovereign immunity, but after its decision in *PennEast Pipeline,* the Supreme Court took review and held that the States waived their sovereign immunity as to matters related to the national armed forces power pursuant to the "plan of the Convention."]

Congress' power to build and maintain the Armed Forces fits *PennEast*'s test. The Constitution's text, its history, and this Court's precedents show that 'when the States entered the federal system, they renounced their right' to interfere with national policy in this area.

For one thing, the Constitution's text, across several Articles, strongly suggests a complete delegation of authority to the Federal Government to provide for the common defense. Unlike most of the powers given to the National Government, the Constitution spells out the war powers not in a single, simple phrase, but in many broad, interrelated provisions. The Preamble makes the "common defence" one of the document's central projects. Article I gives Congress authority to "provide for th[at] common Defence" in six numbered paragraphs: to 'declare War'; 'raise and support Armies'; 'provide and maintain a Navy'; 'make Rules' for the Armed Forces; 'provide for calling forth the Militia'; and 'provide for [their] organizing, arming, and disciplining.' § 8, cls. 1, 11–16. Article II makes the President the 'Commander in Chief of the Army and Navy of the United States, and of the Militia of the several States.' § 2, cl. 1. And the Federal Government is charged with 'protect[ing] each' State 'against Invasion.' Art. IV, § 4.

The Constitution also divests the States of like power. States may not "engage in War, unless actually invaded," "enter into any Treaty," or "keep Troops, or Ships of War in time of Peace." Art. I, § 10, cls. 1, 3. States retain a role in "the Appointment of the Officers" to and the "training [of] the Militia," but that delegation is strictly cabined. Art. I, § 8, cl. 16. States must do so 'according to the discipline prescribed by Congress.' *Ibid.* These substantial limitations on state authority, together with the assignment of sweeping power to the Federal Government, provide strong evidence that the structure of the Constitution prevents States from frustrating national objectives in this field.

History teaches the same lesson. "When the Framers met in Philadelphia in the summer of 1787, they sought to create a cohesive national sovereign in response to the failings of the Articles of Confederation." *PennEast.* The Founders recognized, first and foremost, 'that the confederation produced no security agai[nst] foreign invasion; congress not being permitted to prevent a war nor to support it by the[ir] own authority,' because Congress lacked the power to marshal and maintain a fighting force 'fit for defence.' 1 Records of the Federal Convention of 1787, p. 19 (M. Farrand ed. 1966) (Edmund Randolph opening remarks) (alterations in original).

"[T]he want of power in Congress to raise an army" had left the National Government "dependen[t] upon the States" to supply military forces via a system of quotas and requisition that had nearly cost the Nation victory in the Revolutionary War. *Selective Draft Law Cases*, 245 U.S. 366, 381, 38 S.Ct. 159 (1918). George Washington warned from the battlefield that, unless Congress is "vested with powers by the several States" to raise an army, "our cause is lost." Letter to J. Jones (May 31, 1780), in 8 Writings of George Washington 304 (W. Ford ed. 1890). In short, "[t]he experience of the whole country, during the revolutionary war, established, to the satisfaction of every statesman, the utter inadequacy and impropriety of this system of requisition." 3 J. Story, Commentaries on the Constitution of the United States § 1174, p. 65 (1833) (Story). The need to fix that failing by establishing a strong national power to raise and maintain a military was one of the "recognized necessities" for calling the Constitutional Convention. *Selective Draft Law Cases.*

The Constitution, by design, worked "an entire change in the first principles of the system." The Federalist No. 23, at 148 (A. Hamilton). The Framers gave Congress direct power over the "*formation, direction* or *support* of the NATIONAL FORCES." *Ibid.* (emphasis in original). So "general and indefinite" were these powers vis-à-vis the States that "[o]bjections were made against" them as "subversive of the state governments," which retained "no control on congress" under the new arrangement. 3 Story §§ 1176, 1177, at 67. Some state conventions pitched proposals to limit the reach of Congress' war powers, but those amendments "die[d] away." *Id.*, § 1186, at 74. The States ultimately ratified the Constitution knowing that their sovereignty would give way to national military policy.

Consistent with that structural understanding, Congress has, since the founding era, directed raising and maintaining the national military, including at the expense of state sovereignty. For instance, early Congresses established military bonuses to reward service, even requiring Virginia to give land to some Revolutionary War officers. See Act of Aug. 10, 1790, 1 Stat. 182. Could Virginia have refused to go along? We do not think so.

As President Lincoln reflected while the Civil War raged: The federal power to raise and maintain a military " 'is given fully, completely, unconditionally. It is not a power to raise armies if State authorities consent; . . . it is a power to raise and support armies given to Congress by the Constitution, without an "if." ' " *Lichter v. United States*, 334 U.S. 742, 757, n. 4, 68 S.Ct. 1294 (1948) (quoting 9 J. Nicolay & J. Hay, Complete Works of Abraham Lincoln 75–77 (1894)).

An unbroken line of precedents supports the same conclusion: Congress may legislate at the expense of traditional state sovereignty to raise and support the Armed Forces. [Justice Breyer reviewed the Court's decisions applying federal armed forces laws to supplant state policy and law.]

The lesson we draw from these cases is that " '[t]he power to wage war is the power to wage war successfully.' " *Lichter* (quoting address by C. Hughes, War Powers Under the Constitution (Sept. 5, 1917)). The Framers " 'had emerged from a long struggle which had taught them the weakness of a mere confederation,' " so " 'they established a Union which could fight with the strength of one people under one government entrusted with the common defence.' " *Ibid.* Under our constitutional order, States may not place any " 'limitations inconsistent' " with Congress' power because " 'every resource of the people must be at command.' " *Ibid.* In short, the States agreed to "dives[t]" themselves of "the traditional diplomatic and military tools that . . . sovereigns possess"—to sacrifice their sovereignty for the common defense. *Franchise Tax Bd. of Cal. v. Hyatt*, 587 U.S. ___, ___, 139 S.Ct. 1485, 1496–1497 (2019).

It follows that Congress' power to build and maintain a national military is "complete in itself." *PennEast* (internal quotation marks omitted). Text, history, and precedent show the States agreed that their sovereignty would "yield . . . so far as is necessary" to national policy to raise and maintain the military. And because States committed themselves not to "thwart" the exercise of this federal power, "[t]he consent of a State," including to suit, "can never be a condition precedent to [Congress'] enjoyment" of it. We consequently hold that, as part of the plan of the Convention, the States waived their immunity under Congress' Article I power "[t]o raise and support Armies" and "provide and maintain a Navy." § 8, cls. 12–13. * * *

JUSTICE THOMAS, joined by **JUSTICES ALITO**, **GORSUCH**, and **BARRETT, J.J.**, dissenting.

More than two decades ago, this Court found it "difficult to conceive that the Constitution would have been adopted if it had been understood to strip the States of immunity from suit in their own courts and cede to the Federal Government a power to subject nonconsenting States to private suits in these fora." *Alden v. Maine* (1999). Accordingly, we held—without qualification—that "the powers delegated to Congress under Article I of the United States Constitution *do not include* the power to subject nonconsenting States to private suits for damages in state courts." [Because Torres brought suit in state and not federal court, the dissenters would have rested upon the unqualified holding in *Alden* but also offered their theory of state immunity under the Constitution.]

After declaring independence, the former Colonies "considered themselves fully sovereign nations." *Franchise Tax Bd. of Cal. v. Hyatt*, 139 S.Ct. 1485, 1493 (2019). And, when the States ratified the Constitution, "they entered the Union 'with their sovereignty intact,'" *Federal Maritime Comm'n v. South Carolina Ports Authority*, 535 U.S. 743, 751, 122 S.Ct. 1864 (2002) (quoting *Blatchford v. Native Village of Noatak*, 501 U.S. 775, 779, 111 S.Ct. 2578 (1991)), retaining "a substantial portion of the Nation's primary sovereignty, together with the dignity and essential attributes inhering in that status," *Alden*.

" 'An integral component' of the States' sovereignty was 'their immunity from private suits'" absent consent.) *Franchise Tax Bd.* That "doctrine . . . was universal in the States when the Constitution was drafted and ratified," *Alden*, because "[t]he generation that designed and adopted our federal system considered immunity from private suits central to sovereign dignity," In fact, sovereign immunity was so important that "[t]he Constitution never would have been ratified if the States and their courts were to be stripped of their sovereign authority except as expressly provided by the Constitution itself." *Atascadero State Hospital v. Scanlon*, 473 U.S. 234, 239, n. 2, 105 S.Ct. 3142 (1985).

Although States generally retained their immunity from suit, "in ratifying the Constitution, [they] did surrender a portion of their inherent immunity." *Federal Maritime Comm'n*. As Alexander Hamilton explained in The Federalist, sovereign immunity was part of "the general sense and the general practice of mankind," and the Constitution therefore left it "with the States" unless they had "surrender[ed]" some portion "of this immunity in the plan of the convention." The Federalist No. 81, pp. 487–488 (C. Rossiter ed. 1961).

[During the Nation's first 200 years, the Court recognized only two instances in which the States had surrendered their sovereign immunity in the constitutional plan, both of which involved suits prosecuted by other sovereigns, namely, suits by the United States or by another State against a State. Following precedent, the dissenters maintained that there was nothing close to "compelling evidence" that the Framers intended the constitutional compact to entail state consent to lawsuits. Like the dissenters in *Katz* and *PennEast*, the dissenters here found no explicit evidence that the States would have expected their lawsuit immunity had been given away when they ratified the Constitution.]

PROBLEM 7-3(a):
OTHER CANDIDATES FOR "PLAN OF THE CONVENTION" WAIVER OF ELEVENTH AMENDMENT IMMUNITY?

Like the Armed Forces Clauses, the Copyright Clause of the Constitution of 1789, Art. I, § 8, cl. 8, vests in Congress authority to create a uniform and comprehensive copyright law. If States could not be sued for violating copyright, the national policy would be undermined. Should the reasoning of *Katz/PennEast/Torres* be extended to the Copyright Clause? Note that the Court has found that States retain their Eleventh Amendment immunity in patent cases; the Patent Clause is also found in Art. I, § 8, cl. 8, and so the Court was implicitly rejecting state consent when ratifying the Constitution of 1789. See *Florida Prepaid Postsecondary Education Expense Fund v. College Savings Bank*, 527 U.S. 627 (1999). Should this case be reconsidered in light of *Torres*?

Consider also the Constitution's vesting diplomatic and foreign relations authority exclusively at the national level (in this case, mostly with the President). No State can enter "into and Treaty, Alliance, or Confederation" or, without the consent of Congress, "into any Agreement or Compact * * * with a foreign Power." U.S. Const. art. 1, § 10. *City of Monaco* relied on this structural argument to sustain state immunity from suit by a foreign state, lest the states and the federal judiciary be drawn into delicate foreign relations. But what if Congress adopted a statute permitting and regulating lawsuits by foreign states against states? Cf. Foreign Sovereign Immunities Act of 1976, 28 U.S. 1601 et seq. Would that be constitutional under *Torres* or even under *Principality of Monaco*?

Are there other constitutional provisions, or clusters of them, that might trigger the *Katz/PennEast/Torres* "plan of the Convention" waiver of state immunity from lawsuits?

SECTION 4. BEYOND THE COMMERCE AND CIVIL RIGHTS ENFORCEMENT POWERS

C. THE TREATY POWER

Pages 1005–07. Replace the Notes after *Missouri v. Holland* with the following Notes:

NOTES ON THE TREATY POWER AND ORIGINAL MEANING

Missouri v. Holland is a "nationalist" reading of the Treaty Clause: Treaty obligations entered into by the President, with the advice and consent of the Senate, create domestic law under the Supremacy Clause (Art. VI, cl. 2) even if not supported by an independent Article I ground for federal authority.[1] Through most of our history, there has been a counter vision of the Treaty Clause, a "states' rights" reading: Treaty obligations are not the law of the land unless they fall under one of the powers delegated to the national government under Article I.[2]

As recent scholarship has established, the Framing era and the early Republic also took seriously a third understanding: that neither the state nor federal government had authority to cede the "eminent dominion" that We the People retained over the territory of the states or the country.[3] The Tenth Amendment "reserves" to the states *or* to the people those powers "not delegated to the United States." Indeed, Missouri made precisely this argument in *Holland*: it claimed eminent dominion over the birds within its territory and argued that only a popular ratification could alienate the property of the people of the state.

Justice Holmes dismissed that argument out of hand. By 1920, the imperial ambitions of the United States had overtaken Missouri's argument, which was inconsistent with American annexation of Puerto Rico and other territories after the Spanish-American War of 1898. Under these circumstances, not only was the popular-control argument no longer plausible, but there was an historical thumb on the scale in favor of plenary national authority. See George Sutherland, *Constitutional Power and World Affairs* (1918). Justice Holmes seems friendly to the Sutherland view and cites the Necessary and Proper Clause, which allows Congress "[t]o make all Laws which shall be necessary and proper for carrying into Execution the foregoing Powers [those in Article I], and all other Powers vested by this Constitution in the Government of the United States," including Article II's Treaty Clause. Typically, Holmes did not explain exactly how the constitutional text supported his national-authority holding.

---

[1] David M. Golove, *Treaty-Making and the Nation: The Historic Foundations of the Nationalist Conception of the Treaty Power*, 98 Mich. L. Rev. 1075 (2000).

[2] Curtis A. Bradley, *The Treaty Power and American Federalism*, 97 Mich. L. Rev. 391 (1998).

[3] Brian Richardson, *The Imperial Treaty Power*, 168 U. Pa. L. Rev. 931 (2019).

As Nicholas Rosenkranz has argued, if you put these clauses together, you have the following power of Congress: "To make all Laws which shall be necessary and proper for carrying into Execution * * * [the] Power * * * to make Treaties."[4] Rosenkranz says that the plain meaning of the Constitution reveals that Justice Holmes was flat wrong: the migratory birds statute was *not* needed to carry into execution Congress's power to "make Treaties." Instead, it was a congressional implementation of a treaty already made, but without any basis (in 1921) in the Constitution's delegation of limited authority to Congress. Can the Holmes position be salvaged? David Golove and Louis Henkin, among others, believe that original meaning supports *Missouri v. Holland*. Curtis Bradley and Nick Rosenkranz do not. Consider the evidence.

1.   *Pre-1787 Practice.* In eighteenth-century England, treaties were made by the King, and they were binding on the nation. The Articles of Confederation vested the exclusive right to enter into treaties with Congress, with the proviso that no commercial treaty could interfere with state legislative power to impose equal taxes on foreigners as they impose on their own citizens or from regulating trade in goods or commodities (Art. IX). The Articles also prohibited the states from imposing imposts or duties inconsistent with treaties proposed for France and Spain (Art. VI). These limitations, explicitly recognizing state power as a limit on the national treaty power, bedeviled American negotiators of the Treaty of Peace entered into with Great Britain in 1782. The nationalist-versus-states' rights debate over the treaty power began during this period. Most of the statesmen in the national government— including Jefferson and Madison—took the nationalist position, that Congress could accrue new commerce-regulatory powers through treaties than it was otherwise vested with by the Articles (Golove, *Treaty-Making*). Statesmen at the local level tended to disagree; Virginia, for example, insisted it was not bound to enforce the Treaty of Peace provision enforcing debt obligations to the British. But see *Ware v. Hylton*, 3 U.S. 199 (1796) (upholding Art. IV of the Peace Treaty, requiring restitution of confiscated debts to British citizens). Moreover, other countries doubted the United States had this power either, and refused to enter into commercial treaties with the new country for that reason.

2.   *The Philadelphia Convention and the Ratifying Debates.* The frustrations of the Articles period created consensus at Philadelphia supporting a rule that the national treaty power trumps state law, but there was also a consensus that the national government would be one of limited authority, confined to those powers delegated to it by the Constitution. It is not apparent that anyone gave thought to the proposition that a treaty power in Article II could reach subjects about which Article I did not authorize Congress to legislate. Louis Henkin argues that an early draft of the Necessary and Proper Clause explicitly included the power to "enforce treaties," but that language was struck because it was "superfluous." Rosenkranz responds that

---

[4]   Nicholas Quinn Rosenkranz, *Executing the Treaty Power*, 118 Harv. L. Rev. 1867 (2005).

the language struck was from the Militia Clause and that the Necessary and Proper Clause never had language relating to treaties.[5]

During the state ratifying debates, Anti-Federalists attacked the Constitution's treaty power on the ground that it was unbounded—and therefore represented an important threat to the viability of autonomous states (Golove, *Treaty-Making*). Of particular concern was the possibility that the President and Senate might cede territorial rights over individual state objections. In the Virginia ratifying debates, Madison confessed that the treaty power under both the Articles and the Constitution gave no power of "dismembering" the country, "or alienating any part of it," because that was not a treaty power recognized by the law of nations. (This was an early version of the idea that neither state nor national governments could alienate territory vested in the polity.)

The opponents, particularly Patrick Henry, also argued that the treaty power could override individual rights. The Federalists generally denied that this would be legal, but without detailed reasoning from their constitutional text—except for this defense by George Nicholas: The President and Senate can "make no treaty which shall be repugnant to the spirit of the Constitution, or inconsistent with the delegated powers." Scholars vigorously debate how Nicholas' statement should be interpreted and how broadly to attribute it to other Federalists.[6]

3.   *Early Interpretation and Practice.* The Jay Treaty with Great Britain ignited a great debate between the nationalist and states' rights visions of the treaty power. Article 9 of the treaty overrode state law to assure property rights of British subjects in the American states, and opponents argued that this was beyond the authority of the President and Senate to accomplish. These arguments were rejected by President Washington, who upon the advice of Hamilton signed and supported the treaty; by two-thirds of the Senate, which ratified the treaty; by a slender majority in the House, which voted to give the treaty effect (Golove, *Treaty-Making,* 1154–61); and by the U.S. Supreme Court in *Martin v. Hunter's Lessee*, 14 U.S. 304 (1816), which applied the treaty to override state law. On the other hand, some supporters of the Constitution opined that the treaty power did not authorize national action beyond the powers delegated by Article I. Jefferson opposed the Jay Treaty on this ground and wrote his view into the Senate's earliest manual of parliamentary practice, which said that the treaty power could not extend to objects not normally regulated by treaties, to matters where the Constitution vested the House with a role, or to matters "reserved to the States: for surely the President and Senate cannot do by treaty what the whole government is interdicted from doing in any way" (Bradley, *Treaty Power*, 415, quoting the manual). As President, however, Jefferson was not so particular about the treaty power when he used it to make the Louisiana Purchase (Golove, *Treaty-Making*, 1188–95). Later in

---

[5]   Compare Louis Henkin, *Foreign Affairs and the Constitution* 481 n.111 (2d ed. 1996), with Rosenkranz, *Executing the Treaty Power*, 1912–18.

[6]   Compare Bradley, *Treaty Power*, 413, with Golove, *Treaty-Making*, 1148.

the nineteenth century, Jefferson's private reservations about the legality of the Louisiana Purchase came to light and fueled the argument that neither level of government could alienate territorial or property within the eminent dominion (Richardson, *Imperial Treaty Power*).

Bottom line: Was *Missouri v. Holland* wrongly decided? Should it be overruled? Can *stare decisis* save *Holland*?

SECTION 6. NATIONALIST LIMITATIONS UPON STATE REGULATORY AUTHORITY

B. DORMANT COMMERCE CLAUSE DOCTRINE

3. Exceptions to Dormant Commerce Clause Review

Page 1123. Insert the following right after *Granholm*:

Tennessee Wine & Spirits Ass'n v. Thomas

139 S.Ct. 2449 (2019)

Tennessee law imposes durational-residency requirements on persons and companies wishing to operate retail liquor stores, requiring applicants for an initial license to have resided in the State for the prior two years; requiring an applicant for renewal of a license to reside in the State for 10 consecutive years; and providing that a corporation cannot obtain a license unless all of its stockholders are residents. The lower court invalidated all three requirements, but the state only appealed its loss on the two-year residency requirement. Writing for a 7–2 Court, **Justice Alito** ruled that the residency requirement was a "blatant" violation of the Dormant Commerce Clause and was not saved by the Twenty-First Amendment's savings clause.

Justice Alito started his opinion for the Court with a lengthy apologia for the "Dormant" (i.e., Nontextual) Commerce Clause, which he justified based upon the expectations of the Framers. "[W]ithout the dormant Commerce Clause, we would be left with a constitutional scheme that those who framed and ratified the Constitution would surely find surprising.

"That is so because removing state trade barriers was a principal reason for the adoption of the Constitution. Under the Articles of Confederation, States notoriously obstructed the interstate shipment of goods. "Interference with the arteries of commerce was cutting off the very life-blood of the nation." M. Farrand, The Framing of the Constitution of the United States 7 (1913). The Annapolis Convention of 1786 was convened to address this critical problem, and it culminated in a call for the Philadelphia Convention that framed the Constitution in the summer of 1787. At that Convention, discussion of the power to regulate interstate commerce was almost uniformly linked to the removal of state trade barriers, see Abel, The Commerce Clause in the Constitutional Convention and in Contemporary Comment, 25 Minn. L. Rev.

432, 470–471 (1941), and when the Constitution was sent to the state conventions, fostering free trade among the States was prominently cited as a reason for ratification. In The Federalist No. 7, Hamilton argued that state protectionism could lead to conflict among the States, and in No. 11, he touted the benefits of a free national market. In The Federalist No. 42, Madison sounded a similar theme."

Under the Court's precedents, Justice Alito had no difficulty striking down an open discrimination against interstate commerce, which was not "narrowly tailored" to serve a "legitimate local interest." Tennessee's main defense rested upon § 2 of the Twenty-First Amendment:

> The transportation or importation into any State, Territory, or possession of the United States for delivery or use therein of intoxicating liquors, in violation of the laws thereof, is hereby prohibited.

"Although the interpretation of any provision of the Constitution must begin with a consideration of the literal meaning of that particular provision, reading § 2 to prohibit the transportation or importation of alcoholic beverages in violation of *any* state law would lead to absurd results that the provision cannot have been meant to produce. Under the established rule that a later adopted provision takes precedence over an earlier, conflicting provision of equal stature, such a reading of § 2 would mean that the provision would trump any irreconcilable provision of the original Constitution, the Bill of Rights, the Fourteenth Amendment, and every other constitutional provision predating ratification of the Twenty-first Amendment in 1933. This would mean, among other things, that a state law prohibiting the importation of alcohol for sale to persons of a particular race, religion, or sex would be immunized from challenge under the Equal Protection Clause."

Finding that absurd, Justice Alito looked to the history of the Twenty-First Amendment, which suggested that it was meant to constitutionalize the constitutional status quo that preceded Prohibition—a status quo that *Granholm* (Casebook, p. 1122) had interpreted as barring discriminatory state liquor regulation. Defenders of the Tennessee law argued that *Granholm* only invalidated a discrimination against out-of-state shipments and producers, while their law applied only to in-state distribution of alcohol. The Court rejected that distinction as immaterial for Dormant Commerce Clause purposes. Moreover, the Twenty-First Amendment did not seem to address the Tennessee approach nearly as clearly as it seemed to address the New York approach invalidated in *Granholm*.

Justice Gorsuch, joined by Justice Thomas, dissented. "States may impose residency requirements on those who seek to sell alcohol within their borders to ensure that retailers comply with local laws and norms. In fact, States have enacted residency requirements for at least 150 years, and the Tennessee law at issue before us has stood since 1939. Today and for the first time, the Court claims to have discovered a duty and power to strike down laws like these as unconstitutional. Respectfully, I do not see it."

Picking up themes developed in Justice Thomas's *Granholm* dissent, Justice Gorsuch argued that the Webb-Kenyon Act authorized state regulation of the liquor trade and immunized it from Dormant Commerce Clause attack, which the Twenty-First Amendment constitutionalized. The dissenters were baffled that a nontextual constitutional doctrine was trumping the clear text of the Twenty-First Amendment.

Query: Does the Court's opinion in *Tennessee Wine and Liquor* close the door on the complaints from Justices Thomas and Gorsuch that the Dormant Commerce Clause ought to be retired (Casebook, pp. 1121, 1127–32)? While the *Pike-Kassel* balancing approach for state laws having an "effect" on interstate commerce might have outlived its usefulness, the current Court seems keen on enforcing the Dormant Commerce Clause against explicit state discriminations. Notice that the Court's conservatives and liberals joined the Alito opinion.

CHAPTER 8

SEPARATION OF POWERS

▪ ▪ ▪

SECTION 1. ISSUES OF EXECUTIVE AGGRANDIZEMENT (IMPERIAL PRESIDENCY)

A. THE POST-NEW DEAL FRAMEWORK

Page 1182. Insert the following Case right before Part B:

Financial Oversight & Management Board for Puerto Rico v. Aurelius Investment

140 S.Ct. 1649 (2020)

In 2016, Congress enacted the Puerto Rico Oversight, Management, and Economic Stability Act (PROMESA). 130 Stat. 549, 48 U.S.C. § 2101 *et seq.* The statute created a Financial Oversight and Management Board, whose seven members were appointed by the President without "the advice and consent of the Senate," *i.e.,* without Senate confirmation. A creditor argued that the Board was invalid under Article II, section 2, clause 2's requirement that "Officers of the United States" be appointed by the President, with Senate confirmation.

In an opinion by **Justice Breyer**, the Court nonetheless upheld the statutory appointments scheme. Two provisions of the Constitution empower Congress to create local offices for the District of Columbia and for Puerto Rico and the Territories. See Art. I, § 8, cl. 17; Art. IV, § 3, cl. 2. This structure suggests that when Congress governs a "territory" under Article IV, its officials might be considered "local" officers rather than "Officers of the United States."

As in *Noel Canning*, Justice Breyer looked to history and found that the term "Officers of the United States" had never been understood to cover those whose powers and duties are primarily local in nature and derive from these two constitutional provisions. "When the First Congress legislated for the Northwest Territories, for example, it created a House of Representatives for the Territory with members selected by election. It also created an upper house of the territorial legislature, whose members were appointed by the President (without Senate confirmation) from lists provided by the elected, lower house. And it created magistrates appointed by the Governor." Apparently, no one thought Congress was violating the Appointments Clause in such a scheme of territorial governance. Congress followed that approach for the next 200 years—including its statutes organizing the government of Puerto Rico after the Spanish-American War. Thus, "while the Appointments Clause *does* restrict the appointment of 'Officers of the United States' with duties in or related to the District of Columbia or an Article IV entity, it *does not* restrict the appointment of local officers that Congress vests with primarily local duties under Article IV, § 3, or Article I, § 8, cl. 17." (**Justice Thomas** concurred in the Court's judgment. Based on the Northwest Ordinance, he did not agree with the federal-versus-local duties test.)

Justice Sotomayor criticized the Court's Article IV analysis in light of Puerto Rico's history of self-government under a constitution adopted by its people and ratified by Congress. "Puerto Rico's compact with the Federal Government and its republican form of government may not alter its status as a Territory. But territorial status should not be wielded as a talismanic opt out of prior congressional commitments or constitutional constraints." In light of the congressional super-statute ratifying Puerto Rico's republican governance structure, any statutory adjustment required a clear statement, which PROMESA did not pretend to offer.

"Viewed against that backdrop, the result of these cases seems anomalous. The Board members, tasked with determining the financial fate of a self-governing Territory, exist in a twilight zone of accountability, neither selected by Puerto Rico itself nor subject to the strictures of the Appointments Clause. I am skeptical that the Constitution countenances this freewheeling exercise of control over a population that the Federal Government has explicitly agreed to recognize as operating under a government of their own choosing, pursuant to a constitution of their own choosing. Surely our Founders, having labored to attain such recognition of self-determination, would not view that same recognition with respect to Puerto Rico as a mere act of grace." Because these issues had not been briefed and argued, Justice Sotomayor "reluctantly" concurred in the Court's judgment.

Cross-Reference: For another recent Supreme Court decision interpreting the Appointments Clause, see *Lucia v. SEC* (Casebook, pp. 1308–09).

B.   FOREIGN RELATIONS AND WAR

3.   Presidential Authority in Foreign Relations and Immigration

Page 1212. Insert the following Case at the end of Section 1(B):

Biden v. Texas

142 S.Ct. 2528 (2022)

In January 2019, the Trump Administration's Department of Homeland Security implemented the Migrant Protection Protocols, under which certain non-Mexican nationals arriving by land from Mexico were returned to Mexico to await the results of their removal proceedings under § 1229a of the Immigration and Nationality Act. MPP was implemented pursuant to a provision of the statute that applies to noncitizens "arriving on land . . . from a foreign territory contiguous to the United States" and provides that the Secretary of Homeland Security "may return the alien to that territory pending a proceeding under section 1229a." 8 U. S. C. § 1225(b)(2)(C). The incoming Biden Administration announced that it would suspend the program, and DHL forthwith did so. Writing for a 5–4 Court, **Chief Justice Roberts** upheld the Administration's action as consistent with the statute. Although the Chief Justice did not cite the Jackson opinion in Steel Seizure, he carefully followed its analytical structure—finding both congressional authorization (Category 1) and acquiescence in presidential practice (Category 2).

Section 1225(b)(2)(C) provides: "In the case of an alien . . . who is arriving on land . . . from a foreign territory contiguous to the United States, the [Secretary] may return the alien to that territory pending a proceeding under section 1229a." Section 1225(b)(2)(C), the Court ruled, "confers a discretionary authority to return aliens to Mexico during the pendency of their immigration proceedings. This Court has 'repeatedly observed' that 'the word "may" clearly connotes discretion.' *Opati v. Republic of Sudan*, 590 U.S. ___, ___ (2020); see also *Jama v. Immigration and Customs Enforcement*, 543 U.S. 335, 346 (2005). The use of the word 'may' in section 1225(b)(2)(C) thus makes clear that contiguous-territory return is a tool that the Secretary "has the authority, but not the duty," to use. *Lopez v. Davis*, 531 U.S. 230, 241 (2001)."

Texas relied on § 1225(b)(2)(A), which provides that, "in the case of an alien who is an applicant for admission, if the examining immigration officer determines that an alien seeking admission is not clearly and beyond a doubt entitled to be admitted, the alien shall be detained for a proceeding under section 1229a of this title." Because § 1225(b)(2)(A) makes detention mandatory, Texas (and three dissenting Justices) argued that the otherwise-discretionary return authority in § 1225(b)(2)(C) becomes mandatory when the Secretary violates that detention mandate. The majority was not persuaded.

"Congress's use of the word 'may' is therefore inconsistent with respondents' proposed inference from the statutory structure. If Congress had intended § 1225(b)(2)(C) to operate as a mandatory cure of any noncompliance with the Government's detention obligations, it would not have conveyed that intention through an unspoken inference in conflict with the unambiguous, express term 'may.' It would surely instead have coupled that grant of discretion with some indication of its sometimes mandatory nature—perhaps by providing that the Secretary 'may return' certain aliens to Mexico, 'unless the government fails to comply with its detention obligations, in which case the Secretary must return them.' The statutory grant of discretion here contains no such caveat, and we will not rewrite it to include one."

The Chief Justice confirmed his reading of the statutory structure with its history: "Section 1225(b)(2)(C) was not added to the statute until 1996, in the Illegal Immigration Reform and Immigrant Responsibility Act of 1996

(IIRIRA), § 302, 110 Stat. 300–583—more than 90 years after the Immigration Act of 1903 added the 'shall be detained' language that appears in section 1225(b)(2)(A). And section 1225(b)(2)(C) was enacted in the immediate aftermath of a Board of Immigration Appeals (BIA) decision that specifically called into question the legality of the contiguous-territory return practice. * * * Congress responded mere months later by adding section 1225(b)(2)(C) to IIRIRA and conferring on the Secretary express authority ('may') to engage in the very practice that the BIA had questioned. And INS acknowledged that clarification shortly thereafter, explaining that section 1225(b)(2)(C) and its implementing regulation 'simply add[ ] to the statute and regulation a long-standing practice of the Service.' 62 Fed. Reg. 445 (1997). That modest backstory suggests a more humble role for section 1225(b)(2)(C) than as a mandatory 'safety valve' for any alien who is not detained under section 1225(b)(2)(A).

"In addition to contradicting the statutory text and context, the novelty of respondents' interpretation bears mention. Since IIRIRA's enactment 26 years ago, every Presidential administration has interpreted section 1225(b)(2)(C) as purely discretionary. Indeed, at the time of IIRIRA's enactment and in the decades since, congressional funding has consistently fallen well short of the amount needed to detain all land-arriving inadmissible aliens at the border, yet no administration has ever used section 1225(b)(2)(C) to return all such aliens that it could not otherwise detain.

"And the foreign affairs consequences of mandating the exercise of contiguous-territory return likewise confirm that the Court of Appeals erred. Article II of the Constitution authorizes the Executive to 'engag[e] in direct diplomacy with foreign heads of state and their ministers.' *Zivotofsky v. Kerry*, 576 U.S. 1, 14 (2015). Accordingly, the Court has taken care to avoid 'the danger of unwarranted judicial interference in the conduct of foreign policy,' and declined to 'run interference in [the] delicate field of international relations' without 'the affirmative intention of the Congress clearly expressed.' *Kiobel v. Royal Dutch Petroleum Co.*, 569 U.S. 108, 115–116 (2013). That is no less true in the context of immigration law, where '[t]he dynamic nature of relations with other countries requires the Executive Branch to ensure that enforcement policies are consistent with this Nation's foreign policy.' *Arizona v. United States*, 567 U.S. 387, 397 (2012).

"By interpreting section 1225(b)(2)(C) as a mandate, the Court of Appeals imposed a significant burden upon the Executive's ability to conduct diplomatic relations with Mexico. * * * In attempting to rescind MPP, the Secretary emphasized that '[e]fforts to implement MPP have played a particularly outsized role in diplomatic engagements with Mexico, diverting attention from more productive efforts to fight transnational criminal and smuggling networks and address the root causes of migration.' App. to Pet. for Cert. 262a. Yet under the Court of Appeals' interpretation, section 1225(b)(2)(C) authorized the District Court to force the Executive to the bargaining table with Mexico, over a policy that both countries wish to terminate, and to supervise its continuing negotiations with Mexico to ensure that they are conducted 'in good faith.' That stark consequence confirms our conclusion that Congress did not intend section 1225(b)(2)(C) to tie the hands of the Executive in this manner."

Writing for herself, **Justice Barrett** agreed with the Chief Justice on the merits but (joined by Justices Thomas, Alito, and Gorsuch) dissented on the issue of jurisdiction. Joined by Justices Thomas and Gorsuch, **Justice Alito** dissented on the merits. Like the Court, Justice Alito followed the Jackson approach and rejected the President's directive on the ground that it was foreclosed by Congress's direct command. In fiscal year 2021, there were more than 1.7 million encounters with noncitizens along the Mexican border. What options does the executive branch have to deal with those who are inadmissible? Justice Alito argued that the statute provides clear directives.

"By law, if an alien is 'not clearly and beyond a doubt entitled to be admitted,' the alien 'shall be *detained* for a [removal] proceeding.' 8 U. S. C. § 1225(b)(2)(A) (emphasis added). And if an alien asserts a credible fear of persecution, he or she 'shall be detained for further consideration of the application for asylum,' § 1225(b)(1)(B)(ii) (emphasis added)." Immigration enforcement has two alternatives to detention: "First, if an alien is 'arriving on States,' the Department of Homeland Security (DHS) 'may return the alien to that territory pending a [removal] proceeding.' § 1225(b)(2)(C). Second, DHS may release individual aliens on 'parole,' but 'only on a case-by-case basis for urgent humanitarian reasons or a significant public benefit.' § 1182(d)(5)(A)." The Biden Administration did neither, and the dissenters maintained that the discretionary "may" in § 1225(b)(2)(C) had to be read in light of the limited choices available to the administration under the mandatory "shall" of § 1225(b)(1)(B)(ii) and (2)(A).

Query: As in *Trump v. Hawaii* (2018), the Supreme Court majority read the discretionary language of the immigration law broadly, to give the President a lot of discretion in handling undocumented immigrants. Is this consistent with Justice Jackson's approach? Recall that he ruled against President Truman on a matter the President believed was essential to the conduct of the Korean War. The majority opinion might be understood as applying Jackson's framework, but with the latitude better reflected in Justice Frankfurter's Steel Seizure concurring opinion or Chief Justice Vinson's very deferential dissenting opinion.

C. EXECUTIVE PRIVILEGES AND IMMUNITIES

Page 1228. Insert the following Case right before Problem 8-4:

Donald J. Trump v. Cyrus R. Vance Jr.

591 U.S. ___, 140 S.Ct. 2412 (2020)

The Manhattan District Attorney convened a grand jury to investigate financial transactions that may have violated state law. The office served a subpoena *duces tecum* on Mazars USA, LLP, the personal accounting firm of

President Trump. The subpoena directed Mazars to produce financial records relating to the President and business organizations affiliated with him, including "[t]ax returns and related schedules," from "2011 to the present." The President, acting in his personal capacity but supported by the Department of Justice, sued to enjoin enforcement of the subpoena, on the ground that, under Article II and the Supremacy Clause, a sitting President enjoys absolute immunity from state criminal process. The DA took the position that under *United States v. Nixon* (Casebook, pp. 1212–18), the President had no defense and had to turn over the documents.

Chief Justice Roberts delivered the opinion for the Court, rejecting the President's absolute Article II defense to enforcement of the subpoenas against Mazars. In *United States v. Burr* (1807), Chief Justice Marshall himself granted the defense motion for a *subpoena duces tecum* requiring President Jefferson to produce documents relevant to former Vice-President Aaron Burr's treason trial. Since Jefferson's acquiescence in the subpoena, every President has complied with similar requests in connection with federal criminal trials— until President Nixon refused and was rebuked in *United States v. Nixon* (1974).

Vance's subpoena was the first against a President in connection with *state* (rather than federal) criminal proceedings, and the Department of Justice joined Trump's personal lawyers in arguing that the Supremacy Clause and Article II gave the President absolute immunity from compliance. The Chief Justice did not see any reason to treat state criminal investigations differently from federal ones: in both kind of proceedings, the defendant might need the President's evidence, and no person should be exempt from the law. Roberts rejected the President's claims of distraction and potential harassment for the same reasons the Court had given in *Clinton v. Jones* (1997) (Casebook, pp. 1225–26).

That the President enjoyed no absolute immunity from state grand jury subpoena was an issue on which the Court was *unanimous*. The Court was also *unanimous* in remanding the case back to the district court, which could rule on particular objections the President might have to the subpoenas. The terms of the remand produced divisions within the Court.

The Solicitor General maintained that a state subpoena to the President ought to meet heightened standards, such as a requirement that the requested information was truly "necessary" for the state investigation and could not be secured elsewhere. Speaking for the Court, **Chief Justice Roberts** rejected this contention. "First, such a heightened standard would extend protection designed for official documents to the President's private papers." The Solicitor General's proposed test was derived from executive privilege cases that trace back to *Burr*. But Marshall said this in *Burr*: "If there be a paper in the possession of the executive, which is *not of an official nature*, he must stand, as respects that paper, in nearly the same situation with any other individual." ([E]mphasis added). And it is only "nearly"—and not "entirely"—because the

President retains the right to assert privilege over documents that, while ostensibly private, "partake of the character of an official paper."

Second, Roberts concluded that the Solicitor General had not supplied the Court with sufficient cause to say that "heightened protection against state subpoenas is necessary for the Executive to fulfill his Article II functions." The asserted "risk of harassment" and "unwarranted burdens" were not enough to support President Nixon's opposition to the Watergate subpoenas, and the Court refused in impose a "double standard" on state as opposed to federal subpoenas. "For if the state subpoena is not issued to manipulate, the documents themselves are not protected [by executive privilege], and the Executive is not impaired, then nothing in Article II or the Supremacy Clause supports holding state subpoenas to a higher standard than their federal counterparts."

"Finally, in the absence of a need to protect the Executive, the public interest in fair and effective law enforcement cuts in favor of comprehensive access to evidence. Requiring a state grand jury to meet a heightened standard of need would hobble the grand jury's ability to acquire 'all information that might possibly bear on its investigation.' And, even assuming the evidence withheld under that standard were preserved until the conclusion of a President's term, in the interim the State would be deprived of investigative leads that the evidence might yield, allowing memories to fade and documents to disappear. This could frustrate the identification, investigation, and indictment of third parties (for whom applicable statutes of limitations might lapse). More troubling, it could prejudice the innocent by depriving the grand jury of *exculpatory* evidence."

On remand, Trump could raise the following kinds of objections, if supported by the evidence: (1) "any grounds permitted by state law, which usually include bad faith and undue burden or breadth"; (2) a substantiated claim that the subpoena is "an attempt to influence the performance of his official duties, in violation of the Supremacy Clause"; and (3) a showing that "compliance with a particular subpoena would impede his constitutional duties." As a result, "once the President sets forth and explains a conflict between judicial proceeding and public duties," or shows that an order or subpoena would "significantly interfere with his efforts to carry out" those duties, "the matter changes." [*Clinton v. Jones* (Breyer).] At that point, a court should use its inherent authority to quash or modify the subpoena, if necessary to ensure that such "interference with the President's duties would not occur." [*Id.*]

Justice Kavanaugh (joined by **Justice Gorsuch**) concurred in the Court's judgment and would have directed the district court on remand to quash the subpoena if the prosecutors were not able to satisfy the standards applied to protect "executive privilege" in *Nixon v. United States,* namely, that there is a "demonstrated specific need" for the President's evidence. Although executive privilege was not at stake with regard to the President's tax returns, Article II and Supremacy Clause require such a well-tested burden of proof.

Justice Kavanaugh concluded that the different directives entailed in the Court's and other opinions might in the long term boil down to the same inquiries: "lower courts in cases of this sort involving a President will almost invariably have to begin by delving into why the State wants the information; why and how much the State needs the information, including whether the State could obtain the information elsewhere; and whether compliance with the subpoena would unduly burden or interfere with a President's official duties."

Justice Thomas dissented. In contrast to legislative immunities conferred on speech and debate in Article I, Article II gives the President no absolute immunities, as reflected by the early precedent in *United States v. Burr*. But Justice Thomas would have allowed the President to escape enforcement of the subpoena if he could show on remand that "his duties as chief magistrate demand his whole time for national objects," *United States* v. *Burr*, 25 F. Cas. 30, 34 (No. 14,692d) (CC Va. 1807) (Marshall, C. J.).

Justice Alito also wrote a dissenting opinion. He maintained that the Court neglected the structurally special role of the President in our system. "Constitutionally speaking, the President never sleeps. The President must be ready, at a moment's notice, to do whatever it takes to preserve, protect, and defend the Constitution and the American people." Amar & Katyal, *Executive Privileges and Immunities: The Nixon and Clinton Cases*, 108 Harv. L. Rev. 701, 713 (1995). Alito too the presidential distraction argument very seriously: "Without a President who is able at all times to carry out the responsibilities of the office, our constitutional system could not operate, and the country would be at risk. That is why the Twenty-fifth Amendment created a mechanism for temporarily transferring the responsibilities of the office to the Vice President if the President is incapacitated for even a brief time. The Amendment has been explicitly invoked on only two occasions, each time for a period of about two hours. This mechanism reflects an appreciation that the Nation cannot be safely left without a functioning President for even a brief time."

Another concern arose out of federalism, and the possibility of state and local governments interfering with the presidency—similar to the concern that prevented Maryland from interfering with the Bank of the United States in *McCulloch* (Casebook, pp. 866–76). "Building on this principle of federalism, two centuries of case law prohibit the States from taxing, regulating, or otherwise interfering with the lawful work of federal agencies, instrumentalities, and officers. The Court premised these cases on the principle that 'the activities of the Federal Government are free from regulation by any State. No other adjustment of competing enactments or legal principles is possible.' *Mayo* v. *United States*, 319 U.S. 441, 445 (1943)."

Given these interests, Justice Alito agreed that the President did not enjoy absolute immunity and that the district court should evaluate the President's fact-specific objections—but under the *Nixon* standard suggested by the Solicitor General and not the Court's standard.

Sequelae: Ultimately, the lower federal courts required that the President's tax and other records be turned over to the grand jury. See *Trump v. Vance,* 977 F.3d 198 (2d Cir. 2020) (per curiam) (rejecting questions about the scope etc. of the subpoena and affirming the district court order directing that the records be submitted to the grand jury). In July 2021, the grand jury returned indictments of the Trump company and its chief executive officer for tax fraud. Trump lost an effort to avoid providing a deposition in the case but it currently seems unlikely he will also be charged. The deposition is scheduled for July 15, 2022. In the meantime, a Georgia grand jury has opened an investigation into efforts involving Trump and others to pressure state officials to provide a more supportive vote count. Meanwhile, a House Select Committee is considering whether to make criminal referrals in connection with its investigation of the events of January 6.

Quaere: Address the issues in Problem 8-4 in light of this case as well as the *Clinton* and Nixon cases preceding it in the Casebook. Justice Alito opined that neither state nor federal prosecutors could indict a sitting President. How would the current Court answer the questions in Problem 8-4? If a president *cannot* be prosecuted while in office, would the statute of limitations be tolled for that time? If a president *can* be prosecuted while in office, could he then self-pardon? Is President Trump subject to prosecution in either state or court now that he has left office? Would it matter whether the actions were taken in his official capacity?

DONALD J. TRUMP V. MAZARS USA, LLP
591 U.S. ___, 140 S.Ct. 2019, 207 L.Ed.2d 951 (2020)

[This companion case is excerpted on page 152 of this Supplement.]

SECTION 2. ISSUES OF LEGISLATIVE OVERREACHING

A. "EXCESSIVE" CONGRESSIONAL DELEGATIONS AND THE ARTICLE I, SECTION 7 STRUCTURE FOR LAWMAKING

1. **The Decline and Potential Revival of the Nondelegation Doctrine**

Page 1241. Insert the following Case and Notes to replace Problem 8-7:

GUNDY V. UNITED STATES
588 U.S. ___, 139 S.Ct. 2119, 204 L.Ed.2d 5116 (2019)

JUSTICE KAGAN delivered the judgment of the Court and delivered an opinion in which Justices GINSBURG, BREYER, and SOTOMAYOR joined.

[Herman Avery Gundy was convicted of committing sexual assault in Maryland while on supervised release for a prior federal offense. After serving his sentence for the Maryland sex offense, Gundy was to be transferred to federal custody to serve his sentence for violating his supervised release. As a part of this transfer, Gundy received permission to travel unsupervised by bus from Pennsylvania to New York. Gundy made the trip, but did not register as a sex offender in either Maryland or New York, as required by state law.

[In January 2013, Gundy was indicted under 18 U.S.C. § 2250, the Sex Offender Notification and Registration Act (SORNA), for traveling from Pennsylvania to New York and then staying in New York without registering as a sex offender. Based on rules developed by the Department of Justice to implement SORNA, he was convicted and sentenced to time served, along with five years of supervised release. The Second Circuit affirmed the conviction, and Gundy secured review to determine whether the Department's regulation violated the nondelegation doctrine.

[Under SORNA, 34 U.S.C. § 20913(b), a sex offender must register "before completing a sentence of imprisonment with respect to the offense giving rise to the registration requirement" (or, if the offender is not sentenced to prison, "not later than [three] business days after being sentenced"). Subsection (d) addresses (in its title's words) the "[i]nitial registration of sex offenders unable to comply with subsection (b)":

> The Attorney General shall have the authority to specify the applicability of the requirements of this subchapter to sex offenders convicted before the enactment of this chapter or its implementation in a particular jurisdiction, and to prescribe rules for the registration of any such sex offenders and for other categories of sex offenders who are unable to comply with subsection (b) [relating to the original registration].

The Supreme Court affirmed the conviction and the validity of the Department's regulations, but without an opinion for the Court.]

[A] nondelegation inquiry always begins (and often almost ends) with statutory interpretation. The constitutional question is whether Congress has supplied an intelligible principle to guide the delegee's use of discretion. So the answer requires construing the challenged statute to figure out what task it delegates and what instructions it provides. See, e.g., *Whitman v. American Trucking Assns., Inc.*, 531 U.S. 457, 473 (2001) (construing the text of a delegation to place constitutionally adequate "limits on the EPA's discretion"). Only after a court has determined a challenged statute's meaning can it decide whether the law sufficiently guides executive discretion to accord with Article I. And indeed, once a court interprets the statute, it may find that the constitutional question all but answers itself.

That is the case here, because § 20913(d) does not give the Attorney General anything like the "unguided" and "unchecked" authority that Gundy says. The provision, in Gundy's view, "grants the Attorney General plenary power to determine SORNA's applicability to pre-Act offenders— to require them to register, or not, as she sees fit, and to change her policy for any reason and at any time." If that were so, we would face a nondelegation question. But it is not. This Court has already interpreted § 20913(d) to say something different—to require the Attorney General to apply SORNA to all pre-Act offenders as soon as feasible. [*Reynolds v. United States*, 565 U.S. 432, 442–443 (2012).] And revisiting that issue yet more fully today, we reach the same conclusion. The text, considered alongside its context, purpose, and history, makes clear that the Attorney General's discretion extends only to considering and addressing feasibility issues. [As the Court reasoned in *Reynolds*, SORNA was always intended to regulate pre-Act offenders, but Congress wanted a transition period so that national standards could be devised and then integrated with the state registration systems.]

In that context, the delegation in SORNA easily passes muster (as all eleven circuit courts to have considered the question found). The statute conveyed Congress's policy that the Attorney General require pre-Act offenders to register as soon as feasible. Under the law, the feasibility issues he could address were administrative—and, more specifically, transitional—in nature. Those issues arose, as *Reynolds* explained, from the need to "newly register[ ] or reregister[ ] 'a large number' of pre-Act offenders" not then in the system. And they arose, more technically, from the gap between an initial registration requirement hinged on imprisonment and a set of pre-Act offenders long since released. Even for those limited matters, the Act informed the Attorney General that he did not have forever to work things out. By stating its demand for a "comprehensive" registration system and by defining the "sex offenders" required to register to include pre-Act offenders, Congress conveyed that the Attorney General had only temporary authority. Or again, in the words of *Reynolds*, that he could prevent "*instantaneous* registration" and impose some "implementation delay." That statutory authority, as compared to the delegations we have upheld in the past, is distinctly small-bore. It falls well within constitutional bounds.

Indeed, if SORNA's delegation is unconstitutional, then most of Government is unconstitutional—dependent as Congress is on the need to give discretion to executive officials to implement its programs. Consider again this Court's long-time recognition: "Congress simply cannot do its job absent an ability to delegate power under broad general directives." *Mistretta* [Casebook, pp. 1236–38]. Or as the dissent in that case agreed: "[S]ome judgments . . . must be left to the officers executing the law." Among the judgments often left to executive officials are ones involving feasibility. In fact, standards of that kind are ubiquitous in the U.S. Code. See, *e.g.,* 12 U.S.C. § 1701z–2(a) (providing that the Secretary of Housing and Urban Development "shall require, to the greatest extent feasible, the employment of new and improved technologies, methods, and materials in housing construction[ ] under [HUD] programs"); 47 U.S.C. § 903(d)(1) (providing that "the Secretary of Commerce shall promote efficient and cost-effective use of the spectrum to the maximum extent feasible" in "assigning frequencies for mobile radio services"). In those delegations, Congress gives its delegee the flexibility to deal with real-world constraints in carrying out his charge. So too in SORNA. * * *

JUSTICE ALITO, concurring in the judgment. * * *

If a majority of this Court were willing to reconsider the approach we have taken for the past 84 years, I would support that effort. But because a majority is not willing to do that, it would be freakish to single out the provision at issue here for special treatment.

Because I cannot say that the statute lacks a discernable standard that is adequate under the approach this Court has taken for many years, I vote to affirm.

JUSTICE GORSUCH, with whom the CHIEF JUSTICE and JUSTICE THOMAS join, dissenting. * * *

The breadth of the authority Congress granted to the Attorney General in these few words can only be described as vast. As the Department of Justice itself has acknowledged [in its brief to the Court in *Reynolds*], SORNA "does not require the Attorney General" to impose registration requirements on pre-Act offenders "within a certain time frame or by a date certain; it does not require him to act at all." If the Attorney General does choose to act, he can require all pre-Act offenders to register, or he can "require some but not all to register." For those he requires to register, the Attorney General may impose "some but not all of [SORNA's] registration requirements," as he pleases. And he is free to change his mind on any of these matters "at any given time or over the course of different [political] administrations." Congress thus gave the Attorney General free rein to write the rules for virtually the entire existing sex offender population in this country—a situation that promised to persist for years or decades until pre-Act offenders passed away or fulfilled the terms of their registration obligations and post-Act offenders came to predominate.

[Justice Gorsuch argued that this relatively unfettered delegation of lawmaking authority to the Attorney General was in tension with the Framers' careful structuring of legislative authority in Article I and was not justified by carefully framed allowances for delegations in the early Republic.]

First, we know that as long as Congress makes the policy decisions when regulating private conduct, it may authorize another branch to "fill up the details." In *Wayman* v. *Southard*, [23 U.S. (10 Wheat.) 1 (1825)], this Court upheld a statute that instructed the federal courts to borrow state-court procedural rules but allowed them to make certain "alterations and additions." Writing for the Court, Chief Justice Marshall distinguished between those "important subjects, which must be entirely regulated by the legislature itself," and "those of less interest, in which a general provision may be made, and power given to those who are to act. . . to fill up the details." The Court upheld the statute before it because Congress had announced the controlling general policy when it ordered federal courts to follow state procedures, and the residual authority to make "alterations and additions" did no more than permit courts to fill up the details. * * *

Second, once Congress prescribes the rule governing private conduct, it may make the application of that rule depend on executive fact-finding. Here, too, the power extended to the executive may prove highly consequential. During the Napoleonic Wars, for example, Britain and France each tried to block the United States from trading with the other. Congress responded with a statute instructing that, if the President found that either Great Britain or France stopped interfering with American trade, a trade embargo would be imposed against the other country. In *Cargo of Brig Aurora* v. *United States*, [11 U.S. (7 Cranch) 382, 388 (1813)], this Court explained that it could "see no sufficient reason, why the legislature should not exercise its discretion [to impose an embargo] either expressly or *conditionally*, as their judgment should direct." * * *

Third, Congress may assign the executive and judicial branches certain non-legislative responsibilities. While the Constitution vests all federal legislative power in Congress alone, Congress's legislative authority sometimes overlaps with authority the Constitution separately vests in another branch. So, for example, when a congressional statute confers wide discretion to the executive, no separation-of-powers problem may arise if "the discretion is to be exercised over matters already within the scope of executive power." Though the case was decided on different grounds, the foreign-affairs-related statute in *Cargo of the Brig Aurora* may be an example of this kind of permissible lawmaking, given that many foreign affairs powers are constitutionally vested in the president under Article II. *Wayman* itself might be explained by the same principle as applied to the judiciary: Even in the absence of any statute, courts have the power under Article III "to regulate their practice."

[In the modern era, the "intelligible principle" idea discussed by Chief Justice Taft in *J.W. Hampton* (Casebook, p. 1234) became the governing "test" during and after the New Deal.] We sometimes chide people for treating judicial opinions as if they were statutes, divorcing a passing comment from its context, ignoring all that came before and after, and treating an isolated phrase as if it were controlling. But that seems to be exactly what happened here. For two decades, no one thought to invoke the "intelligible principle" comment as a basis to uphold a statute that would have failed more traditional separation-of-powers tests. In fact, the phrase sat more or less silently entombed until the late 1940s. Only then did lawyers begin digging it up in earnest and arguing to this Court that it had somehow displaced (*sub silentio* of course) all prior teachings in this area [Casebook, pp. 1235–36].

This mutated version of the "intelligible principle" remark has no basis in the original meaning of the Constitution, in history, or even in the decision from which it was plucked. Judges and scholars representing a wide and diverse range of views have condemned it as resting on "misunderst[ood] historical foundations." [*Department of Transp. v. Association of American Railroads*, 135 S.Ct. 1225, 1240–52 (2015) (Thomas, J., dissenting).] * * *

[Justice Gorsuch would abandon the vague and malleable "intelligible principle" test and return to the original allowances discussed above— filling in details, executive fact-finding, and facilitating executive functions. None of those allowances justified SORNA's delegation. Instead, it resembled the delegations in the two New Deal decisions striking down excessive delegations.]

* * * If allowing the President to draft a "cod[e] of fair competition" for slaughterhouses was "delegation running riot," then it's hard to see how giving the nation's chief prosecutor the power to write a criminal code rife with his own policy choices might be permissible. [*Schechter Poultry* (Casebook, p. 1235).] And if Congress may not give the President the discretion to ban or allow the interstate transportation of petroleum, then it's hard to see how Congress may give the Attorney General the discretion to apply or not apply any or all of SORNA's requirements to pre-Act offenders, and then change his mind at any time. [*Panama Refining* (Casebook, p. 1235).] If the separation of powers means anything, it must mean that Congress cannot give the executive branch a blank check to write a code of conduct governing private conduct for a half-million people [the number of pre-Act sex offenders]. * * *

It would be easy enough to let this case go. After all, sex offenders are one of the most disfavored groups in our society. But the rule that prevents Congress from giving the executive *carte blanche* to write laws for sex offenders is the same rule that protects everyone else. Nor is it hard to imagine how the power at issue in this case—the power of a prosecutor to require a group to register with the government on pain of weighty criminal penalties—could be abused in other settings. To allow the nation's chief law enforcement officer to write the criminal laws he is charged with enforcing—to " 'unit[e]' " the " 'legislative and executive powers . . . in the same person' "—would be to mark the end of any meaningful enforcement of our separation of powers and invite the tyranny of the majority that follows when lawmaking and law enforcement responsibilities are united in the same hands.

Nor would enforcing the Constitution's demands spell doom for what some call the "administrative state." The separation of powers does not prohibit any particular policy outcome, let alone dictate any conclusion about the proper size and scope of government. Instead, it is a procedural guarantee that requires Congress to assemble a social consensus before choosing our nation's course on policy questions like those implicated by SORNA. What is more, Congress is hardly bereft of options to accomplish all it might wish to achieve. It may always authorize executive branch officials to fill in even a large number of details, to find facts that trigger the generally applicable rule of conduct specified in a statute, or to exercise non-legislative powers. Congress can also commission agencies or other experts to study and recommend legislative language. Respecting the separation of powers forecloses no substantive outcomes. It only requires us to respect along the way one of the most vital of the procedural protections of individual liberty found in our Constitution. * * *

NEW PROBLEM 8-7:
HOW FAR DOES THE NONDELEGATION
DOCTRINE NOW REACH?

Apparently, Justice Alito voted with the majority so that the Gorsuch dissent could be published; if he had joined the dissenters, the Court would have split 4–4, with no opinions. Justice Kavanaugh did not participate but seems to be a voice for enforcing separation of powers limitations as well, e.g., *PHH Corp. v. Consumer Financial Protection Bureau*, 881 F.3d 75 (D.C. Cir. en banc 2018) (Kavanaugh, J., dissenting), but his vote may be up for grabs. Replacing Justice Ginsburg, Justice Barrett joined the Court later in the year. You are asked to advise Justices Alito, Kavanaugh, and Barrett: How should they vote in the following hypothetical case?

Assume that industry groups challenge the EPA's Ambient Air Quality Standards as a violation of the nondelegation doctrine. The delegation is set forth in this provision of Title 34:

§ 7409. National primary and secondary ambient air quality standards

(a) Promulgation

    (1) The Administrator—

        (A) within 30 days after December 31, 1970, shall publish proposed regulations prescribing a national primary ambient air quality standard and a national secondary ambient air quality standard for each air pollutant for which air quality criteria have been issued prior to such date; and

(B) after a reasonable time for interested persons to submit written comments thereon (but no later than 90 days after the initial publication of such proposed standards) shall by regulation promulgate such proposed national primary and secondary ambient air quality standards with such modifications as he deems appropriate.

(2) With respect to any air pollutant for which air quality criteria are issued after December 31, 1970, the Administrator shall publish, simultaneously with the issuance of such criteria and information, proposed national primary and secondary ambient air quality standards for any such pollutant. The procedure provided for in paragraph (1)(B) of this subsection shall apply to the promulgation of such standards.

(b) Protection of public health and welfare

(1) National primary ambient air quality standards, prescribed under subsection (a) of this section shall be ambient air quality standards the attainment and maintenance of which in the judgment of the Administrator, based on such criteria and allowing an adequate margin of safety, are requisite to protect the public health. Such primary standards may be revised in the same manner as promulgated.

(2) Any national secondary ambient air quality standard prescribed under subsection (a) of this section shall specify a level of air quality the attainment and maintenance of which in the judgment of the Administrator, based on such criteria, is requisite to protect the public welfare from any known or anticipated adverse effects associated with the presence of such air pollutant in the ambient air. Such secondary standards may be revised in the same manner as promulgated.

Does this delegation meet the *Hampton* "intelligible principle" test? The Supreme Court said that it did, in *American Trucking* (Casebook, p. 1238). But Justice Scalia's opinion for the Court did not address the question whether the nondelegation doctrine ought to be reconsidered (Justice Thomas flagged that possibility in a concurring opinion) and so did not apply the approach outlined in Justice Gorsuch's *Gundy* dissent.

So Justices Alito, Kavanaugh, and Barrett face three issues: (1) Should the "intelligible principle" test be retired or tightened? If the latter, how? (2) If the former, should the Court adopt the three-allowances outlined in the Gorsuch dissent, or should there be other allowances for delegated authority? (3) If the Court follows the Gorsuch approach, is the § 7409 delegation constitutional? Should *American Trucking* be overruled? If these Justices join the Gorsuch approach, should the Supreme Court reconsider the SORNA delegation and overrule *Gundy*?

West Virginia v. EPA

142 S.Ct. 2587 (2022)

In 2015, the Environmental Protection Agency (EPA) promulgated the Clean Power Plan rule, which addressed carbon dioxide emissions from existing coal- and natural-gas-fired power plants. For authority, the Agency cited § 111(d) of the Clean Air Act, which authorizes regulation of certain pollutants from existing sources. 42 U. S. C. § 7411(d). Prior to the Clean Power Plan, EPA had used § 111(d) only a handful of times since its enactment in 1970. Under that provision, although the States set the actual enforceable rules governing existing sources (such as power plants), EPA determines the emissions limit with which they will have to comply. The EPA derives that limit by determining the "best system of emission reduction [BSER] that has been adequately demonstrated" for the kind of existing source at issue. The limit then reflects the amount of pollution reduction "achievable through the application of" that system.

In the Clean Power Plan, EPA determined that the BSER for existing coal and natural gas plants included three types of measures, which the Agency called "building blocks." The first building block was "heat rate improvements" at coal-fired plants—essentially practices such plants could undertake to burn coal more cleanly. This sort of source-specific, efficiency-improving measure was similar in kind to those that EPA had previously identified as the BSER in other § 111 rules. Building blocks two and three were quite different, as both involved what EPA called "generation shifting" at the grid level—i.e., a shift in electricity production from higher-emitting to lower-emitting producers. Building block two was a shift in generation from existing coal-fired power plants, which would make less power, to natural-gas-fired plants, which would make more. This would reduce carbon dioxide emissions because natural gas plants produce less carbon dioxide per unit of electricity generated than coal plants. Building block three worked like building block two, except that the shift was from both coal and gas plants to renewables, mostly wind and solar. Building blocks two and three sought to implement a sector-wide shift in electricity production from coal to natural gas and renewables; by 2030, the target was to reduce coal from 38% to 27% of the nation's energy production.

After a change in Administrations (Obama to Trump), the EPA withdrew the Clean Power Plan (before it was ever implemented), because it then believed that Congress had not authorized such a major overhaul in the nation's energy system. The Trump EPA devised the less restrictive Affordable Energy Rule in 2019. Another change in Administrations (Trump to Biden), the EPA withdrew the 2019 Plan and announced that it was working on a revised version of the Clean Power Plan. Writing for a 6–3 Court, **Chief Justice Roberts** ruled that EPA had not been authorized by the Clean Air Act to adopt the Clean Power Plan. He relied on a line of statutory interpretation cases reflecting what the Court now calls the "Major Questions Doctrine," the notion that in "extraordinary cases" in which the "history and the breadth of the authority that [the agency] has asserted," and the "economic and political significance" of that assertion, provide a "reason to hesitate before concluding that Congress" meant to confer such authority. *FDA v. Brown & Williamson Tobacco Corp.*, 529 U.S. 120, 159–60 (2000); accord, *Gonzales v. Oregon*, 546 U.S. 243 (2006).

"Agencies have only those powers given to them by Congress, and 'enabling legislation' is generally not an 'open book to which the agency [may] add pages and change the plot line.' E. Gellhorn & P. Verkuil, Controlling *Chevron*-Based Delegations, 20 Cardozo L. Rev. 989, 1011 (1999). We presume that 'Congress intends to make major policy decisions itself, not leave those decisions to agencies.' *United States Telecom Assn. v. FCC*, 855 F. 3d 381, 419 (CADC 2017) (Kavanaugh, J., dissenting from denial of rehearing en banc). Thus, in certain extraordinary cases, both separation of powers principles and a practical understanding of legislative intent make us 'reluctant to read into ambiguous statutory text' the delegation claimed to be lurking there. [*Utility Air Regulatory Group v. EPA*, 573 U.S. 302, 324 (2015).] To convince us otherwise, something more than a merely plausible textual basis for the agency action is necessary. The agency instead must point to 'clear congressional authorization' for the power it claims. *Ibid.*

"Under our precedents, this is a major questions case. In arguing that § 111(d) empowers it to substantially restructure the American energy market, EPA 'claim[ed] to discover in a long-extant statute an unheralded power' representing a 'transformative expansion in [its] regulatory authority.' *Utility Air*. It located that newfound power in the vague language of an 'ancillary provision[ ]' of the Act, *Whitman*, one that was designed to function as a gap filler and had rarely been used in the preceding decades. And the Agency's discovery allowed it to adopt a regulatory program that Congress had conspicuously and repeatedly declined to enact itself. *Brown & Williamson*; *Gonzales*. Given these circumstances, there is every reason to 'hesitate before concluding that Congress' meant to confer on EPA the authority it claims under § 111(d). *Brown & Williamson*." The Chief Justice found nothing in the Clean Air Act specifically delegating such authority to the EPA.

Joined by Justice Alito, **Justice Gorsuch** concurred in the Court's opinion, but with an elaborate discussion of the Major Questions Doctrine's roots in the constitutional rule of law. "To resolve today's case the Court invokes the major questions doctrine. Under that doctrine's terms, administrative agencies must be able to point to 'clear congressional authorization' when they claim the power to make decisions of vast 'economic and political significance.' Like many parallel clear-statement rules in our law, this one operates to protect foundational constitutional guarantees." The "foundational guarantee" in this case would be the Nondelegation Doctrine, beefed up in the manner suggested by Justice Gorsuch's *Gundy* dissent. But none of the other four majority Justices gestured toward the beefed-up version of the Nondelegation Doctrine and were content to rest on the Major Questions Doctrine.

Joined by Justices Breyer and Sotomayor, **Justice Kagan** dissented. Section 111(a), (d) was a broad delegation of authority to the EPA, which exercised measured discretion in carrying forth Congress's project.

NOTES ON THE *MAJOR QUESTIONS DOCTRINE AS A QUASI-CONSTITUTIONAL CLEAR STATEMENT RULE*

1. *Quasi-Constitutional Clear Statement Rules.* More than 30 years ago, it was clear to scholars that the Supreme Court was creating new "clear statement rules" to give teeth to "underenforced" constitutional values—including separation of powers, federalism, and the nondelegation doctrine. William Eskridge Jr. & Philip Frickey, *Quasi-Constitutional Law: Clear Statement Rules as Constitutional Lawmaking*, 45 Vand. L. Rev. 593, 606–07 (1992) (anticipating the Major Questions Doctrine by noting the Court's rule against "excessive legislative delegation"). Scholars such as Eskridge and Frickey believed that the Court was unlikely to enforce the nondelegation doctrine directly, by striking down statutes, but was moving toward an indirect enforcement by narrow statutory interpretations. It is striking that Justice Gorsuch, who pushed for aggressive judicial review in *Gundy*, pushes for aggressive quasi-constitutional canons in *West Virginia v. EPA*.

Like the famous "avoidance doctrine" (judges should interpret statutes to avoid constitutional difficulties), the emerging clear statement rules had the virtue of avoiding constitutional conflict between Congress and the Court and respected Congress by giving it the benefit of any constitutional doubts. The danger of such rules, as with the avoidance doctrine, was that it would encourage what Eskridge and Frickey dubbed "stealth constitutionalism," where the Court would undermine the regulatory state through lower-visibility narrowing constructions that would not attract as much attention and controversy ("judicial activism") as striking down statutes. See Eskridge & Frickey, *The Supreme Court, 1993 Term: Foreword—Law as Equilibrium*, 108 Harv. L. Rev. 26, 81–87 (1994).

2. *The Evolution of the Major Questions Canon.* Following Eskridge and Frickey, the dissenters in *West Virginia v. EPA* claim that the *Supreme* Court majority has altered the earlier version of the MQD. In the 1990s, it wasn't even a "doctrine," was just a caution against reading a lot into modest congressional delegations of authority, as in the FDA Tobacco Case, upon which the majority relies. As late as *King v. Burwell*, 576 U.S. 473, 486 (2015), Chief Justice Roberts invoked the MQD simply as a reason why courts ought not give special deference to agencies delegated lawmaking authority by Congress (what is known as *Chevron* deference). The agency prevailed in that case—notwithstanding some pretty clear statutory text that had to be explained away—but without any special deference.

Starting no later than in Justice Scalia's opinion in *Utility Air*, the Roberts Court altered the Rehnquist Court's *Chevron* avoidance into an anti-deference clear statement rule, much like the rule of lenity: in case of a tie or close case, the government loses. In the 2021 Term of the Court, the MQD has become what Eskridge and Frickey dubbed "super-strong clear statement rules," requiring ever-greater specificity from a gridlocked Congress that is hard-put to vote through the most general delegations. In *NFIB v. OSHA*, 142 S.Ct. (2022) (*per curiam*), for a dramatic example, the 6–3 (GOP-Dem) Court overruled OSHA's mandate for large employers to implement measures to protect worker "safety," the precise mandate of the statute. The *per curiam* opinion invoked the MQD not only to reject *Chevron* deference to the agency (the Court did not even mention *Chevron*, which it usually ignores completely), and not only to inject anti-deference into the case (the government loses in close cases), but to raise the bar for what counts as a super-strong clear statement. "Safety" was not clear enough for the Court, even though COVID-19 was, and is, sweeping through workplaces, making workers sick, and killing some of them.

3. *Quo Vadis Nondelegation Doctrine?* Justice Gorsuch's concurring opinion was a big shout-out for the MQD. Read together with his concurring opinion in *West Virginia v. EPA,* is he abandoning his *Gundy* crusade in favor of a statutory approach? If so, consider the ongoing relevance of his *Gundy* dissent, which may command majority support on the 6–3 (GOP-Dem) Roberts Court.

B. CONGRESSIONAL AND PRESIDENTIAL POWER TO CONTROL "EXECUTIVE" OFFICIALS

Pages 1291–95. Replace *PHH Corp.* with the following Supreme Court decision and notes:

SEILA LAW LLC v. CONSUMER FINANCIAL PROTECTION BUREAU
591 U.S. ___, 140 S.Ct. 2183, 207 L.Ed.2d 194 (2020)

CHIEF JUSTICE ROBERTS delivered the opinion of the Court with respect to Parts I, II, and III.

[In the Dodd-Frank Wall Street Reform and Consumer Protection Act of 2010, P.L. 111–203, Congress established the Consumer Financial Protection Bureau (CFPB). The CFPB is a financial regulator that applies a set of preexisting statutes to financial services marketed "primarily for personal, family, or household purposes." 12 U.S.C. § 5481(5)(A); *see also id.* §§ 5481(4), (6), (15). Congress has historically given a modicum of independence to financial regulators like the Federal Reserve, the FTC, and the Office of the Comptroller of the Currency. Rather than a multi-member commission, the CFPB's chief decision-maker is its Director, who is appointed by the President for a five-year term. The Director in 2017 would have seen his term expire in 2018; the next expiration date would be 2023, and so forth. The Director may be fired only for "inefficiency, neglect of duty, or malfeasance in office," 12 U.S.C. § 5491(c)(3)—the same language the Supreme Court approved for the independent commission in *Humphrey's.*

[The Director has a considerable amount of authority. He or she sets the agency's general agenda; determines what proposed rules ought to be advanced for public comment; decides whether to issue a final rule, after notice and comment; manages the agency's budget; and accepts or rejects adjudicatory decisions rendered by administrative law judges (ALJs), who conduct the formal hearings and draft proposed orders and decisions. The primary issue on appeal was whether the CFPB's structure violated the Constitution's separation of powers and/or Article II.]

[III.A] Article II provides that "[t]he executive Power shall be vested in a President," who must "take Care that the Laws be faithfully executed." Art. II, § 1, cl. 1; *id.,* § 3. The entire "executive Power" belongs to the President alone. But because it would be "impossib[le]" for "one man" to "perform all the great business of the State," the Constitution assumes that lesser executive officers will "assist the supreme Magistrate in discharging the duties of his trust." 30 Writings of George Washington 334 (J. Fitzpatrick ed. 1939).

These lesser officers must remain accountable to the President, whose authority they wield. As Madison explained, "[I]f any power whatsoever is in its nature Executive, it is the power of appointing, overseeing, and controlling those who execute the laws." 1 Annals of Cong. 463 (1789). That power, in turn, generally includes the ability to remove executive officials, for it is "only the authority that can remove" such officials that they "must fear and, in the performance of [their] functions, obey." *Bowsher.*

The President's removal power has long been confirmed by history and precedent. It "was discussed extensively in Congress when the first executive departments were created" in 1789. *Free Enterprise Fund.* "The view that 'prevailed, as most consonant to the text of the Constitution' and 'to the requisite responsibility and harmony in the Executive Department,' was that the executive power included a power to oversee executive officers through removal." *Ibid.* (quoting Letter from James Madison to Thomas Jefferson (June 30, 1789), 16 Documentary History of the First Federal Congress 893 (2004)). [The First Congress recognized this as a constitutional rule in the Decision of 1789, as did the Court's decision in *Myers* and subsequent precedents, culminating in *Free Enterprise Fund*, where the Court declined to extend earlier allowances of congressional removal restrictions to "a new situation not yet encountered by the Court"—an official insulated by *two* layers of for-cause removal protection.]

Free Enterprise Fund left in place two exceptions to the President's unrestricted removal power. First, in *Humphrey's Executor*, decided less than a decade after *Myers*, the Court upheld a statute that protected the

Commissioners of the FTC from removal except for "inefficiency, neglect of duty, or malfeasance in office." In reaching that conclusion, the Court stressed that Congress's ability to impose such removal restrictions "will depend upon the character of the office."

Because the Court limited its holding "to officers of the kind here under consideration," the contours of the *Humphrey's Executor* exception depend upon the characteristics of the agency before the Court. Rightly or wrongly, the Court viewed the FTC (as it existed in 1935) as exercising "no part of the executive power." Instead, it was "an administrative body" that performed "specified duties as a legislative or as a judicial aid." It acted "as a legislative agency" in "making investigations and reports" to Congress and "as an agency of the judiciary" in making recommendations to courts as a master in chancery. "To the extent that [the FTC] exercise[d] any executive *function*[,] as distinguished from executive *power* in the constitutional sense," it did so only in the discharge of its "quasi-legislative or quasi-judicial powers." * * *

We have recognized a second exception for *inferior* officers in two cases, *United States* v. *Perkins* and *Morrison* v. *Olson*. In *Perkins*, we upheld tenure protections for a naval cadet-engineer. And, in *Morrison*, we upheld a provision granting good-cause tenure protection to an independent counsel appointed to investigate and prosecute particular alleged crimes by high-ranking Government officials. Backing away from the reliance in *Humphrey's Executor* on the concepts of "quasi-legislative" and "quasi-judicial" power, we viewed the ultimate question as whether a removal restriction is of "such a nature that [it] impede[s] the President's ability to perform his constitutional duty." Although the independent counsel was a single person and performed "law enforcement functions that typically have been undertaken by officials within the Executive Branch," we concluded that the removal protections did not unduly interfere with the functioning of the Executive Branch because "the independent counsel [was] an inferior officer under the Appointments Clause, with limited jurisdiction and tenure and lacking policymaking or significant administrative authority."

These two exceptions—one for multimember expert agencies that do not wield substantial executive power, and one for inferior officers with limited duties and no policymaking or administrative authority— "represent what up to now have been the outermost constitutional limits of permissible congressional restrictions on the President's removal power." *PHH*, 881 F.3d at 196 (Kavanaugh, J., dissenting). [In Part III.B, the Chief Justice found both *Humphrey's* and *Morrison* distinguishable. So the issue was whether or not their exceptions should be extended to the CFPB.]

[III.C] "Perhaps the most telling indication of [a] severe constitutional problem" with an executive entity "is [a] lack of historical precedent" to support it. Free *Enterprise Fund.* An agency with a structure like that of the CFPB is almost wholly unprecedented.

After years of litigating the agency's constitutionality, the Courts of Appeals, parties, and *amici* have identified "only a handful of isolated" incidents in which Congress has provided good-cause tenure to principal officers who wield power alone rather than as members of a board or commission. "[T]hese few scattered examples"—four to be exact—shed little light. *Noel Canning.* [The Comptroller of the Currency enjoyed removal protection for one year during the Civil War. The Office of Special Counsel, enforcing certain rules governing federal employment since 1978, has a single director, but Presidents Carter and Reagan objected to the constitutionality of its removal protections. Also controversially, the Social Security Administration (SSA) has been run by a single Administrator since 1994. Created in 2008 in response to the same crisis as the CFPB, the Federal Housing Finance Agency (FHFA), took responsibility for Fannie Mae and Freddie Mac, government-sponsored enterprises. The Fifth Circuit recently held its removal protections unconstitutional.]

With the exception of the one-year blip for the Comptroller of the Currency, these isolated examples are modern and contested. And they do not involve regulatory or enforcement authority remotely comparable to that exercised by the CFPB. The CFPB's single-Director structure is an innovation with no foothold in history or tradition.

In addition to being a historical anomaly, the CFPB's single-Director configuration is incompatible with our constitutional structure. Aside from the sole exception of the Presidency, that structure scrupulously avoids concentrating power in the hands of any single individual. [See The Federalist No. 51; *Chadha.*]

The Executive Branch is a stark departure from all this division. The Framers viewed the legislative power as a special threat to individual liberty, so they divided that power to ensure that "differences of opinion" and the "jarrings of parties" would "promote deliberation and circumspection" and "check excesses in the majority." See The Federalist No. 70, at 475 (A. Hamilton); see also *id.*, No. 51, at 350. By contrast, the Framers thought it necessary to secure the authority of the Executive so that he could carry out his unique responsibilities. See *id.*, No. 70, at 475–478. As Madison put it, while "the weight of the legislative authority requires that it should be . . . divided, the weakness of the executive may require, on the other hand, that it should be fortified." *Id.*, No. 51, at 350.

The Framers deemed an energetic executive essential to "the protection of the community against foreign attacks," "the steady administration of the laws," "the protection of property," and "the security of liberty." *Id.*, No. 70, at 471. Accordingly, they chose not to bog the Executive down with the "habitual feebleness and dilatoriness" that comes with a "diversity of views and opinions." *Id.*, at 476. Instead, they gave the Executive the "[d]ecision, activity, secrecy, and dispatch" that "characterise the proceedings of one man." *Id.*, at 472.

To justify and check *that* authority—unique in our constitutional structure—the Framers made the President the most democratic and politically accountable official in Government. Only the President (along with the Vice President) is elected by the entire Nation. And the President's political accountability is enhanced by the solitary nature of the Executive Branch, which provides "a single object for the jealousy and watchfulness of the people." *Id.*, at 479. The President "cannot delegate ultimate responsibility or the active obligation to supervise that goes with it," because Article II "makes a single President responsible for the actions of the Executive Branch." *Free Enterprise Fund.*

The resulting constitutional strategy is straightforward: divide power everywhere except for the Presidency, and render the President directly accountable to the people through regular elections. In that scheme, individual executive officials will still wield significant authority, but that authority remains subject to the ongoing supervision and control of the elected President. Through the President's oversight, "the chain of dependence [is] preserved," so that "the lowest officers, the middle grade, and the highest" all "depend, as they ought, on the President, and the President on the community." 1 Annals of Cong. 499 (J. Madison).

The CFPB's single-Director structure contravenes this carefully calibrated system by vesting significant governmental power in the hands of a single individual accountable to no one. The Director is neither elected by the people nor meaningfully controlled (through the threat of removal) by someone who is. The Director does not even depend on Congress for annual appropriations. See The Federalist No. 58, at 394 (J. Madison) (describing the "power over the purse" as the "most compleat and effectual weapon" in representing the interests of the people). Yet the Director may *unilaterally*, without meaningful supervision, issue final regulations, oversee adjudications, set enforcement priorities, initiate prosecutions, and determine what penalties to impose on private parties. With no colleagues to persuade, and no boss or electorate looking over her shoulder, the Director may dictate and enforce policy for a vital segment of the economy affecting millions of Americans.

The CFPB Director's insulation from removal by an accountable President is enough to render the agency's structure unconstitutional. But several other features of the CFPB combine to make the Director's removal protection even more problematic. In addition to lacking the most direct method of presidential control—removal at will—the agency's unique structure also forecloses certain indirect methods of Presidential control.

Because the CFPB is headed by a single Director with a five-year term, some Presidents may not have any opportunity to shape its leadership and thereby influence its activities. A President elected in 2020 would likely not appoint a CFPB Director until 2023, and a President elected in 2028 may *never* appoint one. That means an unlucky President might get elected on a consumer-protection platform and enter office only to find herself saddled with a holdover Director from a competing political party who is dead set *against* that agenda. To make matters worse, the agency's single-Director structure means the President will not have the opportunity to appoint any other leaders—such as a chair or fellow members of a Commission or Board—who can serve as a check on the Director's authority and help bring the agency in line with the President's preferred policies.

The CFPB's receipt of funds outside the appropriations process further aggravates the agency's threat to Presidential control. The President normally has the opportunity to recommend or veto spending bills that affect the operation of administrative agencies. See Art. I, § 7, cl. 2; Art. II, § 3. And, for the past century, the President has annually submitted a proposed budget to Congress for approval. See Budget and Accounting Act, 1921, ch. 18, § 201, 42 Stat. 20. Presidents frequently use these budgetary tools "to influence the policies of independent agencies." *PHH* (Henderson, J., dissenting) (citing Pasachoff, The President's Budget as a Source of Agency Policy Control, 125 Yale L. J. 2182, 2191, 2203–2204 (2016)). But no similar opportunity exists for the President to influence the CFPB Director. Instead, the Director receives over $500 million per year to fund the agency's chosen priorities. And the Director receives that money from the Federal Reserve, which is itself funded outside of the annual appropriations process. This financial freedom makes it even more likely that the agency will "slip from the Executive's control, and thus from that of the people." *Free Enterprise Fund.*

[In Part IV, the Chief Justice, writing only for himself and Justices Alito and Kavanaugh, ruled that the invalid nonremovability provision was severable form the remainder of Dodd-Frank, including those provisions creating the CFPB. The Chief Justice emphasized the *Alaska Airlines* (and *Sebelius*) presumption in favor of severability, which was buttressed by Dodd-Frank's general severability provision. Justices Ginsburg, Breyer, Sotomayor, and Kagan agreed with the Chief Justice on severability. So the CFPB survived, and the Court remanded the case to the lower courts to determine what relief should be granted Seila Law.]

JUSTICE THOMAS, joined by **JUSTICE GORSUCH,** concurring in part and dissenting in part.

[Justice Thomas would not have severed the nonremoval provisions from the remainder of Dodd-Frank that created and defined the CFPB; he objected to the Court's severability jurisprudence, as inviting judges to reach beyond their narrow Article III powers and revise legislation. He would also have overruled *Humphrey's Executor*. Its quasi-legislative, quasi-judicial reasoning was rejected in *Morrison*, and its holding was inconsistent with the structural analysis in *Free Enterprise Fund* and the opinion for the Court here.] In light of these decisions, it is not clear what is left of *Humphrey's Executor*'s rationale. But if any remnant of that decision is still standing, it certainly is not enough to justify the numerous, unaccountable independent agencies that currently exercise vast executive power outside the bounds of our constitutional structure.

Continued reliance on *Humphrey's Executor* to justify the existence of independent agencies creates a serious, ongoing threat to our Government's design. Leaving these unconstitutional agencies in place does not enhance this Court's legitimacy; it subverts political accountability and threatens individual liberty. We have a "responsibility to 'examin[e] without fear, and revis[e] without reluctance,' any 'hasty and crude decisions' rather than leaving 'the character of [the] law impaired, and the beauty and harmony of the [American constitutional] system destroyed by the perpetuity of error.'" *Gamble* v. *United States*, 139 S.Ct. 1960, 1984, 204 L.Ed.2d 322 (2019) (Thomas, J., concurring) (quoting 1 J. Kent, Commentaries on American Law 444 (1826); some alterations in original). We simply cannot compromise when it comes to our Government's structure. Today, the Court does enough to resolve this case, but in the future, we should reconsider *Humphrey's Executor in toto*. And I hope that we will have the will to do so.

JUSTICE KAGAN, joined by JUSTICES GINSBURG, BREYER, and SOTOMAYOR, concurring in the judgment with respect to severability and dissenting in part.

* * * The Court today fails to respect its proper role. It recognizes that this Court has approved limits on the President's removal power over heads of agencies much like the CFPB. Agencies possessing similar powers, agencies charged with similar missions, agencies created for similar reasons. The majority's explanation is that the heads of those agencies fall within an "exception"—one for multimember bodies and another for inferior officers—to a "general rule" of unrestricted presidential removal power. And the majority says the CFPB Director does not. That account, though, is wrong in every respect. The majority's general rule does not exist. Its exceptions, likewise, are made up for the occasion—gerrymandered so the CFPB falls outside them. And the distinction doing most of the majority's work—between multimember bodies and single directors—does not respond to the constitutional values at stake. If a removal provision violates the separation of powers, it is because the measure so deprives the President of control over an official as to impede his own constitutional functions. But with or without a for-cause removal provision, the President has at least as much control over an individual as

over a commission—and possibly more. That means the constitutional concern is, if anything, ameliorated when the agency has a single head. Unwittingly, the majority shows why courts should stay their hand in these matters. "Compared to Congress and the President, the Judiciary possesses an inferior understanding of the realities of administration" and the way "political power[ ] operates." *Free Enterprise Fund* (Breyer, J., dissenting).

[I.A. Justice Kagan maintained that the Court overread the separation of powers, by neglecting the checks and balances contained in the Constitution's text.] One way the Constitution reflects that vision is by giving Congress broad authority to establish and organize the Executive Branch. Article II presumes the existence of "Officer[s]" in "executive Departments." § 2, cl. 1. But it does not, as you might think from reading the majority opinion, give the President authority to decide what kinds of officers—in what departments, with what responsibilities—the Executive Branch requires. See *ante* ("The entire 'executive Power' belongs to the President alone"). Instead, Article I's Necessary and Proper Clause puts those decisions in the legislature's hands. Congress has the power "[t]o make all Laws which shall be necessary and proper for carrying into Execution" not just its own enumerated powers but also "all other Powers vested by this Constitution in the Government of the United States, or in any Department or Officer thereof." § 8, cl. 18. Similarly, the Appointments Clause reflects Congress's central role in structuring the Executive Branch. Yes, the President can appoint principal officers, but only as the legislature "shall . . . establish[ ] by Law" (and of course subject to the Senate's advice and consent). Art. II, § 2, cl. 2. And Congress has plenary power to decide not only what inferior officers will exist but also who (the President or a head of department) will appoint them. So as Madison told the first Congress, the legislature gets to "create[ ] the office, define[ ] the powers, [and] limit[ ] its duration." 1 Annals of Cong. 582 (1789). The President, as to the construction of his own branch of government, can only try to work his will through the legislative process.

The majority relies for its contrary vision on Article II's Vesting Clause, but the provision can't carry all that weight. Or as Chief Justice Rehnquist wrote of a similar claim in *Morrison*, "extrapolat[ing]" an unrestricted removal power from such "general constitutional language"—which says only that "[t]he executive Power shall be vested in a President"—is "more than the text will bear." Dean John Manning has well explained why, even were it not obvious from the Clause's "open-ended language." Separation of Powers as Ordinary Interpretation, 124 Harv. L. Rev. 1939, 1971 (2011). The Necessary and Proper Clause, he writes, makes it impossible to "establish a constitutional violation simply by showing that Congress has constrained the way '[t]he executive Power' is implemented"; that is exactly what the Clause gives Congress the power to do. *Id.*, at 1967. Only "a *specific* historical understanding" can bar Congress from enacting a given constraint. *Id.*, at 2024. And nothing of that sort broadly prevents Congress from limiting the President's removal power. * * * [N]ote two points about practice before the Constitution's drafting. First, in that era, Parliament often restricted the King's power to remove royal officers—and the President, needless to say, wasn't supposed to be a king. See Birk, Interrogating the Historical Basis for a Unitary Executive, 73 Stan. L. Rev. (forthcoming 2021). Second, many States at the time allowed limits on gubernatorial removal power even though their constitutions had similar vesting clauses. See Shane, The Originalist Myth of the Unitary Executive, 19 U. Pa. J. Const. L. 323, 334–344 (2016). Historical understandings thus belie the majority's "general rule."

Nor can the Take Care Clause come to the majority's rescue. That Clause cannot properly serve as a "placeholder for broad judicial judgments" about presidential control. Goldsmith & Manning, The Protean Take Care Clause, 164 U. Pa. L. Rev. 1835, 1867 (2016). To begin with, the provision—"he shall take Care that the Laws be faithfully executed"— speaks of duty, not power. Art. II, § 3. New scholarship suggests the language came from English and colonial oaths taken by, and placing fiduciary obligations on, all manner and rank of executive officers. See Kent, Leib, & Shugerman, Faithful Execution and Article II, 132 Harv. L. Rev. 2111, 2121–2178 (2019). To be sure, the imposition of a duty may imply a grant of power sufficient to carry it out. But again, the majority's view of that power ill comports with founding-era practice, in which removal limits were common. See, *e.g.,* Corwin, Tenure of Office and the Removal Power Under the Constitution, 27 Colum. L. Rev. 353, 385 (1927) (noting that New York's Constitution of 1777 had nearly the same clause, though the State's executive had "very little voice" in removals). And yet more important, the text of the Take Care Clause requires only enough authority to make sure "the laws [are] faithfully executed"—meaning with fidelity to the law itself, not to every presidential policy preference. As this Court has held, a President can ensure " 'faithful execution' of the laws"— thereby satisfying his "take care" obligation—with a removal provision like the one here. *Morrison.* A for-cause standard gives him "ample authority to assure that [an official] is competently performing [his] statutory responsibilities in a manner that comports with the [relevant legislation's] provisions."

Finally, recall the Constitution's telltale silence: Nowhere does the text say anything about the President's power to remove subordinate officials at will. The majority professes unconcern. After all, it says, "neither is there a 'separation of powers clause' or a 'federalism clause.' " But those concepts are carved into the Constitution's text—the former in its first three articles separating powers, the latter in its enumeration of federal powers and its reservation of all else to the States. And anyway, at-will removal is hardly such a "foundational doctrine[ ]," *ibid.*: You won't find it on a civics class syllabus. That's because removal is a *tool*—one means among many, even if sometimes an important one, for a President to control executive officials. See generally *Free Enterprise Fund* (Breyer, J., dissenting). To find that authority hidden in the Constitution as a "general rule" is to discover what is nowhere there.

[In Part I.B, Justice Kagan offered a counter-history of congressional regulation of presidential removal authority. To begin, with virtually no reliable historians agree with Chief Justice Taft's inaccurate account of the Decision of 1789. Most believe that Congress left the matter of its authority to limit removal unresolved. See Prakash, New Light on the Decision of 1789, 91 Cornell L. Rev. 1021, 1072 (2006). But however ambiguous was that decision, early legislation resolved the matter in favor of such authority.]

Take first Congress's decision in 1816 to create the Second Bank of the United States—"the first truly independent agency in the republic's history." Of the twenty-five directors who led the Bank, the President could appoint and remove only five. See Act of Apr. 10, 1816, § 8, 3 Stat. 269. Yet the Bank had a greater impact on the Nation than any but a few institutions, regulating the Nation's money supply in ways anticipating what the Federal Reserve does today. Of course, the Bank was controversial—in large part because of its freedom from presidential control. Andrew Jackson chafed at the Bank's independence and eventually fired his Treasury Secretary for keeping public moneys there (a dismissal that itself provoked a political storm). No matter. Innovations in governance always have opponents; administrative independence predictably (though by no means invariably) provokes presidential ire. The point is that by the early 19th century, Congress established a body wielding enormous financial power mostly outside the President's dominion.

The Civil War brought yet further encroachments on presidential control over financial regulators. In response to wartime economic pressures, President Lincoln (not known for his modest view of executive power) asked Congress to establish an office called the Comptroller of the Currency. The statute he signed made the Comptroller removable only with the Senate's consent—a version of the old Hamiltonian idea, though this time required not by the Constitution itself but by Congress. See Act of Feb. 25, 1863, ch. 58, 12 Stat. 665. A year later, Congress amended the statute to permit removal by the President alone, but only upon "reasons to be communicated by him to the Senate." Act of June 3, 1864, § 1, 13 Stat. 100. The majority dismisses the original version of the statute as an "aberration." But in the wake of the independence given first to the Comptroller of the Treasury and then to the national Bank, it's hard to conceive of this newest Comptroller position as so great a departure. And even the second iteration of the statute preserved a constraint on the removal power, requiring a President in a firing mood to explain himself to Congress—a demand likely to make him sleep on the subject. In both versions of the law, Congress responded to new financial challenges with new regulatory institutions, alert to the perils in this area of political interference.

And then, nearly a century and a half ago, the floodgates opened. In 1887, the growing power of the railroads over the American economy led Congress to create the Interstate Commerce Commission. Under that legislation, the President could remove the five Commissioners only "for inefficiency, neglect of duty, or malfeasance in office"—the same standard Congress applied to the CFPB Director. Act of Feb. 4, 1887, § 11, 24 Stat. 383. More—many more—for-cause removal provisions followed. In 1913, Congress gave the Governors of the Federal Reserve Board for-cause protection to ensure the agency would resist political pressure and promote economic stability. See Act of Dec. 23, 1913, ch. 6, 38 Stat. 251. The next year, Congress provided similar protection to the FTC in the interest of House] incumbency." 51 Cong. Rec. 10376 (1914). The Federal Deposit Insurance Corporation (FDIC), the Securities and Exchange Commission (SEC), the Commodity Futures Trading Commission. In the financial realm, "independent agencies have remained the bedrock of the institutional framework governing U. S. markets." Gadinis, From Independence to Politics in Financial Regulation, 101 Cal. L. Rev. 327, 331 (2013). By one count, across all subject matter areas, 48 agencies have heads (and below them hundreds more inferior officials) removable only for cause. See *Free Enterprise Fund* (Breyer, J., dissenting). So year by year by year, the broad sweep of history has spoken to the constitutional question before us: Independent agencies are everywhere.

[I.C] What is more, the Court's precedents before today have accepted the role of independent agencies in our governmental system. To be sure, the line of our decisions has not run altogether straight. But we have repeatedly upheld provisions that prevent the President from firing regulatory officials except for such matters as neglect or malfeasance. In those decisions, we sounded a caution, insisting that Congress could not impede through removal restrictions the President's performance of his own constitutional duties. (So, to take the clearest example, Congress could not curb the President's power to remove his close military or diplomatic advisers.) But within that broad limit, this Court held, Congress could protect from at-will removal the officials it deemed to need some independence from political pressures. Nowhere do those precedents suggest what the majority announces today: that the President has an "unrestricted removal power" subject to two bounded exceptions.

[Thus, Justice Kagan viewed *Humphrey's* and not *Myers* as the foundational precedent, and rejected the Court's apparent view that the Court's virtually unanimous decision in *Morrison* was an aberration.]

[I.D] The deferential approach this Court has taken gives Congress the flexibility it needs to craft administrative agencies. Diverse problems of government demand diverse solutions. They call for varied measures and mixtures of democratic accountability and technical expertise, energy and efficiency. Sometimes, the arguments push toward tight presidential control of agencies. The President's engagement, some people say, can disrupt bureaucratic stagnation, counter industry capture, and make agencies more responsive to public interests. See, well, Kagan, Presidential Administration, 114 Harv. L. Rev. 2245, 2331–2346 (2001). At other times, the arguments favor greater independence from presidential involvement. Insulation from political pressure helps ensure impartial adjudications. It places technical issues in the hands of those most capable of addressing them. It promotes continuity, and prevents short-term electoral interests from distorting policy. (Consider, for example, how the Federal Reserve's independence stops a President trying to win a second term from manipulating interest rates.) Of course, the right balance between presidential control and independence is often uncertain, contested, and value-laden. No mathematical formula governs institutional design; trade-offs are endemic to the enterprise. But that is precisely why the issue is one for the political branches to debate—and then debate again as times change. And it's why courts should stay (mostly) out of the way. Rather than impose rigid rules like the majority's, they should let Congress and the President figure out what blend of independence and political control will best enable an agency to perform its intended functions.

Judicial intrusion into this field usually reveals only how little courts know about governance. Even everything I just said is an over-simplification. It suggests that agencies can easily be arranged on a spectrum, from the most to the least presidentially controlled. But that is not so. A given agency's independence (or lack of it) depends on a wealth of features, relating not just to removal standards, but also to appointments practices, procedural rules, internal organization, oversight regimes, historical traditions, cultural norms, and (inevitably) personal relationships. It is hard to pinpoint how those factors work individually, much less in concert, to influence the distance between an agency and a President. In that light, even the judicial opinions' perennial focus on removal standards is a bit of a puzzle. Removal is only the most obvious, not necessarily the most potent, means of control. See generally *Free Enterprise Fund* (Breyer, J., dissenting). That is because informal restraints can prevent Presidents from firing at-will officers—and because other devices can keep officers with for-cause protection under control. Of course no court, as *Free Enterprise Fund* noted, can accurately assess the "bureaucratic minutiae" affecting a President's influence over an agency. But that is yet more reason for courts to defer to the branches charged with fashioning administrative structures, and to hesitate before ruling out agency design specs like for-cause removal standards.

Our Constitution, as shown earlier, entrusts such decisions to more accountable and knowledgeable actors. The document—with great good sense—sets out almost no rules about the administrative sphere. As Chief Justice Marshall wrote when he upheld the first independent financial agency: "To have prescribed the means by which government should, in all future time, execute its powers, would have been to change, entirely, the character of the instrument." *McCulloch*, 4 Wheat. at 415. That would have been, he continued, "an unwise attempt to provide, by immutable rules, for exigencies which, if foreseen at all, must have been seen dimly." *Ibid.* And if the Constitution, for those reasons, does not lay out immutable rules, then neither should judges. This Court has usually respected that injunction. It has declined to second-guess the work of the political branches in creating independent agencies like the CFPB. In reversing course today—in spurning a "pragmatic, flexible approach to American governance" in favor of a dogmatic, inflexible one, the majority makes a serious error. * * *

NOTES ON SEILA LAW AND ITS SEQUELS

1. *The Constitutional Debate in* Seila Law. Building upon the learned analysis in Justice Breyer's *Free Enterprise* dissent, Justice Kagan's *Seila Law* dissenting opinion lays out a strong assault on the legal reasoning of the Chief Justice's opinion for the Court in this case and in *Free Enterprise*. As you read these criticisms, consider how Chief Justice Roberts would respond:

- *Constitutional Text: Gerrymandered.* The Court overreads the Vesting Clause of Article II, which never says "all" executive power, and ignores the Necessary and Proper Clause of Article I, which gives Congress authority to structure the executive branch. There is no "removal" authority granted the President in Article II. For any judge who reads the constitutional text, this is odd. Victoria Nourse dubs this "Textual Gerrymandering.". What is Roberts' theory of Article II?

- *Law Office Pseudo-History.* Legal historians such as the Professor Prakash have demonstrated that the majority Justices have misunderstood the Decision of 1789 and have turned it into a much bigger deal that it was at the time. For a general critique of the Justices' inability to carry out genuinely "historicist" analysis, see Jonathan Gienapp, *Historicism and Holism: Failures of Originalist Translation*, 84 Fordham L. Rev. 935 (2015). If Roberts were right about the import of the Decision of 1789, how could the Second Bank have been adopted—and why would President Madison (the bulwark of the Roberts opinion) have signed it without objection? Is the Second Bank materially different from the CFPB? From independent agencies today?

- *Constitutional Structure and Plan: Where Is the Violation?* There can be no denying that the Constitution established checks and balances—which the Court in cases like *Chadha* and *Myers* (where Congress required Senate consent to discharge the postal official) has augmented with cautions against congressional power grabs. But the CFPB structure, like that of the Fed, seeks independence from the political process—both Congress and the President. Why is the CFPB in violation of the constitutional plan? The Chief Justice imagines the plan somewhat differently: Can you articulate his vision, which emphasizes separation of powers?

- *The Novelty Argument: Why Does This Carry Weight?* The majority and dissent argue about how "novel" the CFPB arrangement is, and students can form their own opinion about who "wins." But why does that carry any weight? As the Court said in *McCulloch*, the generally phrased Constitution has lasted a long time and constantly addresses new circumstances and innovations. Why is innovation a bad thing?

- *Practice and Precedent Cut Every Which Way.* The Roberts-Kagan debate is a classic example of how two lines of cases can be deployed to support a variety of results—and hence create no rule of law, only a rule of which lawyers have a majority. Until *Free Enterprise Fund* and *Seila Law,* the dominant line of cases allowed a great deal of congressional latitude, so long as there was no self-aggrandizement (arguably the best way to reconcile *Myers, Humphrey's,* and *Morrison*). After *Free Enterprise Fund,* the reverse is the case. Does precedent really limit the Court— or is using precedent like looking out over the crowd and picking out your friends?

- *Representation-Reinforcing Review: Bickel vs. Ely?* The dissent sounds Bickelian themes: Who do we think we are? Justices are not competent to micromanage the Congress-President competition. Many academics would read the majority as making moves that serve the interests of Corporate America: limit Congress's ability to impose regulations on corporations and rich people. We believe that at least some of the Justices were impressed by the President's ability to impose coherence in regulatory policies across the board—and be accountable for his/her/their policy regime at election time (the President either runs for reelection or supports her/his party's nominee). Does the Roberts opinion serve this purpose? (Compare it to the Chief's opinion in *Shelby County*.)

The elephant in the opinions is whether this line of cases, combined with a revived nondelegation doctrine, will result in a frontal challenge to the constitutionality of "independent" agencies—which the FTC, SEC, Fed, etc. still are. See the next note.

2. *The Fate of Independent Agencies Following* Seila Law. The result in *Seila Law* might be a tweak in the existing case law, which the Court expands to cover the unusual structure of the CFPB. See Ian Millhiser, *The Supreme Court's Big Decision on the CFPB and the "Unitary Executive," Explained*, Vox (June 29, 2020). Or the decision might be the next step in a larger campaign to undermine or restructure independent agencies. Recall the D.C. Circuit's en banc decision upholding the constitutionality of the CFPB structure in *PHH Corp. v. CFPB*, 881 F.3d 75 (D.C. Cir. en banc 2018). Then-Judge Kavanaugh wrote a powerful dissent in *PHH Corp.*, discussing how the Supreme Court's exception in *Humphrey's Executor* threatened individual freedom—especially the freedom of corporations and businesses. Consistent with his critique, the Federalist Society and allied judges and professors have waged a long battle against limitations on executive authority over the administrative state. In an odd move (from the perspective of the rule of law and stare decisis), they treat Justice Scalia's solo dissent in *Morrison v. Olson* as citable precedent.

Seila Law does not overrule *Morrison*, but it does suggest that there may be new limits on Congress's power to structure independent agencies. For example, what are the consequences of *Seila Law* for independent agencies with a multi-member structure? Might congressional fixed terms (like five years, which extend beyond the presidential term) be vulnerable? Statutory requirements of partisan balance?

3. *Extending* Seila Law. In *Collins v. Yellen*, 141 S.Ct. 1761 (2020), the Supreme Court applied *Seila Law* to hold that the restriction on removal of the Federal Housing Finance Agency (FHFA) Director was unconstitutional. After the 2008 housing crisis placed Fannie Mae and Freddie Mac in a precarious financial situation, Congress created the FHFA to regulate these companies. Congress structured the agency to be headed by a single director removable only for good cause. *Seila Law* had noted that the FHFA was a "companion of the CFPB, established in response to the same financial crisis," but observed that the FHFA did not "involve regulatory or enforcement authority remotely comparable to that exercised by the CFPB."

In *Collins*, Justice Alito's majority opinion ruled that *Seila Law* was "all but dispositive" to the outcome. The Court held that the constitutionality of an agency's structure is not dependent on the scope of its power. Citing *Free Enterprise Fund*, Alito asserted that the President's removal power is essential to maintain a degree of political accountability in Executive Branch action. Additionally, while a for-good-cause restriction on removal appeared to be more modest than the one at issue for the CFPB, the Court cited *Seila Law* in holding that "even 'modest restrictions' on the President's power to remove the head of an agency with a single top officer" are unconstitutional.

Regarding remedy, the agency's unconstitutional structure did not invalidate its agreement with Treasury that plaintiffs were challenging. The Acting Director of the FHFA (as opposed to a confirmed director) had implemented the agreement; the FHFA's authorizing statute provided no removal protection for acting directors, and the Court reasoned that the Acting Director's authority and actions were constitutionally valid. The Court remanded to the lower court to determine if the shareholders suffered any harm due to the previous, confirmed Director's tenure protection. Agreeing with Justice Alito, Justice Thomas argued that even if the agreement had been made by a Director, private parties could not invalidate her/his/their actions: such a Director was legitimately appointed, and under the Constitution the President could remove her/him/them at any time. In other words, only the President could benefit from invalidating the for-good-cause restriction. Justice Gorsuch disagreed with Justices Alito and Thomas and refused to join that part of the Court's opinion, on the ground that the Acting Director was unconstitutionally constituted and so all actions were illegal.

The liberal Justices joined the majority's discussion of the proper remedy while objecting in two separate opinions to the extension of *Seila Law*. They criticized the majority for abandoning its prior emphasis on single-director agencies that wielded significant executive power, thereby concluding in effect that any agency led by a single director is subject to at-will removal. Justice Kagan found the Court's extension unnecessary given its analysis of the FHFA as in fact wielding significant executive power. Justice Sotomayor (joined by Justice Breyer) disagreed that the FHFA has significant executive power remotely comparable to the CFPB. She argued that in regulating only governmental actors, not private entities, the FHFC is more like the independent counsel whose tenure protections were held to be constitutional in *Morrison*. And with its regulatory authority limited mainly to certain non-executive powers (like acting as a conservator or gathering specified forms of information), the FHFC is more like the 1935 FTC for which the Court upheld removal provisions in *Humphrey's Executor*.

The Social Security Administration and the Office of Special Counsel are headed by single directors with limited duties and jurisdictions. Both directors are subject to removal for cause-related reasons. Can these for-cause provisions survive *Collins*? If you were the current White House Counsel or the Assistant Attorney General for the Office of Legal Counsel, would you advise President Biden that he can dismiss these directors at will? Is there any way Congress can fix this problem?

4. *Identifying "Inferior Officers."* In *United States v. Arthrex, Inc.*, 141 S.Ct. 1970 (2021), the Supreme Court grappled with the President's right to appoint agency officers. The President appoints the Director of the Patent and Trademark Office (PTO), an executive agency inside the Commerce Department. Within the PTO, the Commerce Secretary appoints more than 200 Administrative Patent Judges (APJs) who comprise the Patent Trial and Appeal Board (PTAB). The Director designates PTAB panels to oversee inter partes (adversarial) proceedings reviewing challenges to previously issued patents. The PTAB must issue a final decision within a specified time frame, and that is the final decision within the executive branch. Parties may then

seek judicial review in the Federal Circuit, at which point the Director may intervene to defend or disavow the PTAB decision.

Chief Justice Roberts's opinion for the *Arthrex* Court held that the APJs serving on the PTAB were "principal" and not "inferior" officers, because they wielded unreviewable authority during inter partes proceedings. Accordingly, their appointment by the Commerce Secretary rather than the President was unconstitutional under the Appointments Clause of Article II, which presumes that the President appoint executive "Officers" but allows Congress to vest appointment of "inferior Officers" in cabinet heads. Even though the PTO Director (appointed by the President) can select APJs to decide particular cases, providing some oversight, she/he/they would still be shielded from the fallout of a given PTAB decision. Citing *Free Enterprise*, Chief Justice Roberts concluded that conferring final decisionmaking power within the executive branch on the APJs contravenes Article II's principles of legitimacy and public accountability.

Rather than invalidate the entire inter partes review procedure, however, Roberts (writing for a plurality) determined that the panel appointments process was unenforceable "insofar as it prevents the Director from reviewing the decisions of the PTAB on his own." The Court remanded the case to the Acting Director to determine if a rehearing was warranted in this particular dispute. The Chief Justice's remedial analysis was joined by Justices Alito, Kavanaugh, and Barrett; the remedial result was also endorsed by Justices Breyer, Sotomayor, and Kagan.

Agreeing on the constitutional merits, Justice Gorsuch disagreed with the Chief Justice's remedial analysis. The Court could have achieved the same result by requiring that the President appoint APJs, or by moving the inter partes review process to the judiciary. Because Congress did not indicate a preferred way for the Court to resolve the issue, Gorsuch viewed the remedial holding as a naked policy choice—one that "gifts the Director a new power that he/she/they never before enjoyed, a power Congress expressly * * * gave to someone else." Is it fair to expect Congress to include "fallback" provisions instructing courts on how to remedy an unconstitutional provision in the agency's authorizing statute? Is it more appropriate, as a matter of statutory interpretation, for the Court to ask what the past Congress would have done if confronted with a constitutional conundrum it presumably never anticipated?

Justice Breyer (joined by Justices Sotomayor and Kagan) dissented on the constitutional issue. He contended that as a functional matter, the Director has ample discretion to make policy and the PTAB simply applies that policy. By imposing a review mechanism on the PTAB structure, the Court undermined Congress' intention to give APJs a degree of independence over their technical decisionmaking. Breyer argued that the Executive Branch and Congress are more likely than unelected judges to understand "the nature of different mechanisms of bureaucratic control that may apply to the many thousands of administrators who will carry out the tasks" Congress has written into legislation.

Justice Thomas in dissent (joined by the three liberals) expressed dismay at the Court's unprecedented invalidation of a statutory structure vesting the appointment of a federal officer in the head of a department. "Just who are these 'principal' officers that Congress unsuccessfully sought to smuggle into the Executive Branch without Senate confirmation? About 250 administrative patent judges who sit at the bottom of an organizational chart, nestled under at least two levels of authority." Thomas found that APJs are surely "inferior Officers" in that they serve the Director's policy goals and the Director can remove them from a case if they defy his/her/their authority. He objected to the invention of an Appointments Clause doctrine centered on policing the way that Congress distributes executive power among an agency's officers. Instead, the Court should adhere to precedent by labeling officers "inferior" where their supervisor was appointed by the President and confirmed by the Senate.

When Congress accords mid-level officers a certain amount of independence, is Thomas's bright line approach of dubbing them "inferior" because the President appointed their boss preferable to the approach the Court took in *Arthrex*? Should courts judge inferior officer status on a case-by-case basis or by using a bright-line rule? Does Article II, Section 2 have anything to contribute on this question?

5. *The Inspectors General.* Congress in the Inspector General Act of 1978 created 12 departmental inspectors general (IGs), appointed by the President and confirmed by the Senate. IGs are charged with identifying, auditing, and investigating fraud, waste, abuse, and mismanagement within their assigned department. Presidents from Reagan to Obama dismissed IGs, with mixed results (Reagan fired 16 IGs and then re-hired five after Congress objected). In April/May 2020, President Trump dismissed the IGs of five cabinet departments within six weeks: Intelligence, Defense, HHS, Transportation, and State. The President expressed dislike for actions taken by several of the IGs, which led to the dismissals being seen as retaliatory. These concerns grew after it came to light that at least two firings may have related to ongoing IG investigations into the conduct of the cabinet secretaries in charge of those departments. See Ian Duncan & Michael Laris, *Democrats Open Investigation into Trump's Replacement of Acting Transportation Department Inspector General*, Wash. Post, May 19, 2020.

Under current law, IGs continue to serve at the pleasure of the President. An IG law enacted in 2008 required the President to communicate in writing to Congress "the reasons for such removal" at least 30 days before removing a Senate-confirmed IG. Responding to the Trump firings, House Democrats introduced legislation in 2020 to give IGs for-cause removal protections and seven-year terms. In 2021, Senator Grassley introduced the Securing Inspector General Independence Act of 2021, with bipartisan support. The Grassley bill would require the President to provide to Congress in writing "the substantive rationale, including detailed and case-specific reasons" at least 15 days before removing an IG. The bill provides an exception to the notice requirement if the President determines that the continued presence of an IG poses a threat to legitimate government interests. Does this proposed change from communicating "reasons" under current law to requiring "detailed and case-specific reasons" in advance really restrict the President's removal powers?

Rebecca Jones, policy counsel at the Project on Government Oversight, contends that the structure and work of IGs align more closely with cases where the Court upheld for-cause removal protections. Although these officials do not appear to fit cleanly into either the *Humphrey's Executor* or *Morrison* exceptions, Jones argues that the nature and work of these watchdogs "belong[s] in a middle ground, pulling from both exceptions." Rebecca Jones, Seila Law v. CFPB*: What's Unconstitutional for One May Not Be Unconstitutional for All*, POGO (July 1, 2020). One reason is the fact that IGs are designed to be nonpartisan and to act with impartiality, and that their duties are neither political nor executive, like the FTC in *Humphrey's Executor*. And the Court could make a similar distinction as in *Morrison* about the work and scope of IGs, who investigate misconduct related to federal programs and spending, often involving high-level officials, and do not have enforcement power. Are you persuaded? Would the Grassley bill survive the holding and reasoning in *Seila Law*?

Page 1296. Insert the following Supreme Court decision and notes right before Part C:

DONALD J. TRUMP V. MAZARS USA, LLP
591 U.S. ___, 140 S.Ct. 2019, 207 L.Ed.2d 951 (2020)

CHIEF JUSTICE ROBERTS delivered the opinion of the Court.

[In April 2019, three committees of the U. S. House of Representatives issued four subpoenas seeking information about the finances of President Donald Trump, his children, and affiliated businesses. The House Committee on Financial Services issued a subpoena to Deutsche Bank seeking any document related to account activity, due diligence, foreign transactions, business statements, debt schedules, statements of net worth, tax returns, and suspicious activity identified by Deutsche Bank. The Permanent Select Committee on Intelligence issued a similar subpoena to Deutsche Bank. And the House Committee on Oversight and Reform issued a subpoena to the President's personal accounting firm, Mazars, demanding information related to the President and several affiliated businesses. Although each of the committees sought overlapping sets of financial documents, each supplied different justifications for the requests, explaining that the information would help guide legislative reform in areas ranging from money laundering and terrorism to foreign involvement in U. S. elections.

President Trump et al. contested the subpoena issued by the Oversight Committee in the District Court for the District of Columbia and the subpoenas issued by the Financial Services and Intelligence Committees in the Southern District of New York. The courts of appeals sustained the authority of the district courts to enforce the subpoenas under the regular rules for such enforcement. The Supreme Court reversed, on the ground that the courts of appeals should have applied a heightened standard, reflecting the separation of powers concerns raised by the subpoenas.]

[II.A] The question presented is whether the subpoenas exceed the authority of the House under the Constitution. Historically, disputes over congressional demands for presidential documents have not ended up in court. Instead, they have been hashed out in the "hurly-burly, the give-and-take of the political process between the legislative and the executive." Hearings on S. 2170 et al. before the Subcommittee on Intergovernmental Relations of the Senate Committee on Government Operations, 94th Cong., 1st Sess., 87 (1975) (A. Scalia, Assistant Attorney General, Office of Legal Counsel).

That practice began with George Washington and the early Congress. In 1792, a House committee requested Executive Branch documents pertaining to General St. Clair's campaign against the Indians in the Northwest Territory, which had concluded in an utter rout of federal forces when they were caught by surprise near the present-day border between Ohio and Indiana. See T. Taylor, Grand Inquest: The Story of Congressional Investigations 19–23 (1955). Since this was the first such request from Congress, President Washington called a Cabinet meeting, wishing to take care that his response "be rightly conducted" because it could "become a precedent." 1 Writings of Thomas Jefferson 189 (P. Ford ed. 1892).

The meeting, attended by the likes of Alexander Hamilton, Thomas Jefferson, Edmund Randolph, and Henry Knox, ended with the Cabinet of "one mind": The House had authority to "institute inquiries" and "call for papers" but the President could "exercise a discretion" over disclosures, "communicat[ing] such papers as the public good would permit" and "refus[ing]" the rest. President Washington then dispatched Jefferson to speak to individual congressmen and "bring them by persuasion into the right channel." The discussions were apparently fruitful, as the House later narrowed its request and the documents were supplied without recourse to the courts.

[The Chief Justice provided subsequent examples where the branches had worked out demands for executive department information through a negotiated settlement. This case is the first one where the Supreme Court was called upon to resolve the legality of a congressional subpoena against the President.]

[II.B] Congress has no enumerated constitutional power to conduct investigations or issue subpoenas, but we have held that each House has power "to secure needed information" in order to legislate. *McGrain* v. *Daugherty*, 273 U.S. 135, 161 (1927). This "power of inquiry—with process to enforce it—is an essential and appropriate auxiliary to the legislative function." Without information, Congress would be shooting in the dark, unable to legislate "wisely or effectively." The congressional power to obtain information is "broad" and "indispensable." *Watkins* v. *United States*, 354 U.S. 178, 187, 215 (1957). It encompasses inquiries into the administration of existing laws, studies of proposed laws, and "surveys of defects in our social, economic or political system for the purpose of enabling the Congress to remedy them." *Id.*

Because this power is "justified solely as an adjunct to the legislative process," it is subject to several limitations. *Watkins.* Most importantly, a congressional subpoena is valid only if it is "related to, and in furtherance of, a legitimate task of the Congress." The subpoena must serve a "valid legislative purpose," *Quinn* v. *United States*, 349 U.S. 155, 161 (1955); it must "concern[ ] a subject on which legislation 'could be had,' " *Eastland* v. *United States Servicemen's Fund*, 421 U.S. 491, 506 (1975) (quoting *McGrain*).

Furthermore, Congress may not issue a subpoena for the purpose of "law enforcement," because "those powers are assigned under our Constitution to the Executive and the Judiciary." *Quinn.* Thus Congress may not use subpoenas to "try" someone "before [a] committee for any crime or wrongdoing." *McGrain.* Congress has no " 'general' power to inquire into private affairs and compel disclosures," and "there is no congressional power to expose for the sake of exposure," *Watkins.* "Investigations conducted solely for the personal aggrandizement of the investigators or to 'punish' those investigated are indefensible." *Id.*

Finally, recipients of legislative subpoenas retain their constitutional rights throughout the course of an investigation. See *id.* And recipients have long been understood to retain common law and constitutional privileges with respect to certain materials, such as attorney-client communications and governmental communications protected by executive privilege. See, *e.g.*, Congressional Research Service, *supra,* at 16–18 (attorney-client privilege); *Senate Select Committee*, 498 F. 2d, at 727, 730–731 (executive privilege).

[In Part II.C, the Chief Justice rejected the President's position, that the subpoena should have been governed by *Nixon*'s "demonstrated, specific need" for the financial information, just as the Watergate special prosecutor was required to do in order to obtain the tapes. See also *Senate Select Committee* (D.C. Circuit case refusing to enforce the Senate subpoena for the tapes).] Unlike the cases before us, *Nixon* and *Senate Select Committee* involved Oval Office communications over which the President asserted executive privilege. That privilege safeguards the public interest in candid, confidential deliberations within the Executive Branch; it is "fundamental to the operation of Government." *Nixon.* As a result, information subject to executive privilege deserves "the greatest protection consistent with the fair administration of justice." *Id.* We decline to transplant that protection root and branch to cases involving nonprivileged, private information, which by definition does not implicate sensitive Executive Branch deliberations.

The standards proposed by the President and the Solicitor General— if applied outside the context of privileged information—would risk seriously impeding Congress in carrying out its responsibilities. The President and the Solicitor General would apply the same exacting standards to *all* subpoenas for the President's information, without recognizing distinctions between privileged and nonprivileged information, between official and personal information, or between various legislative objectives. Such a categorical approach would represent a significant departure from the longstanding way of doing business between the branches, giving short shrift to Congress's important interests in conducting inquiries to obtain the information it needs to legislate effectively. * * *

[In Part II.D, the Chief Justice rejected the House's position and that of the courts of appeals, that enforcement of the subpoenas should be governed by the rules generally applicable to subpoenas. Such a rule did not take account of the sensitive separation of powers concerns presented here but not in the ordinary subpoena case.]

[II.E The Chief Justice considered the practicalities of this kind of dispute and balanced the interests of each branch to produce the following guidelines for the lower courts on remand:]

First, courts should carefully assess whether the asserted legislative purpose warrants the significant step of involving the President and his papers. " '[O]ccasion[s] for constitutional confrontation between the two branches' should be avoided whenever possible." *Cheney* v. *United States Dist. Court for D. C.*, 542 U.S. 367, 389–390 (2004) (quoting *Nixon*). Congress may not rely on the President's information if other sources could reasonably provide Congress the information it needs in light of its particular legislative objective. The President's unique constitutional position means that Congress may not look to him as a "case study" for general legislation.

Unlike in criminal proceedings, where "[t]he very integrity of the judicial system" would be undermined without "full disclosure of all the facts," *Nixon*, efforts to craft legislation involve predictive policy judgments that are "not hamper[ed] . . . in quite the same way" when every scrap of potentially relevant evidence is not available, *Cheney*. While we certainly recognize Congress's important interests in obtaining information through appropriate inquiries, those interests are not sufficiently powerful to justify access to the President's personal papers when other sources could provide Congress the information it needs.

Second, to narrow the scope of possible conflict between the branches, courts should insist on a subpoena no broader than reasonably necessary to support Congress's legislative objective. The specificity of the subpoena's request "serves as an important safeguard against unnecessary intrusion into the operation of the Office of the President." *Cheney*.

Third, courts should be attentive to the nature of the evidence offered by Congress to establish that a subpoena advances a valid legislative purpose. The more detailed and substantial the evidence of Congress's legislative purpose, the better. See *Watkins* (preferring such evidence over "vague" and "loosely worded" evidence of Congress's purpose). That is particularly true when Congress contemplates legislation that raises sensitive constitutional issues, such as legislation concerning the Presidency. In such cases, it is "impossible" to conclude that a subpoena is designed to advance a valid legislative purpose unless Congress adequately identifies its aims and explains why the President's information will advance its consideration of the possible legislation. *Id.*

Fourth, courts should be careful to assess the burdens imposed on the President by a subpoena. We have held that burdens on the President's time and attention stemming from judicial process and litigation, without more, generally do not cross constitutional lines. See *Vance*; *Clinton*. But burdens imposed by a congressional subpoena should be carefully scrutinized, for they stem from a rival political branch that has an ongoing relationship with the President and incentives to use subpoenas for institutional advantage.

Other considerations may be pertinent as well; one case every two centuries does not afford enough experience for an exhaustive list. * * *

[JUSTICE THOMAS dissented, on the ground that neither chamber of Congress has subpoena power ancillary to its legislative powers under Article I. "At the time of the founding, the power to subpoena private, nonofficial documents was not included by necessary implication in any of Congress' legislative powers," a precept consistent with *Kilbourn* v. *Thompson*, 103 U.S. 168 (1881), which refused to enforce a subpoena against private documents. Justice Thomas would have overruled *McGrain*, which did sustain such a power, because it was inconsistent with legislative powers as understood in 1789. The House has authority under its impeachment power to issue such subpoenas, an authority not invoked for these cases.]

[JUSTICE ALITO agreed with the remand but dissented from the formulation of the standard to be applied.] Specifically, the House should provide a description of the type of legislation being considered, and while great specificity is not necessary, the description should be sufficient to permit a court to assess whether the particular records sought are of any special importance. The House should also spell out its constitutional authority to enact the type of legislation that it is contemplating, and it should justify the scope of the subpoenas in relation to the articulated legislative needs. In addition, it should explain why the subpoenaed information, as opposed to information available from other sources, is needed. Unless the House is required to make a showing along these lines, I would hold that enforcement of the subpoenas cannot be ordered.

NOTE ON THE TRUMP TAX SUBPOENA CASES AND SEPARATION OF POWERS

The House Subpoena Case, read in conjunction with the State Grand Jury Subpoena Case and the cases in this Section 2, exploring separation of powers limits on Congress's authority, offer the student an opportunity to reflect on the Supreme Court's methodology in these cases, where Congress (or one chamber) is at loggerheads with the President. Consider some themes:

- *Justiciable but Still Political.* The Supreme Court declined to consider any of these cases "political questions" (not justiciable under Article III, as we explore in Casebook, pages 1360–80), and so the federal courts now stand as arbiters of clashes between Congress and the President. Although the Chief Justice emphasized the need for Congress and the President to resolve most of these information-generating disputes through interbranch bargaining, the Supreme Court and the judiciary assume power as 'neutral' arbiters. Notice that the Court gave the state grand jury proceedings a much easier path to the Trump tax records than it gave Congress.

- *Relevance of History.* Only Justice Thomas revealed interest in applying the original public meaning of Articles I and II to this controversy, or to the parallel controversy between the Manhattan District Attorney and President Trump over the grand jury subpoena. The other justices were interested in post-1789 history, carefully hewing to the Court's precedents (some of which Thomas questioned) and considering historic practice as they figured out what standard should be applied on remand. Recall the Jackson concurring opinion in the Steel Seizure Cases. It is by now a hallmark of Chief Justice Roberts' jurisprudence that he approaches constitutional "novelty" (issues of first impression) with extreme caution: he is reluctant to sanction novelty without reservation but is protective of the Court's political capital by refusing to make 'big moves'.

- *Balancing and the Critical Role of Process.* At bottom, both tax subpoena cases boiled down to judicial balancing—and process emerged as the big winner. Getting stuff from a President who does not want to give it up is going to require a lot of process—

and this reinforces the already huge institutional advantages of the presidency: even a renegade president can slow down the processes of impeachment and congressional fact-finding so much that Congress shrinks further into irrelevance. Are there other themes that strike you as important in the Trump Tax Subpoena Cases? In the end, the House did not secure the documents requested from the President, but in January 2021 the House voted Articles of Impeachment for the President's alleged role in instigating a riot that sacked the U.S. Capitol on January 6, 2021. After President Trump left office, the Senate voted 57–43 to convict the President, ten votes short of the number needed to disqualify him from future service as President. At this writing, he and others are under investigation by a House Select Committee investigating the January 6 events, which may result in criminal referrals.

SECTION 3. SEPARATION OF POWERS, DUE PROCESS, RELIGION, AND THE WAR ON TERROR

Page 1342. Insert the following Note right before Problem 8-10:

NOTE ON THE UNAVAILABILITY OF HABEAS FOR IMMIGRANTS DENIED ASYLUM

In *Department of Homeland Security v. Thuraissigiam*, 140 S.Ct. 1959 (2020), the Court ruled that the Suspension of Habeas Clause did not apply to federal detention of noncitizens who had entered the United States seeking asylum from persecution. (By treaty and by statute, the United States is supposed to grant asylum to persons fleeing from a "well-founded fear of persecution.") In *INS v. St. Cyr*, 533 U.S. 289 (2001), the Court had ruled that habeas was available to immigrants who had entered the country but were being detained as a prelude to deportation. But in *Thuraissigiam,* the Court declined to require habeas review of a statutory bar to factual review of executive denial of asylum claims.

Justice Alito's opinion for the Court held that the Suspension Clause's protection for habeas as it existed when the Constitution was adopted in 1789 (the test the majority deduced from *Boumedienne*) did not apply to asylum petitioners, who were seeking a mandamus or an injunction rather than a traditional habeas remedy of release from detention. The United States was detaining the asylum-seeker here but was happy to release him to an "airplane cabin" taking him back to his home country. **Justices Breyer** and **Ginsburg** concurred in the Court's judgment on narrow, fact-specific grounds.

Justice Sotomayor, joined by **Justice Kagan**, dissented. She charged the Court with a biased framing of the case: the immigrant was seeking review of executive detention resting upon a legally erroneous interpretation of the immigration laws—the classic function of habeas review. The dissenters also maintained that the statutory denial of judicial review violated the Due Process Clause of the Fifth Amendment.

CHAPTER 9

LIMITS ON THE JUDICIAL POWER

■ ■ ■

SECTION 1. THE POLITICAL QUESTION DOCTRINE

Page 1380. Insert the following before the heading for Section 2:

RUCHO V. COMMON CAUSE

588 U.S. ___, 139 S.Ct. 2484, 204 L.Ed.2d 931 (2019)

CHIEF JUSTICE ROBERTS delivered the opinion of the Court.

Voters and other plaintiffs in North Carolina and Maryland challenged their States' congressional districting maps as unconstitutional partisan gerrymanders. The North Carolina plaintiffs complained that the State's districting plan discriminated against Democrats; the Maryland plaintiffs complained that their State's plan discriminated against Republicans. The plaintiffs alleged that the gerrymandering violated the First Amendment, the Equal Protection Clause of the Fourteenth Amendment, the Elections Clause, and Article I, § 2, of the Constitution. The District Courts in both cases ruled in favor of the plaintiffs, and the defendants appealed directly to this Court.

These cases require us to consider once again whether claims of excessive partisanship in districting are "justiciable"—that is, properly suited for resolution by the federal courts. This Court has not previously struck down a districting plan as an unconstitutional partisan gerrymander, and has struggled without success over the past several decades to discern judicially manageable standards for deciding such claims. The districting plans at issue here are highly partisan, by any measure. The question is whether the courts below appropriately exercised judicial power when they found them unconstitutional as well. * * *

In considering whether partisan gerrymandering claims are justiciable, we are mindful of Justice Kennedy's counsel in *Vieth* [*v. Jubelirer,* 541 U.S. 267 (2004)]: Any standard for resolving such claims must be grounded in a "limited and precise rationale" and be "clear, manageable, and politically neutral."). An important reason for those careful constraints is that, as a Justice with extensive experience in state and local politics put it, "[t]he opportunity to control the drawing of electoral boundaries through the legislative process of apportionment is a critical and traditional part of politics in the United States. An expansive standard requiring "the correction of all election district lines drawn for partisan reasons would commit federal and state courts to unprecedented intervention in the American political process."

As noted, the question is one of degree: How to "provid[e] a standard for deciding how much partisan dominance is too much.".). And it is vital in such circumstances that the Court act only in accord with especially clear standards: "With uncertain limits, intervening courts—even when proceeding with best intentions—would risk assuming political, not legal, responsibility for a process that often produces ill will and distrust." If federal courts are to "inject [themselves] into the most heated partisan issues" by adjudicating partisan gerrymandering claims, they must be armed with a standard that can reliably differentiate unconstitutional from "constitutional political gerrymandering."

Partisan gerrymandering claims rest on an instinct that groups with a certain level of political support should enjoy a commensurate level of political power and influence. Explicitly or implicitly, a districting map is alleged to be unconstitutional because it makes it too difficult for one party to translate statewide support into seats in the legislature. But such a claim is based on a "norm that does not exist" in our electoral system— "statewide elections for representatives along party lines."

Partisan gerrymandering claims invariably sound in a desire for proportional representation. As Justice O'Connor put it, such claims are based on "a conviction that the greater the departure from proportionality, the more suspect an apportionment plan becomes." "Our cases, however, clearly foreclose any claim that the Constitution requires proportional representation or that legislatures in reapportioning must draw district lines to come as near as possible to allocating seats to the contending parties in proportion to what their anticipated statewide vote will be."

The Founders certainly did not think proportional representation was required. For more than 50 years after ratification of the Constitution, many States elected their congressional representatives through at-large or "general ticket" elections. Such States typically sent single-party delegations to Congress That meant that a party could garner nearly half of the vote statewide and wind up without any seats in the congressional delegation. The Whigs in Alabama suffered that fate in 1840: "their party garnered 43 percent of the statewide vote, yet did not receive a single seat." When Congress required single-member districts in the Apportionment Act of 1842, it was not out of a general sense of fairness, but instead a (mis)calculation by the Whigs that such a change would improve their electoral prospects.

Unable to claim that the Constitution requires proportional representation outright, plaintiffs inevitably ask the courts to make their own political judgment about how much representation particular political parties *deserve*—based on the votes of their supporters—and to rearrange the challenged districts to achieve that end. But federal courts are not equipped to apportion political power as a matter of fairness, nor is there any basis for concluding that they were authorized to do so. As Justice Scalia put it for the plurality in *Vieth*:

> " 'Fairness' does not seem to us a judicially manageable standard. . . . Some criterion more solid and more demonstrably met than that seems to us necessary to enable the state legislatures to discern the limits of their districting discretion, to meaningfully constrain the discretion of the courts, and to win public acceptance for the courts' intrusion into a process that is the very foundation of democratic decision-making."

The initial difficulty in settling on a "clear, manageable and politically neutral" test for fairness is that it is not even clear what fairness looks like in this context. There is a large measure of "unfairness" in any winner-take-all system. Fairness may mean a greater number of competitive districts. Such a claim seeks to undo packing and cracking so that supporters of the disadvantaged party have a better shot at electing their preferred candidates. But making as many districts as possible more competitive could be a recipe for disaster for the disadvantaged party. As Justice White has pointed out, "[i]f all or most of the districts are competitive . . . even a narrow statewide preference for either party would produce an overwhelming majority for the winning party in the state legislature."

On the other hand, perhaps the ultimate objective of a "fairer" share of seats in the congressional delegation is most readily achieved by yielding to the gravitational pull of proportionality and engaging in cracking and packing, to ensure each party its "appropriate" share of "safe" seats. Such an approach, however, comes at the expense of competitive districts and of individuals in districts allocated to the opposing party.

Or perhaps fairness should be measured by adherence to "traditional" districting criteria, such as maintaining political subdivisions, keeping communities of interest together, and protecting incumbents. But protecting incumbents, for example, enshrines a particular partisan distribution. And the "natural political geography" of a State—such as the fact that urban electoral districts are often dominated by one political party—can itself lead to inherently packed districts. As Justice Kennedy has explained, traditional criteria such as compactness and contiguity "cannot promise political neutrality when used as the basis for relief.

Instead, it seems, a decision under these standards would unavoidably have significant political effect, whether intended or not."

Deciding among just these different visions of fairness (you can imagine many others) poses basic questions that are political, not legal. There are no legal standards discernible in the Constitution for making such judgments, let alone limited and precise standards that are clear, manageable, and politically neutral. Any judicial decision on what is "fair" in this context would be an "unmoored determination" of the sort characteristic of a political question beyond the competence of the federal courts.

And it is only after determining how to define fairness that you can even begin to answer the determinative question: "How much is too much?" At what point does permissible partisanship become unconstitutional? If compliance with traditional districting criteria is the fairness touchstone, for example, how much deviation from those criteria is constitutionally acceptable and how should map drawers prioritize competing criteria? Should a court "reverse gerrymander" other parts of a State to counteract "natural" gerrymandering caused, for example, by the urban concentration of one party? If a districting plan protected half of the incumbents but redistricted the rest into head to head races, would that be constitutional? A court would have to rank the relative importance of those traditional criteria and weigh how much deviation from each to allow.

If a court instead focused on the respective number of seats in the legislature, it would have to decide the ideal number of seats for each party and determine at what point deviation from that balance went too far. If a 5–3 allocation corresponds most closely to statewide vote totals, is a 6–2 allocation permissible, given that legislatures have the authority to engage in a certain degree of partisan gerrymandering? Which seats should be packed and which cracked? Or if the goal is as many competitive districts as possible, how close does the split need to be for the district to be considered competitive? Presumably not all districts could qualify, so how to choose? Even assuming the court knew which version of fairness to be looking for, there are no discernible and manageable standards for deciding whether there has been a violation. The questions are "unguided and ill-suited to the development of judicial standards," and "results from one gerrymandering case to the next would likely be disparate and inconsistent."

Appellees contend that if we can adjudicate one-person, one-vote claims, we can also assess partisan gerrymandering claims. But the one-person, one-vote rule is relatively easy to administer as a matter of math. The same cannot be said of partisan gerrymandering claims, because the Constitution supplies no objective measure for assessing whether a districting map treats a political party fairly. It hardly follows from the principle that each person must have an equal say in the election of representatives that a person is entitled to have his political party achieve representation in some way commensurate to its share of statewide support. * * *

Nor do our racial gerrymandering cases provide an appropriate standard for assessing partisan gerrymandering. "[N]othing in our case law compels the conclusion that racial and political gerrymanders are subject to precisely the same constitutional scrutiny. In fact, our country's long and persistent history of racial discrimination in voting—as well as our Fourteenth Amendment jurisprudence, which always has reserved the strictest scrutiny for discrimination on the basis of race—would seem to compel the opposite conclusion." Unlike partisan gerrymandering claims, a racial gerrymandering claim does not ask for a fair share of political power and influence, with all the justiciability conundrums that entails. It asks instead for the elimination of a racial classification. A partisan gerrymandering claim cannot ask for the elimination of partisanship.

Appellees and the dissent propose a number of "tests" for evaluating partisan gerrymandering claims, but none meets the need for a limited and precise standard that is judicially discernible and manageable. And none provides a solid grounding for judges to take the extraordinary step of reallocating power and influence between political parties. * * *

The dissent proposes using a State's own districting criteria as a neutral baseline from which to measure how extreme a partisan gerrymander is. The dissent would have us line up all the possible maps drawn using those criteria according to the partisan distribution they would produce. Distance from the "median" map would indicate whether a particular districting plan harms supporter of one party to an unconstitutional extent.

As an initial matter, it does not make sense to use criteria that will vary from State to State and year to year as the baseline for determining whether a gerrymander violates the Federal Constitution. The degree of partisan advantage that the Constitution tolerates should not turn on criteria offered by the gerrymanderers themselves. It is easy to imagine how different criteria could move the median map toward different partisan distributions. As a result, the same map could be constitutional or not depending solely on what the mapmakers said they set out to do. That possibility illustrates that the dissent's proposed constitutional test is indeterminate and arbitrary.

Even if we were to accept the dissent's proposed baseline, it would return us to "the original unanswerable question (How much political motivation and effect is too much?)." Would twenty percent away from the median map be okay? Forty percent? Sixty percent? Why or why not? (We appreciate that the dissent finds all the unanswerable questions annoying, but it seems a useful way to make the point.) The dissent's answer says it all: "This much is too much." That is not even trying to articulate a standard or rule.

The dissent argues that there are other instances in law where matters of degree are left to the courts. True enough. But those instances typically involve constitutional or statutory provisions or common law confining and guiding the exercise of judicial discretion. For example, the dissent cites the need to determine "substantial anticompetitive effect[s]" in antitrust law. That language, however, grew out of the Sherman Act, understood from the beginning to have its "origin in the common law" and to be "familiar in the law of this country prior to and at the time of the adoption of the [A]ct." Judges began with a significant body of law about what constituted a legal violation. In other cases, the pertinent statutory terms draw meaning from related provisions or statutory context. Here, on the other hand, the Constitution provides no basis whatever to guide the exercise of judicial discretion. Common experience gives content to terms such as "substantial risk" or "substantial harm," but the same cannot be said of substantial deviation from a median map. There is no way to tell whether the prohibited deviation from that map should kick in at 25 percent or 75 percent or some other point. The only provision in the Constitution that specifically addresses the matter assigns it to the political branches. See Art. I, § 4, cl. 1.

The North Carolina District Court further concluded that the 2016 Plan violated the Elections Clause and Article I, § 2. We are unconvinced by that novel approach.

Article I, § 2, provides that "[t]he House of Representatives shall be composed of Members chosen every second Year by the People of the several States." The Elections Clause provides that "[t]he Times, Places and Manner of holding Elections for Senators and Representatives, shall be prescribed in each State by the Legislature thereof; but the Congress may at any time by Law make or alter such Regulations, except as to the Places of choosing Senators." Art. I, § 4, cl. 1.

The District Court concluded that the 2016 Plan exceeded the North Carolina General Assembly's Elections Clause authority because, among other reasons, "the Elections Clause did not empower State legislatures to disfavor the interests of supporters of a particular candidate or party in drawing congressional districts." 318 F.Supp.3d at 937. The court further held that partisan gerrymandering infringes the right of "the People" to select their representatives. Before the District Court's decision, no court had reached a similar conclusion. In fact, the plurality in *Vieth* concluded— without objection from any other Justice—that neither § 2 nor § 4 of Article I "provides a judicially enforceable limit on the political considerations that the States and Congress may take into account when districting."

The District Court nevertheless asserted that partisan gerrymanders violate "the core principle of [our] republican government" preserved in Art. I, § 2, "namely, that the voters should choose their representatives, not the other way around." That seems like an objection more properly grounded in the Guarantee Clause of Article IV, § 4, which "guarantee[s] to every State in [the] Union a Republican Form of Government." This Court has several times concluded, however, that the Guarantee Clause does not provide the basis for a justiciable claim.

Excessive partisanship in districting leads to results that reasonably seem unjust. But the fact that such gerrymandering is "incompatible with democratic principles," does not mean that the solution lies with the federal judiciary. We conclude that partisan gerrymandering claims present political questions beyond the reach of the federal courts. Federal judges have no license to reallocate political power between the two major political parties, with no plausible grant of authority in the Constitution, and no legal standards to limit and direct their decisions.

JUSTICE KAGAN, with whom **JUSTICES GINSBURG**, **BREYER** and **SOTOMAYOR** join, dissenting.

The majority gives two reasons for thinking that the adjudication of partisan gerrymandering claims is beyond judicial capabilities. First and foremost, the majority says, it cannot find a neutral baseline—one not based on contestable notions of political fairness—from which to measure injury. According to the majority, "[p]artisan gerrymandering claims invariably sound in a desire for proportional representation." But the Constitution does not mandate proportional representation. So, the majority contends, resolving those claims "inevitably" would require courts to decide what is "fair" in the context of districting. They would have "to make their own political judgment about how much representation particular political parties *deserve*" and "to rearrange the challenged districts to achieve that end." And second, the majority argues that even after establishing a baseline, a court would have no way to answer "the determinative question: 'How much is too much?'" No "discernible and manageable" standard is available, the majority claims—and so courts could willy-nilly become embroiled in fixing every districting plan.

I'll give the majority this one—and important—thing: It identifies some dangers everyone should want to avoid. Judges should not be apportioning political power based on their own vision of electoral fairness, whether proportional representation or any other. And judges should not be striking down maps left, right, and center, on the view that every smidgen of politics is a smidgen too much. Respect for state legislative processes—and restraint in the exercise of judicial authority—counsels' intervention in only egregious cases.

But in throwing up its hands, the majority misses something under its nose: What it says can't be done *has* been done. Over the past several years, federal courts across the country—including, but not exclusively, in the decisions below—have largely converged on a standard for adjudicating partisan gerrymandering claims (striking down both Democratic and Republican districting plans in the process). And that standard does what the majority says is impossible. The standard does not use any judge-made conception of electoral fairness—either proportional representation or any other; instead, it takes as its baseline a State's *own* criteria of fairness, apart from partisan gain. And by requiring plaintiffs to make difficult showings relating to both purpose and effects, the standard invalidates the most extreme, but only the most extreme, partisan gerrymanders. * * *

Start with the standard the lower courts used. * * * As many legal standards do, that test has three parts: (1) intent; (2) effects; and (3) causation. First, the plaintiffs challenging a districting plan must prove that state officials' "predominant purpose" in drawing a district's lines was to "entrench [their party] in power" by diluting the votes of citizens favoring its rival. Second, the plaintiffs must establish that the lines drawn in fact have the intended effect by "substantially" diluting their votes. And third, if the plaintiffs make those showings, the State must come up with a legitimate, non-partisan justification to save its map. If you are a lawyer, you know that this test looks utterly ordinary. It is the sort of thing courts work with every day.

Turn now to the test's application. First, did the North Carolina and Maryland districters have the predominant purpose of entrenching their own party in power? Here, the two District Courts catalogued the overwhelming direct evidence that they did. To remind you of some highlights, North Carolina's redistricting committee used "Partisan Advantage" as an official criterion for drawing district lines. And from the first to the last, that committee's chair (along with his mapmaker) acted to ensure a 10–3 partisan split, whatever the statewide vote, because he thought that "electing Republicans is better than electing Democrats." For their part, Maryland's Democrats—the Governor, senior Congressman, and State Senate President alike—openly admitted to a single driving purpose: flip the Sixth District from Republican to Democratic. They did not blanch from moving some 700,000 voters into new districts (when one-person-one-vote rules required relocating just 10,000) for that reason and that reason alone.

The majority's response to the District Courts' purpose analysis is discomfiting. The majority does not contest the lower courts' findings; how could it? Instead, the majority says that state officials' intent to entrench their party in power is perfectly "permissible," even when it is the predominant factor in drawing district lines. But that is wrong. True enough, that the intent to inject "political considerations" into districting may not raise any constitutional concerns. * * * But when political actors have a specific and predominant intent to entrench themselves in power by manipulating district lines, that goes too far. * * *

On to the second step of the analysis, where the plaintiffs must prove that the districting plan substantially dilutes their votes. The majority fails to discuss most of the evidence the District Courts relied on to find that the plaintiffs had done so. But that evidence—particularly from North Carolina—is the key to understanding both the problem these cases present and the solution to it they offer. The evidence reveals just how bad the two gerrymanders were (in case you had any doubts). And it shows how the same technologies and data that today facilitate extreme partisan gerrymanders also enable courts to discover them, by exposing just how much they dilute votes.

Consider the sort of evidence used in North Carolina first. There, the plaintiffs demonstrated the districting plan's effects mostly by relying on what might be called the "extreme outlier approach." (Here's a spoiler: the State's plan was one.) The approach—which also has recently been used in Michigan and Ohio litigation—begins by using advanced computing technology to randomly generate a large collection of districting plans that incorporate the State's physical and political geography and meet its declared districting criteria, *except* for partisan gain. For each of those maps, the method then uses actual precinct-level votes from past elections to determine a partisan outcome (*i.e.*, the number of Democratic and Republican seats that map produces). Suppose we now have 1,000 maps, each with a partisan outcome attached to it. We can line up those maps on a continuum—the most favorable to Republicans on one end, the most favorable to Democrats on the other. We can then find the median outcome—that is, the outcome smack dab in the center—in a world with no partisan manipulation. And we can see where the State's actual plan falls on the spectrum—at or near the median or way out on one of the tails? The further out on the tail, the more extreme the partisan distortion and the more significant the vote dilution.

Using that approach, the North Carolina plaintiffs offered a boatload of alternative districting plans—all showing that the State's map was an out-out-out-outlier. One expert produced 3,000 maps, adhering in the way described above to the districting criteria that the North Carolina redistricting committee had used, other than partisan advantage. To calculate the partisan outcome of those maps, the expert also used the same election data (a composite of seven elections) that Hofeller had employed when devising the North Carolina plan in the first instance. The results were, shall we say, striking. Every single one of the 3,000 maps would have produced at least one more Democratic House Member than the State's actual map, and 77% would have elected three or four more. A second expert obtained essentially the same results with maps conforming to more generic districting criteria (*e.g.,* compactness and contiguity of districts). Over 99% of that expert's 24,518 simulations would have led to the election of at least one more Democrat, and over 70% would have led to two or three more. Based on those and other findings, the District Court determined that the North Carolina plan substantially dilutes the plaintiffs' votes.

* * * Contrary to the majority's suggestion, the District Courts did not have to—and in fact did not—choose among competing visions of electoral fairness. That is because they did not try to compare the State's actual map to an "ideally fair" one (whether based on proportional representation or some other criterion). Instead, they looked at the difference between what the State did and what the State would have done if politicians hadn't been intent on partisan gain. * * * Under their approach, in other words, the State selected its own fairness baseline in the form of its other districting criteria. All the courts did was determine how far the State had gone off that track because of its politicians' effort to entrench themselves in office.

The North Carolina litigation well illustrates the point. The thousands of randomly generated maps I've mentioned formed the core of the plaintiffs' case that the North Carolina plan was an "extreme[ ] outlier." Those maps took the State's political landscape as a given. In North Carolina, for example, Democratic voters are highly concentrated in cities. That fact was built into all the maps; it became part of the baseline. On top of that, the maps took the State's legal landscape as a given. * * * The point is that the assemblage of maps, reflecting the characteristics and judgments of the State itself, creates a neutral baseline from which to assess whether partisanship has run amok. Extreme outlier as to what? As to the other maps the State could have produced given its unique political geography and its chosen districting criteria. *Not* as to the maps a judge, with his own view of electoral fairness, could have dreamed up. * * *

The majority's sole response misses the point. According to the majority, "it does not make sense to use" a State's own (non-partisan) districting criteria as the baseline from which to measure partisan gerrymandering because those criteria "will vary from State to State and year to year." But that is a virtue, not a vice—a feature, not a bug. Using the criteria the State itself has chosen at the relevant time prevents any judicial predilections from affecting the analysis—exactly what the majority claims it wants. At the same time, using those criteria enables a court to measure just what it should: the extent to which the pursuit of partisan advantage—by these legislators at this moment—has distorted the State's districting decisions. Sure, different non-partisan criteria could result, as the majority notes, in different partisan distributions to serve as the baseline. But that in itself raises no issue: Everyone agrees that state officials using non-partisan criteria (*e.g.,* must counties be kept together? should districts be compact?) have wide latitude in districting. The problem arises only when legislators or mapmakers substantially deviate from the baseline distribution by manipulating district lines for partisan gain. So once again, the majority's analysis falters because it equates the demand to eliminate partisan gerrymandering with a demand for a single partisan distribution—the one reflecting proportional representation. But those two demands are different, and only the former is at issue here.

The majority's "how much is too much" critique fares no better than its neutrality argument. How about the following for a first-cut answer: This much is too much? By any measure, a map that produces a greater partisan skew than any of 3,000 randomly generated maps (all with the State's political geography and districting criteria built in) reflects "too much" partisanship. Think about what I just said: The absolute worst of 3,001 possible maps. The *only one* that could produce a 10–3 partisan split even as Republicans got a bare majority of the statewide vote. And again: How much is too much? This much is too much: A map that without any evident non-partisan districting reason (to the contrary) shifted the composition of a district from 47% Republicans and 36% Democrats to 33% Republicans and 42% Democrats. A map that in 2011 was responsible for the largest partisan swing of a congressional district in the country. Even the majority acknowledges that "[t]hese cases involve blatant examples of partisanship driving districting decisions." If the majority had done nothing else, it could have set the line here. How much is too much? At the least, any gerrymanders as bad as these.

This Court has long understood that it has a special responsibility to remedy violations of constitutional rights resulting from politicians' districting decisions. Over 50 years ago, we committed to providing judicial review in that sphere, recognizing as we established the one-person-one-vote rule that "our oath and our office require no less.". Of course, our oath and our office require us to vindicate all constitutional rights. But the need for judicial review is at its most urgent in cases like these. "For here, politicians' incentives conflict with voters' interests, leaving citizens without any political remedy for their constitutional harms."). Those harms arise because politicians want to stay in office. No one can look to them for effective relief. * * *

[G]errymandering is, as so many Justices have emphasized before, anti-democratic in the most profound sense. In our government, "all political power flows from the people." And that means, as Alexander Hamilton once said, "that the people should choose whom they please to govern them." 2 *Debates on the Constitution* 257 (J. Elliot ed. 1891). But in Maryland and North Carolina they cannot do so. In Maryland, election in and election out, there are 7 Democrats and 1 Republican in the congressional delegation. In North Carolina, however the political winds blow, there are 10 Republicans and 3 Democrats. Is it conceivable that someday voters will be able to break out of that prefabricated box? Sure. But everything possible has been done to make that hard. To create a world in which power does not flow from the people because they do not choose their governors.

Of all times to abandon the Court's duty to declare the law, this was not the one. The practices challenged in these cases imperil our system of government. Part of the Court's role in that system is to defend its foundations. None is more important than free and fair elections. With respect but deep sadness, I dissent.

NOTES ON RUCHO

1. *Judicially Unmanageable Standards?* Is the test suggested by the dissent truly vaguer or less rooted in the Constitution than tests the Court has used in other contexts? For instance, in the one-person, one-vote context, the Court has not required mathematical equality but instead has given legislatures reasonable leeway to consider traditional voting factors. Or consider the middle-tier scrutiny applied in some Equal Protection and First Amendment contexts, which also involve judgment calls by courts. Does the majority make a persuasive argument that the dissent's standard is qualitatively different than those standards? Or is the real thrust of the majority opinion that the need for clear, neutral standards is heightened in this context because of the inherently political nature of the issues? Does *Rucho* represent the triumph of Justice Frankfurter's desire to stay out of the "political thicket"?

2. *Congressional Remedies.* The majority suggests that as to federal elections, Congress may have the power to limit political gerrymandering. (Of course, the political difficulty is that the House is elected from districts that are shaped by state gerrymandering.) Imagine, for instance, a federal statute prohibiting state maps that are in the five ten percent of partisanship using the dissent's approach. Would such a federal statute be constitutional?

The two available sources of power seem to be the Guaranty Clause and section 5 of the Fourteenth Amendment. The extent of congressional power under the Guaranty Clause remains unclear, as is whether a court could review the exercise of that power. As to the Fourteenth Amendment, *Rucho* creates a bit of the puzzle. Assuming that extreme gerrymandering does violate the Fourteenth Amendment but that there is no judicially manageable standard, there must be "congruence and proportionality" between a statute and the underlying constitutional violation in order to satisfy section 5. But how can that test be applied unless the court is able to identify those underlying violations when it sees them? To put it another way, is the scope of congressional power to address political gerrymandering itself a nonjusticiable political question?

3. *The Future of Process Theory.* In *Rucho*, the Court seems to have abandoned or reached the limits of its role in ensuring the representativeness of the political process. How should its acceptance of limits to representative democracy process bear on constitutional doctrine more generally? Should the

Court's willingness to overturn legislative decisions be affected by flaws in the representative nature of legislatures, as footnote four of *Carolene Products* and the work of John Hart Ely would suggest?

SECTION 2. "CASES" OR "CONTROVERSIES"

Page 1413. Insert the following before the Note heading:

CALIFORNIA V. TEXAS
593 U.S. ___, 141 S.Ct. 2104, 210 L.Ed.2d 230 (2021)

[This is a sequel to *National Federation of Independent Business v. Sebelius* on p. 1053 of the casebook. In the case, the Supreme Court upheld the "individual mandate" in the Affordable Care Act as an exercise of the taxing power. Subsequently, Congress repealed the provision imposing the penalty for violation of the mandate. As a result, although the statute still contained language in § 5000A(a) stating that individuals must purchase insurance, that language no longer had any legal consequences. In litigation later joined by two individuals, Texas and seventeen other states claimed that the individual mandate was unconstitutional because it was no longer a valid exercise of the taxing power, that it was inseverable from the remainder of the statute, and that therefore the entire Affordable Care Act was invalid.]

JUSTICE BREYER delivered the opinion of the Court.

* * * We proceed no further than standing. The Constitution gives federal courts the power to adjudicate only genuine "Cases" and "Controversies." Art. III, § 2. That power includes the requirement that litigants have standing. A plaintiff has standing only if he can "allege personal injury fairly traceable to the defendant's allegedly unlawful conduct and likely to be redressed by the requested relief. Neither the individual nor the state plaintiffs have shown that the injury they will suffer or have suffered is "fairly traceable" to the "allegedly unlawful conduct" of which they complain.

We begin with the two individual plaintiffs. They claim a particularized individual harm in the form of payments they have made and will make each month to carry the minimum essential coverage that § 5000A(a) requires. The individual plaintiffs point to the statutory language, which, they say, commands them to buy health insurance. But even if we assume that this pocketbook injury satisfies the injury element of Article III standing, the plaintiffs nevertheless fail to satisfy the traceability requirement.

Their problem lies in the fact that the statutory provision, while it tells them to obtain that coverage, has no means of enforcement. With the penalty zeroed out, the IRS can no longer seek a penalty from those who fail to comply. Because of this, there is no possible Government action that is causally connected to the plaintiffs' injury—the costs of purchasing health insurance. Or to put the matter conversely, that injury is not "fairly traceable" to any "allegedly unlawful conduct" of which the plaintiffs complain. They have not pointed to any way in which the defendants, the Commissioner of Internal Revenue and the Secretary of Health and Human Services, will act to enforce § 5000A(a). They have not shown how any other federal employees could do so either. In a word, they have not shown that any kind of Government action or conduct has caused or will cause the injury they attribute to § 5000A(a). * * *

To consider the matter from the point of view of another standing requirement, namely, redressability, makes clear that the statutory language alone is not sufficient. To determine whether an injury is redressable, a court will consider the relationship between "the judicial relief requested" and the "injury" suffered. The plaintiffs here sought injunctive relief and a declaratory judgment. The injunctive relief, however, concerned the Act's other provisions that they say are inseverable from the minimum essential coverage requirement. The relief they sought in respect to the only provision they attack as unconstitutional—the minimum essential coverage provision—is declaratory relief, namely, a judicial statement that the provision they attacked is unconstitutional.

* * * The Declaratory Judgment Act, 28 U.S.C. § 2201, alone does not provide a court with jurisdiction. At a minimum, this means that the dispute must "be 'real and substantial' and 'admit of specific relief through a decree of a conclusive character, as distinguished from an opinion advising what the law would be upon a hypothetical state of facts.' Thus, to satisfy Article III standing, we must look elsewhere to find a remedy that will redress the individual plaintiffs' injuries.

What is that relief? The plaintiffs did not obtain damages. Nor, as we just said, did the plaintiffs obtain an injunction in respect to the provision they attack as unconstitutional. But, more than that: How could they have sought any such injunction? The provision is unenforceable. There is no one, and nothing, to enjoin. They cannot enjoin the Secretary of Health and Human Services, because he has no power to enforce § 5000A(a) against them. And they do not claim that they might enjoin Congress. In these circumstances, injunctive relief could amount to no more than a declaration that the statutory provision they attack is unconstitutional, i.e., a declaratory judgment. But once again, that is the very kind of relief that cannot alone supply jurisdiction otherwise absent.

The matter is not simply technical. To find standing here to attack an unenforceable statutory provision would allow a federal court to issue what would amount to "an advisory opinion without the possibility of any judicial relief." It would threaten to grant unelected judges a general authority to conduct oversight of decisions of the elected branches of Government. * * *

Next, we turn to the state plaintiffs. We conclude that Texas and the other state plaintiffs have similarly failed to show that they have alleged an "injury fairly traceable to the defendant's allegedly unlawful conduct." They claim two kinds of pocketbook injuries. First, they allege an indirect injury in the form of the increased use of (and therefore cost to) state-operated medical insurance programs. Second, they claim a direct injury resulting from a variety of increased administrative and related expenses required, they say, by the minimum essential coverage provision, along with other provisions of the Act that, they add, are inextricably "'interwoven'" with it.

First, the state plaintiffs claim that the minimum essential coverage provision has led state residents subject to it to enroll in state-operated or state-sponsored insurance programs such as Medicaid the Children's Health Insurance Program (CHIP), and health insurance programs for state employees. The state plaintiffs say they must pay a share of the costs of serving those new enrollees. As with the individual plaintiffs, the States also have failed to show how this injury is directly traceable to any actual or possible unlawful Government conduct in enforcing § 5000A(a). That alone is enough to show that they, like the individual plaintiffs, lack Article III standing.

But setting aside that pure issue of law, we need only examine the initial factual premise of their claim to uncover another fatal weakness: The state plaintiffs have failed to show that the challenged minimum essential coverage provision, without any prospect of penalty, will harm them by leading more individuals to enroll in these programs.

We have said that, where a causal relation between injury and challenged action depends upon the decision of an independent third party (here an individual's decision to enroll in, say, Medicaid), "standing is not precluded, but it is ordinarily 'substantially more difficult' to establish." To satisfy that burden, the plaintiff must show at the least "that third parties will likely react in predictable ways." And, "at the summary judgment stage, such a party can no longer rest on . . . mere allegations, but must set forth . . . specific facts" that adequately support their contention. The state plaintiffs have not done so.

The programs to which the state plaintiffs point offer their recipients many benefits that have nothing to do with the minimum essential coverage provision of § 5000A(a). Given these benefits, neither logic nor intuition suggests that the presence of the minimum essential coverage requirement would lead an individual to enroll in one of those programs that its absence would lead them to ignore. A penalty might have led some inertia-bound individuals to enroll. But without a penalty, what incentive could the provision provide?

The evidence that the state plaintiffs introduced in the District Court does not show the contrary. That evidence consists of 21 statements (from state officials) about how new enrollees will increase the costs of state health insurance programs, along with one statement taken from a 2017 Congressional Budget Office (CBO) Report. [The Court found all of these statements too conclusory to satisfy the requirement of traceability.]

Unsurprisingly, the States have not demonstrated that an unenforceable mandate will cause their residents to enroll in valuable benefits programs that they would otherwise forgo. It would require far stronger evidence than the States have offered here to support their counterintuitive theory of standing, which rests on a "highly attenuated chain of possibilities."

The state plaintiffs add that § 5000A(a)'s minimum essential coverage provision also causes them to incur additional costs directly. They point to the costs of providing beneficiaries of state health plans with information about their health insurance coverage, as well as the cost of furnishing the IRS with that related information.

The problem with these claims, however, is that other provisions of Act, not the minimum essential coverage provision, impose these other requirements. Nothing in the text of these form provisions suggests that they would not operate without § 5000A(a). To show that the minimum essential coverage requirement is unconstitutional would not show that enforcement of any of these other provisions violates the Constitution. The state plaintiffs do not claim the contrary. The Government's conduct in question is therefore not "fairly traceable" to enforcement of the "allegedly unlawful" provision of which the plaintiffs complain—§ 5000A(a).

The state plaintiffs complain of other pocketbook injuries. They say, for example, that, in order to avoid a "substantial tax penalty," they will have to "offer their full-time employees (and qualified dependents) minimum essential coverage under an eligible employer-sponsored plan." They say that the Act's insistence that they "expand Medicaid eligibility" has led to "increas[ed] . . . Medicaid expenditures." And they argue that "the [Act]'s vast and complex rules and regulations" will require additional expenditures. They seem to argue that they will have to pay more to expand coverage for employees who work 30–39 hours per week, and for those who become too old to remain in foster care.

Again, the problem for the state plaintiffs is that these other provisions also operate independently of § 5000A(a). At most, those provisions pick up only § 5000A(f)'s definition of minimum essential coverage in related subsections. No one claims these other provisions violate the Constitution. Rather, the state plaintiffs attack the constitutionality of only the minimum essential coverage provision. They have not alleged that they have suffered an "injury fairly traceable to the defendant's allegedly unlawful conduct."

* * *

For these reasons, we conclude that the plaintiffs in this suit failed to show a concrete, particularized injury fairly traceable to the defendants' conduct in enforcing the specific statutory provision they attack as unconstitutional. They have failed to show that they have standing to attack as unconstitutional the Act's minimum essential coverage provision. Therefore, we reverse the Fifth Circuit's judgment in respect to standing, vacate the judgment, and remand the case with instructions to dismiss.

NOTES ON CALIFORNIA V. TEXAS

1. *Severability and Remedies.* The Court says that the individual plaintiffs do not have standing because they have no possible remedy: since the individual mandate is unenforceable, there is no one they could sue to halt enforcement. That being the case, there is no case or controversy between them and the government. The states, on the other hand, do not have standing because their injuries would presumably be the same even if the individual mandate didn't exist.

2. *Severability and Traceability.* The majority viewed severability as a remedial question. That is, in the majority's view, if a plaintiff is entitled to a remedy directed toward Provision 1, the Court then expands relief to include Provision 2 because Congress would not want Provision 2 to remain operative. Since none of the plaintiffs were injured by Provision 1 (the mandate), none of them could get relief against that provision, and hence none could ask for broader relief.

In dissent, Justice Alito (joined by Justice Gorsuch) maintained a different theory of severability. On that theory, Provision 2 is simply inoperative, as if the statute said: "Provision 2 shall apply only if Provision A is constitutional." Under Alito's theory, someone who is injured by Provision 2 can bring a claim that it is inoperative because Provision A is unconstitutional. Because Congress has made Provision B conditional on the constitutionality of Provision 1, a court must necessarily determine that issue in order to resolve the plaintiff's claim that Provision 2 is inoperative. Alito argued that previous cases adopted his view of standing. The majority declined to consider this argument because it was made only belatedly, and then by the federal government as amicus rather than by the plaintiffs. Under Alito's view, does anyone who has been impacted by any provision of a law have standing to challenge every other provision so long as there's a possibility that a court might find them inseverable?

3. *Congressional Power over Standing.* The logic of Alito's argument is clear, but wouldn't it give Congress the power to create standing simply by adding conditions to statutory provisions? Suppose Congress passed a law after

Clapper adding a dollar to the taxes of every federal taxpayer "conditional on the constitutionality of the government's surveillance program." Or if that seems too artificial, suppose Congress levied a one dollar tax on all telephone users to support the surveillance program challenged in *Clapper*? Is the payment of the tax "fairly traceable" to the surveillance program? (This situation doesn't seem to fall under the general rule against taxpayer standing, but if that concerns you, assume instead that Congress told phone companies to charge all customers an extra dollar to cover any additional costs that a company might have due to the surveillance program.) Would Alito agree that Congress can extend standing in this way? We return to the question of congressional control over standing below.

Page 1418. Replace *Spokeo* and the Notes after the Case with the following:

TransUnion LLC v. Ramirez

594 U.S. ___, 141 S.Ct. 2190, 210 L.Ed.2d 568 (2021)

JUSTICE KAVANAUGH delivered the opinion of the Court.

To have Article III standing to sue in federal court, plaintiffs must demonstrate, among other things, that they suffered a concrete harm. No concrete harm, no standing. Central to assessing concreteness is whether the asserted harm has a "close relationship" to a harm traditionally recognized as providing a basis for a lawsuit in American courts—such as physical harm, monetary harm, or various intangible harms including (as relevant here) reputational harm. *Spokeo, Inc. v. Robins*, 578 U.S. 330, 340–341 (2016).

In this case, a class of 8,185 individuals sued TransUnion, a credit reporting agency, in federal court under the Fair Credit Reporting Act. The plaintiffs claimed that TransUnion failed to use reasonable procedures to ensure the accuracy of their credit files, as maintained internally by TransUnion. For 1,853 of the class members, TransUnion provided misleading credit reports to third-party businesses. We conclude that those 1,853 class members have demonstrated concrete reputational harm and thus have Article III standing to sue on the reasonable-procedures claim. The internal credit files of the other 6,332 class members were not provided to third-party businesses during the relevant time period. We conclude that those 6,332 class members have not demonstrated concrete harm and thus lack Article III standing to sue on the reasonable-procedures claim.

In two other claims, all 8,185 class members complained about formatting defects in certain mailings sent to them by TransUnion. But the class members other than the named plaintiff Sergio Ramirez have not demonstrated that the alleged formatting errors caused them any concrete harm. Therefore, except for Ramirez, the class members do not have standing as to those two claims. * * *

In 1970, Congress passed and President Nixon signed the Fair Credit Reporting Act. The Act seeks to promote "fair and accurate credit reporting" and to protect consumer privacy. To achieve those goals, the Act regulates the consumer reporting agencies that compile and disseminate personal information about consumers.

The Act "imposes a host of requirements concerning the creation and use of consumer reports." Three of the Act's requirements are relevant to this case. First, the Act requires consumer reporting agencies to "follow reasonable procedures to assure maximum possible accuracy" in consumer reports. Second, the Act provides that consumer reporting agencies must, upon request, disclose to the consumer "[a]ll information in the consumer's file at the time of the request." Third, the Act compels consumer reporting agencies to "provide to a consumer, with each written disclosure by the agency to the consumer," a "summary of rights" prepared by the Consumer Financial Protection Bureau.

The Act creates a cause of action for consumers to sue and recover damages for certain violations. The Act provides: "Any person who willfully fails to comply with any requirement imposed under this subchapter with respect to any consumer is liable to that consumer" for actual damages or for statutory damages not less than $100 and not more than $1,000, as well as for punitive damages and attorney's fees. § 1681n(a).

TransUnion is one of the "Big Three" credit reporting agencies, along with Equifax and Experian. As a credit reporting agency, TransUnion compiles personal and financial information about individual consumers to create consumer reports. TransUnion then sells those consumer reports for use by entities such as banks, landlords, and car dealerships that request information about the creditworthiness of individual consumers.

Beginning in 2002, TransUnion introduced an add-on product called OFAC Name Screen Alert. OFAC is the U. S. Treasury Department's Office of Foreign Assets Control. OFAC maintains a list of "specially designated nationals" who threaten America's national security. Individuals on the OFAC list are terrorists, drug traffickers, or other serious criminals. It is generally unlawful to transact business with any person on the list. TransUnion created the OFAC Name Screen Alert to help businesses avoid transacting with individuals on OFAC's list.

When this litigation arose, Name Screen worked in the following way: When a business opted into the Name Screen service, TransUnion would conduct its ordinary credit check of the consumer, and it would also use third-party software to compare the consumer's name against the OFAC list. If the consumer's first and last name matched the first and last name of an individual on OFAC's list, then TransUnion would place an alert on the credit report indicating that the consumer's name was a "potential match" to a name on the OFAC list. TransUnion did not compare any data other than first and last names. Unsurprisingly, TransUnion's Name Screen product generated many false positives. Thousands of law-abiding Americans happen to share a first and last name with one of the terrorists, drug traffickers, or serious criminals on OFAC's list of specially designated nationals.

Sergio Ramirez learned the hard way that he is one such individual. On February 27, 2011, Ramirez visited a Nissan dealership in Dublin, California, seeking to buy a Nissan Maxima. Ramirez was accompanied by his wife and his father-in-law. After Ramirez and his wife selected a color and negotiated a price, the dealership ran a credit check on both Ramirez and his wife. Ramirez's credit report, produced by TransUnion, contained the following alert: "***OFAC ADVISOR ALERT—INPUT NAME MATCHES NAME ON THE OFAC DATABASE." App. 84. A Nissan salesman told Ramirez that Nissan would not sell the car to him because his name was on a " 'terrorist list.' " Ramirez's wife had to purchase the car in her own name.

The next day, Ramirez called TransUnion and requested a copy of his credit file. TransUnion sent Ramirez a mailing that same day that included his credit file and the statutorily required summary of rights prepared by the CFPB. The mailing did not mention the OFAC alert in Ramirez's file. The following day, TransUnion sent Ramirez a second mailing—a letter alerting him that his name was considered a potential match to names on the OFAC list. The second mailing did not include an additional copy of the summary of rights. Concerned about the mailings, Ramirez consulted a lawyer and ultimately canceled a planned trip to Mexico. TransUnion eventually removed the OFAC alert from Ramirez's file. * * *

[Ramirez sued TransUnion. He also sought to certify a class of all people in the United States to whom TransUnion sent a mailing during the period from January 1, 2011, to July 26, 2011, that was like the second mailing Ramirez received. TransUnion opposed certification. The district court certified the class.]

Before trial, the parties stipulated that the class contained 8,185 members, including Ramirez. The parties also stipulated that only 1,853 members of the class (including Ramirez) had their credit reports disseminated by TransUnion to potential creditors during the period from January 1, 2011, to July 26, 2011. * * *

The question in this case focuses on the Article III requirement that the plaintiff's injury in fact be "concrete"—that is, "real, and not abstract."

What makes a harm concrete for purposes of Article III? As a general matter, the Court has explained that "history and tradition offer a meaningful guide to the types of cases that Article III empowers federal courts to consider." And with respect to the concrete-harm requirement in particular, this Court's opinion in Spokeo v. Robins indicated that courts should assess whether the alleged injury to the plaintiff has a "close relationship" to a harm "traditionally" recognized as providing a basis for a lawsuit in American courts. That inquiry asks whether plaintiffs have identified a close historical or common-law analogue for their asserted injury. Spokeo does not require an exact duplicate in American history and tradition. But Spokeo is not an open-ended invitation for federal courts to loosen Article III based on contemporary, evolving beliefs about what kinds of suits should be heard in federal courts.

As Spokeo explained, certain harms readily qualify as concrete injuries under Article III. The most obvious are traditional tangible harms, such as physical harms and monetary harms. If a defendant has caused physical or monetary injury to the plaintiff, the plaintiff has suffered a concrete injury in fact under Article III.

Various intangible harms can also be concrete. Chief among them are injuries with a close relationship to harms traditionally recognized as providing a basis for lawsuits in American courts. Those include, for example, reputational harms, disclosure of private information, and intrusion upon seclusion. And those traditional harms may also include harms specified by the Constitution itself. [Citing a free speech case and a free exercise case.]

In determining whether a harm is sufficiently concrete to qualify as an injury in fact, the Court in Spokeo said that Congress's views may be "instructive." Courts must afford due respect to Congress's decision to impose a statutory prohibition or obligation on a defendant, and to grant a plaintiff a cause of action to sue over the defendant's violation of that statutory prohibition or obligation. In that way, Congress may "elevate to the status of legally cognizable injuries concrete, de facto injuries that were previously inadequate in law." But even though "Congress may 'elevate' harms that 'exist' in the real world before Congress recognized them to actionable legal status, it may not simply enact an injury into existence, using its lawmaking power to transform something that is not remotely harmful into something that is."

Importantly, this Court has rejected the proposition that "a plaintiff automatically satisfies the injury-in-fact requirement whenever a statute grants a person a statutory right and purports to authorize that person to sue to vindicate that right." As the Court emphasized in Spokeo, "Article III standing requires a concrete injury even in the context of a statutory violation."

Congress's creation of a statutory prohibition or obligation and a cause of action does not relieve courts of their responsibility to independently decide whether a plaintiff has suffered a concrete harm under Article III any more than, for example, Congress's enactment of a law regulating speech relieves courts of their responsibility to independently decide whether the law violates the First Amendment.

For standing purposes, therefore, an important difference exists between (i) a plaintiff's statutory cause of action to sue a defendant over the defendant's violation of federal law, and (ii) a plaintiff's suffering concrete harm because of the defendant's violation of federal law. Congress may enact legal prohibitions and obligations. And Congress may create causes of action for plaintiffs to sue defendants who violate those legal prohibitions or obligations. But under Article III, an injury in law is not an injury in fact. Only those plaintiffs who have been concretely harmed by a defendant's statutory violation may sue that private defendant over that violation in federal court. As then-Judge Barrett succinctly summarized, "Article III grants federal courts the power to redress harms that defendants cause plaintiffs, not a freewheeling power to hold defendants accountable for legal infractions."

To appreciate how the Article III "concrete harm" principle operates in practice, consider two different hypothetical plaintiffs. Suppose first that a Maine citizen's land is polluted by a nearby factory. She sues the company, alleging that it violated a federal environmental law and damaged her property. Suppose also that a second plaintiff in Hawaii files a federal lawsuit alleging that the same company in Maine violated that same environmental law by polluting land in Maine. The violation did not personally harm the plaintiff in Hawaii.

Even if Congress affords both hypothetical plaintiffs a cause of action (with statutory damages available) to sue over the defendant's legal violation, Article III standing doctrine sharply distinguishes between those two scenarios. The first lawsuit may of course proceed in federal court because the plaintiff has suffered concrete harm to her property. But the second lawsuit may not proceed because that plaintiff has not suffered any physical, monetary, or cognizable intangible harm traditionally recognized as providing a basis for a lawsuit in American courts. An uninjured plaintiff who sues in those circumstances is, by definition, not seeking to remedy any harm to herself but instead is merely seeking to ensure a defendant's "compliance with regulatory law" (and, of course, to obtain some money via the statutory damages). Those are not grounds for Article III standing.[1]

---

[1]   The lead dissent notes that the terminology of injury in fact became prevalent only in the latter half of the 20th century. That is unsurprising because until the 20th century, Congress did not often afford federal "citizen suit"-style causes of action to private plaintiffs who did not suffer concrete harms. For example, until the 20th century, Congress generally did not create "citizen suit" causes of action for private plaintiffs to sue the Government. Moreover, until *Abbott Laboratories* v. *Gardner*, 387 U. S. 136 (1967), a plaintiff often could not bring a pre-enforcement suit against a Government agency or official under the Administrative Procedure Act arguing that an agency rule was unlawful; instead, a party could raise such an argument only in an enforcement action. Likewise, until the 20th century, Congress rarely created "citizen suit"-style causes of action for suits against private parties by private plaintiffs who had not suffered a concrete harm. All told, until the 20th century, this Court had little reason to emphasize the injury-in-fact

As those examples illustrate, if the law of Article III did not require plaintiffs to demonstrate a "concrete harm," Congress could authorize virtually any citizen to bring a statutory damages suit against virtually any defendant who violated virtually any federal law. Such an expansive understanding of Article III would flout constitutional text, history, and precedent. In our view, the public interest that private entities comply with the law cannot "be converted into an individual right by a statute that denominates it as such, and that permits all citizens (or, for that matter, a subclass of citizens who suffer no distinctive concrete harm) to sue."

A regime where Congress could freely authorize unharmed plaintiffs to sue defendants who violate federal law not only would violate Article III but also would infringe on the Executive Branch's Article II authority. We accept the "displacement of the democratically elected branches when necessary to decide an actual case." But otherwise, the choice of how to prioritize and how aggressively to pursue legal actions against defendants who violate the law falls within the discretion of the Executive Branch, not within the purview of private plaintiffs (and their attorneys). Private plaintiffs are not accountable to the people and are not charged with pursuing the public interest in enforcing a defendant's general compliance with regulatory law. See *Lujan*, 504 U.S., at 577.

In sum, the concrete-harm requirement is essential to the Constitution's separation of powers. To be sure, the concrete-harm requirement can be difficult to apply in some cases. Some advocate that the concrete-harm requirement be ditched altogether, on the theory that it would be more efficient or convenient to simply say that a statutory violation and a cause of action suffice to afford a plaintiff standing. But as the Court has often stated, "the fact that a given law or procedure is efficient, convenient, and useful in facilitating functions of government, standing alone, will not save it if it is contrary to the Constitution." So it is here.

We now apply those fundamental standing principles to this lawsuit. We must determine whether the 8,185 class members have standing to sue TransUnion for its alleged violations of the Fair Credit Reporting Act. The plaintiffs argue that TransUnion failed to comply with statutory obligations (i) to follow reasonable procedures to ensure the accuracy of credit files so that the files would not include OFAC alerts labeling the plaintiffs as potential terrorists; and (ii) to provide a consumer, upon request, with his or her complete credit file, including a summary of rights.
* * *

---

requirement because, until the 20th century, there were relatively few instances where litigants without concrete injuries had a cause of action to sue in federal court. The situation has changed markedly, especially over the last 50 years or so. During that time, Congress has created many novel and expansive causes of action that in turn have required greater judicial focus on the requirements of Article III.

We first address the plaintiffs' claim that TransUnion failed to "follow reasonable procedures to assure maximum possible accuracy" of the plaintiffs' credit files maintained by TransUnion. 15 U. S. C. § 1681e(b). In particular, the plaintiffs argue that TransUnion did not do enough to ensure that OFAC alerts labeling them as potential terrorists were not included in their credit files.

Assuming that the plaintiffs are correct that TransUnion violated its obligations under the Fair Credit Reporting Act to use reasonable procedures in internally maintaining the credit files, we must determine whether the 8,185 class members suffered concrete harm from TransUnion's failure to employ reasonable procedures.

Start with the 1,853 class members (including the named plaintiff Ramirez) whose reports were disseminated to third-party businesses. The plaintiffs argue that the publication to a third party of a credit report bearing a misleading OFAC alert injures the subject of the report. The plaintiffs contend that this injury bears a "close relationship" to a harm traditionally recognized as providing a basis for a lawsuit in American courts—namely, the reputational harm associated with the tort of defamation.

We agree with the plaintiffs. Under longstanding American law, a person is injured when a defamatory statement "that would subject him to hatred, contempt, or ridicule" is published to a third party. TransUnion provided third parties with credit reports containing OFAC alerts that labeled the class members as potential terrorists, drug traffickers, or serious criminals. The 1,853 class members therefore suffered a harm with a "close relationship" to the harm associated with the tort of defamation. We have no trouble concluding that the 1,853 class members suffered a concrete harm that qualifies as an injury in fact.

TransUnion counters that those 1,853 class members did not suffer a harm with a "close relationship" to defamation because the OFAC alerts on the disseminated credit reports were only misleading and not literally false. TransUnion points out that the reports merely identified a consumer as a "potential match" to an individual on the OFAC list—a fact that TransUnion says is not technically false.

In looking to whether a plaintiff's asserted harm has a "close relationship" to a harm traditionally recognized as providing a basis for a lawsuit in American courts, we do not require an exact duplicate. The harm from being labeled a "potential terrorist" bears a close relationship to the harm from being labeled a "terrorist." In other words, the harm from a misleading statement of this kind bears a sufficiently close relationship to the harm from a false and defamatory statement.

In short, the 1,853 class members whose reports were disseminated to third parties suffered a concrete injury in fact under Article III.

The remaining 6,332 class members are a different story. To be sure, their credit files, which were maintained by TransUnion, contained misleading OFAC alerts. But the parties stipulated that TransUnion did not provide those plaintiffs' credit information to any potential creditors during the class period from January 2011 to July 2011. Given the absence of dissemination, we must determine whether the 6,332 class members suffered some other concrete harm for purposes of Article III.

The initial question is whether the mere existence of a misleading OFAC alert in a consumer's internal credit file at TransUnion constitutes a concrete injury. As Judge Tatel phrased it in a similar context, "if inaccurate information falls into" a consumer's credit file, "does it make a sound?"

* * * Judge Tatel answered no. Publication is "essential to liability" in a suit for defamation. And there is "no historical or common-law analog where the mere existence of inaccurate information, absent dissemination, amounts to concrete injury." "Since the basis of the action for words was the loss of credit or fame, and not the insult, it was always necessary to show a publication of the words." Other Courts of Appeals have similarly recognized that, as Judge Colloton summarized, the "retention of information lawfully obtained, without further disclosure, traditionally has not provided the basis for a lawsuit in American courts," meaning that the mere existence of inaccurate information in a database is insufficient to confer Article III standing.

The standing inquiry in this case thus distinguishes between (i) credit files that consumer reporting agencies maintain internally and (ii) the consumer credit reports that consumer reporting agencies disseminate to third-party creditors. The mere presence of an inaccuracy in an internal credit file, if it is not disclosed to a third party, causes no concrete harm. In cases such as these where allegedly inaccurate or misleading information sits in a company database, the plaintiffs' harm is roughly the same, legally speaking, as if someone wrote a defamatory letter and then stored it in her desk drawer. A letter that is not sent does not harm anyone, no matter how insulting the letter is. So too here.

Because the plaintiffs cannot demonstrate that the misleading information in the internal credit files itself constitutes a concrete harm, the plaintiffs advance a separate argument based on an asserted risk of future harm. They say that the 6,332 class members suffered a concrete injury for Article III purposes because the existence of misleading OFAC alerts in their internal credit files exposed them to a material risk that the information would be disseminated in the future to third parties and thereby cause them harm. The plaintiffs rely on language from Spokeo where the Court said that "the risk of real harm" (or as the Court otherwise stated, a "material risk of harm") can sometimes "satisfy the requirement of concreteness."

To support its statement that a material risk of future harm can satisfy the concrete-harm requirement, Spokeo cited this Court's decision in Clapper. But importantly, Clapper involved a suit for injunctive relief. As this Court has recognized, a person exposed to a risk of future harm may pursue forward-looking, injunctive relief to prevent the harm from occurring, at least so long as the risk of harm is sufficiently imminent and substantial.

But a plaintiff must "demonstrate standing separately for each form of relief sought." [Friends of the Earth] Therefore, a plaintiff's standing to seek injunctive relief does not necessarily mean that the plaintiff has standing to seek retrospective damages.

TransUnion advances a persuasive argument that in a suit for damages, the mere risk of future harm, standing alone, cannot qualify as a concrete harm—at least unless the exposure to the risk of future harm itself causes a separate concrete harm. TransUnion contends that if an individual is exposed to a risk of future harm, time will eventually reveal whether the risk materializes in the form of actual harm. If the risk of future harm materializes and the individual suffers a concrete harm, then the harm itself, and not the pre-existing risk, will constitute a basis for the person's injury and for damages. If the risk of future harm does not materialize, then the individual cannot establish a concrete harm sufficient for standing, according to TransUnion.

Consider an example. Suppose that a woman drives home from work a quarter mile ahead of a reckless driver who is dangerously swerving across lanes. The reckless driver has exposed the woman to a risk of future harm, but the risk does not materialize and the woman makes it home safely. As counsel for TransUnion stated, that would ordinarily be cause for celebration, not a lawsuit. But if the reckless driver crashes into the woman's car, the situation would be different, and (assuming a cause of action) the woman could sue the driver for damages. * * *

Even apart from that fundamental problem with their argument based on the risk of future harm, the plaintiffs did not factually establish a sufficient risk of future harm to support Article III standing. As Judge McKeown explained in her dissent, the risk of future harm that the 6,332 plaintiffs identified—the risk of dissemination to third parties—was too speculative to support Article III standing. The plaintiffs claimed that TransUnion could have divulged their misleading credit information to a third party at any moment. But the plaintiffs did not demonstrate a sufficient likelihood that their individual credit information would be requested by third-party businesses and provided by TransUnion during the relevant time period. Nor did the plaintiffs demonstrate that there was a sufficient likelihood that TransUnion would otherwise intentionally or accidentally release their information to third parties. "Because no evidence in the record establishes a serious likelihood of disclosure, we cannot simply presume a material risk of concrete harm."

Moreover, the plaintiffs did not present any evidence that the 6,332 class members even knew that there were OFAC alerts in their internal TransUnion credit files. If those plaintiffs prevailed in this case, many of them would first learn that they were "injured" when they received a check compensating them for their supposed "injury." It is difficult to see how a risk of future harm could supply the basis for a plaintiff's standing when the plaintiff did not even know that there was a risk of future harm.

Finally, the plaintiffs advance one last argument for why the 6,332 class members are similarly situated to the other 1,853 class members and thus should have standing. The 6,332 plaintiffs note that they sought damages for the entire 46-month period permitted by the statute of limitations, whereas the stipulation regarding dissemination covered only 7 of those months. They argue that the credit reports of many of those 6,332 class members were likely also sent to third parties outside of the period covered by the stipulation because all of the class members requested copies of their reports, and consumers usually do not request copies unless they are contemplating a transaction that would trigger a credit check.

That is a serious argument, but in the end, we conclude that it fails to support standing for the 6,332 class members. The plaintiffs had the burden to prove at trial that their reports were actually sent to third-party businesses. The inferences on which the argument rests are too weak to demonstrate that the reports of any particular number of the 6,332 class members were sent to third-party businesses. The plaintiffs' attorneys could have attempted to show that some or all of the 6,332 class members were injured in that way. They presumably could have sought the names and addresses of those individuals, and they could have contacted them. In the face of the stipulation, which pointedly failed to demonstrate dissemination for those class members, the inferences on which the plaintiffs rely are insufficient to support standing.

In sum, the 6,332 class members whose internal TransUnion credit files were not disseminated to third-party businesses did not suffer a concrete harm. By contrast, the 1,853 class members (including Ramirez) whose credit reports were disseminated to third-party businesses during the class period suffered a concrete harm. [In the final portion of the opinion, the Court concluded that the defendant's error of sending required notices in two mailings rather than one had not been shown to create any harm to class members.]

* * *

No concrete harm, no standing. The 1,853 class members whose credit reports were provided to third-party businesses suffered a concrete harm and thus have standing as to the reasonable-procedures claim. The 6,332 class members whose credit reports were not provided to third-party businesses did not suffer a concrete harm and thus do not have standing as to the reasonable-procedures claim. As for the claims pertaining to the format of TransUnion's mailings, none of the 8,185 class members other than the named plaintiff Ramirez suffered a concrete harm.

JUSTICE THOMAS, with whom JUSTICE BREYER, JUSTICE SOTOMAYOR, and JUSTICE KAGAN join, dissenting.

TransUnion generated credit reports that erroneously flagged many law-abiding people as potential terrorists and drug traffickers. In doing so, TransUnion violated several provisions of the Fair Credit Reporting Act (FCRA) that entitle consumers to accuracy in credit-reporting procedures; to receive information in their credit files; and to receive a summary of their rights. Yet despite Congress' judgment that such misdeeds deserve redress, the majority decides that TransUnion's actions are so insignificant that the Constitution prohibits consumers from vindicating their rights in federal court. The Constitution does no such thing. * * *

Key to the scope of the judicial power, then, is whether an individual asserts his or her own rights. At the time of the founding, whether a court possessed judicial power over an action with no showing of actual damages depended on whether the plaintiff sought to enforce a right held privately by an individual or a duty owed broadly to the community. Where an individual sought to sue someone for a violation of his private rights, such as trespass on his land, the plaintiff needed only to allege the violation. But where an individual sued based on the violation of a duty owed broadly to the whole community, such as the overgrazing of public lands, courts required "not only *injuria* [legal injury] but also *damnum* [damage]."

This distinction mattered not only for traditional common-law rights, but also for newly created statutory ones. The First Congress enacted a law defining copyrights and gave copyright holders the right to sue infringing persons in order to recover statutory damages, even if the holder "could not show monetary loss." In the patent context, a defendant challenged an infringement suit brought under a similar law. Along the lines of what TransUnion argues here, the infringer contended that "the making of a machine cannot be an offence, because no action lies, except for actual damage, and there can be no actual damages, or even a rule for damages, for an infringement by making a machine." Riding circuit, Justice Story rejected that theory, noting that the plaintiff could sue in federal court merely by alleging a violation of a private right: "[W]here the law gives an action for a particular act, the doing of that act imports of itself a damage

to the party" because "[e]very violation of a right imports some damage."
* * *

The Court chooses a different approach. Rejecting this history, the majority holds that the mere violation of a personal legal right is not—and never can be—an injury sufficient to establish standing. What matters for the Court is only that the "injury in fact be 'concrete.' " "No concrete harm, no standing."

That may be a pithy catchphrase, but it is worth pausing to ask why "concrete" injury in fact should be the sole inquiry. After all, it was not until 1970—"180 years after the ratification of Article III"—that this Court even introduced the "injury in fact" (as opposed to injury in law) concept of standing. And the concept then was not even about constitutional standing; it concerned a statutory cause of action under the Administrative Procedure Act.

The Court later took this statutory requirement and began to graft it onto its constitutional standing analysis. But even then, injury in fact served as an additional way to get into federal court. Article III injury still could "exist solely by virtue of 'statutes creating legal rights, the invasion of which creates standing.' " So the introduction of an injury-in-fact requirement, in effect, "represented a substantial broadening of access to the federal courts." A plaintiff could now invoke a federal court's judicial power by establishing injury by virtue of a violated legal right or by alleging some other type of "personal interest."

In the context of public rights, the Court continued to require more than just a legal violation. In *Lujan,* for example, the Court concluded that several environmental organizations lacked standing to challenge a regulation about interagency communications, even though the organizations invoked a citizen-suit provision allowing " 'any person [to] commence a civil suit . . . to enjoin any person . . . who is alleged to be in violation of' " the law. Echoing the historical distinction between duties owed to individuals and those owed to the community, the Court explained that a plaintiff must do more than raise "a generally available grievance about government—claiming only harm to his and every citizen's interest in proper application of the Constitution and laws." "Vindicating the public interest (including the public interest in Government observance of the Constitution and laws) is the function of Congress and the Chief Executive." " 'The province of the court,' " in contrast, " 'is, solely, to decide on the rights of individuals.' " * * *

In *Spokeo,* the Court built on this approach. Based on a few sentences from *Lujan* and *Summers,* the Court concluded that a plaintiff does not automatically "satisf[y] the injury-in-fact requirement whenever a statute grants a person a statutory right and purports to authorize that person to sue to vindicate that right." But the Court made clear that "Congress is well positioned to identify intangible harms that meet minimum Article III requirements" and explained that "the violation of a procedural right granted by statute *can be* sufficient in some circumstances to constitute injury in fact." (emphasis added). * * *

The majority today, however, takes the road less traveled: "[U]nder Article III, an injury in law is not an injury in fact." No matter if the right is personal or if the legislature deems the right worthy of legal protection, legislatures are constitutionally unable to offer the protection of the federal courts for anything other than money, bodily integrity, and anything else that this Court thinks looks close enough to rights existing at common law. The 1970s injury-in-fact theory has now displaced the traditional gateway into federal courts.

This approach is remarkable in both its novelty and effects. Never before has this Court declared that legal injury is *inherently* insufficient to support standing. And never before has this Court declared that legislatures are constitutionally precluded from creating legal rights enforceable in federal court if those rights deviate too far from their common-law roots. According to the majority, courts alone have the power to sift and weigh harms to decide whether they merit the Federal Judiciary's attention. In the name of protecting the separation of powers, this Court has relieved the legislature of its power to create and define rights.

Even assuming that this Court should be in the business of second-guessing private rights, this is a rather odd case to say that Congress went too far. TransUnion's misconduct here is exactly the sort of thing that has long merited legal redress.

* * * But even setting aside everything already mentioned—the Constitution's text, history, precedent, financial harm, libel, the risk of publication, and actual disclosure to a third party—one need only tap into common sense to know that receiving a letter identifying you as a potential drug trafficker or terrorist is harmful. All the more so when the information comes in the context of a credit report, the entire purpose of which is to demonstrate that a person can be trusted.

And if this sort of confusing and frustrating communication is insufficient to establish a real injury, one wonders what could rise to that level. If, instead of falsely identifying Ramirez as a potential drug trafficker or terrorist, TransUnion had flagged him as a "potential" child molester, would that alone still be insufficient to open the courthouse doors? What about falsely labeling a person a racist? Including a slur on the report? Or what about openly reducing a person's credit score by several points because of his race? If none of these constitutes an injury in fact, how can that possibly square with our past cases indicating that the inability to "observe an animal species, even for purely esthetic purposes, ...

undeniably" is? Had the class members claimed an aesthetic interest in viewing an accurate report, would this case have come out differently?

And if some of these examples do cause sufficiently "concrete" and "real"—though "intangible"—harms, how do we go about picking and choosing which ones do and which do not? I see no way to engage in this "inescapably value-laden" inquiry without it "devolv[ing] into [pure] policy judgment." Weighing the harms caused by specific facts and choosing remedies seems to me like a much better fit for legislatures and juries than for this Court.

Finally, it is not just the harm that is reminiscent of a constitutional case or controversy. So too is the remedy. Although statutory damages are not necessarily a proxy for unjust enrichment, they have a similar flavor in this case. TransUnion violated consumers' rights in order to create and sell a product to its clients. Reckless handling of consumer information and bungled responses to requests for information served a means to an end. And the end was financial gain. "TransUnion could not confirm that a single OFAC alert sold to its customers was accurate." Yet thanks to this Court, it may well be in a position to keep much of its ill-gotten gains.[9]

Ultimately, the majority seems to pose to the reader a single rhetorical question: Who could possibly think that a person is harmed when he requests and is sent an incomplete credit report, or is sent a suspicious notice informing him that he may be a designated drug trafficker or terrorist, or is not sent anything informing him of how to remove this inaccurate red flag? The answer is, of course, legion: Congress, the President, the jury, the District Court, the Ninth Circuit, and four Members of this Court.

NOTES ON TRANSUNION

1. *Disagreement Among the Dissenters.* Justice Kagan also filed a separate dissent, joined by Justices Breyer and Sotomayor. She disagreed with Justice Thomas's view that violations of a plaintiff's statutory rights give rise to standing without the need to prove the existence of a concrete injury. In her view, a concrete injury is required, but courts should defer to Congress's view of when such injury exists. Consequently, "[o]verriding an authorization to sue is appropriate when but only when Congress could not reasonably have thought that a suit will contribute to compensating or preventing the harm at issue."

---

[9] Today's decision might actually be a pyrrhic victory for TransUnion. The Court does not prohibit Congress from creating statutory rights for consumers; it simply holds that federal courts lack jurisdiction to hear some of these cases. That combination may leave state courts—which "are not bound by the limitations of a case or controversy or other federal rules of justiciability even when they address issues of federal law," *ASARCO Inc. v. Kadish,* 490 U. S. 605, 617 (1989)—as the sole forum for such cases, with defendants unable to seek removal to federal court. By declaring that federal courts lack jurisdiction, the Court has thus ensured that state courts will exercise exclusive jurisdiction over these sorts of class actions.

2. *Constitutional Limits on Common Law Actions.* Cases based on the state law would also be governed by *TransUnion*. Thus, it would seem that a state statutory cause of action or common law rule would be governed by the same rule. Some states recognize a cause of action for the enhanced risk of developing cancer when someone has been exposed to a toxic chemical when the increased risk is high enough or the defendant's conduct is willful. In other states, when individuals have been exposed to a carcinogen and require medical monitoring to determine whether the disease has developed, they can sue for the costs of monitoring. Note that the Court seems to suggest at points that the question is not whether an effect qualifies as a concrete harm in general, but whether there is an analogous established cause of caution involving the concrete harm. Under the Court's rule, in a case involving diversity of citizenship, could claims of either type be brought in federal court? There are also questions in state courts about whether claims for future risks can be brought if the toxic chemical has caused changes in the plaintiff's body that could lead to future problems but do not cause any symptoms ("subclinical effects"). Under the Court's view of Article III, would those changes qualify as concrete harms? Is that really an issue to which the Constitution should speak?

3. *The Debate Within the Court.* Justice Thomas's view is simple: if the defendant violated a legal duty owed to the plaintiff, Congress can give the plaintiff the right to sue for damages. That seems at least superficial like common sense. However, he is the only member of the Court who seems to take that position. Both the majority and the three liberal dissenters say that there must also be a concrete harm, although the liberal dissenters are willing to defer greatly to Congress on this point. Who has the better of this debate?

4. *Risks as Harms.* Justice Kavanaugh says that a mere risk doesn't qualify as a basis for harm, but he also says that pocketbook losses do qualify. What if the two were tied together? Suppose that the increased risk translates into increased insurance premiums, or suppose the plaintiff has invested in increased precautions due to the risk. Under those circumstances, would a concrete risk be present? For instance, suppose on learning that TransUnion's files contain false information, the plaintiff incurs expenses in having the information removed and in contacting other credit agencies to ensure that their fails do not contain the falsehood. Would this pocketbook loss provide a basis for standing?

SECTION 3. REMEDIAL LIMITATIONS

Page 1435. Insert the following before the heading for Section 4:

The Court limited the scope of *Boumedienne*'s ruling on the Suspension Clause in Department of Homeland Security v. Thuraissigiam, 140 S.Ct. 1959, 207 L.Ed.2d 247 (2020), which is discussed in somewhat more detail in Chapter 8. Thuraissigiam crossed the U.S. Border and was immediately detained. He sought asylum, claiming that he had a credible fear of persecution. In an expedited removal proceeding, that claim was rejected by immigration officials. A statute prohibited review of that claim by habeas. The Court ruled that habeas only authorized immediate release during the Founding era, which was not the relief that he sought. (*Boumedienne*, in contrast, involved a challenge to detention.) The Court also held that he had no due process right to a hearing on his claim of credible fear of prosecution. The law is well-settled, the Court said, that aliens seeking admission into the United States have no due process rights. The fact that Thuraissigiam made it twenty-five yards into U.S. territory before he was caught made no difference.